COMIC LAUGHTER

A Philosophical Essay

COMIC LAUGHTER

A Philosophical Essay

BY MARIE COLLINS SWABEY

Archon Books, 1970

BH 301
C7
S9
1970

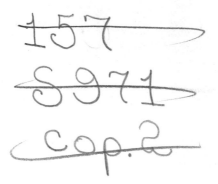

157
S971
cop.2

ISBN: 0 208 00825 X
Library of Congress Catalog Card Number: 78-113019
Printed in the United States of America

Preface

IT IS a misplaced hope to expect to find here a comic treatment of the comic. While the subject has been approached from many angles in recent years, it has rarely been dealt with from a strictly philosophical point of view. The title of the present essay is meant to distinguish comic laughter from such varieties as infantile, drunken, hysterical, or nonsense laughter. Considerations of the natural origin and practical purposes of laughter, as we see it, are irrelevant to its essential comicality. What is genuinely funny in words, character, or situation must have a logical point, drift, nub, or pertinence and yield some insight into values.

Our treatment, being philosophical, differs strikingly from the biological view of laughter as a release of suppressed energy, a reversion to infantilism, or as an expression of basic organic drives. Similarly, it stands in contrast to the sociological view of laughter as a means of social control to punish nonconformists. Nor does it resemble the psychological accounts which find in merriment an outlet for frustration, aggression, liberation of the libido or the unconscious mind. What is really important, in our opinion, is that in the laughter of comic insight we achieve a logical moment of truth; while metaphysically, through some darting thought, we detect an incongruence as cancelled by an underlying congruence. We gain an inkling, as it were, of the hang of things, sometimes even a hint of cosmic beneficence. In short, perception of the ludicrous helps us to comprehend both ourselves and the world, making us, at least in the highest reaches of humor, feel more at home in the universe by aiding in the discernment of values.

Although wit and the comic in the narrower sense focus for the most part upon matters of politics, sex, manners, and the foibles of the day, humor in its higher forms may concern itself to a degree with issues of the soul and ultimate destiny. To be sure, in the history of comedy on the stage, love, for instance, has been in large part mockingly and carnally treated, being, as an experience of the soul, reserved for tragedy. Nevertheless, as regards the summits of comedy this is not the case. Farce, of course, in taking life cheaply, tends to destroy faith in love along with other values. But men like Shakespeare, while laughing at love as a ridiculous trick of nature, a strange blindness or magic spell fallen upon its victims, have a great fondness for lovers. Far from being a mere hallucination, true love for them involves a revelation of the ideal, of genuine perfections disclosed to the lover, by which his egotism is breached. Possessing body and soul, it tries the mettle of a man, so that the intimations of beauty and goodness glimpsed in another may suffice to induce the loyalty of a lifetime.

In conclusion, may I express my thanks to the authors, editors, and publishers to whom I am indebted for quotations, especially to the Directors of the *Journal of Philosophy* for permission to reprint as Chapter 2 an essay of mine, "The Comic as Nonsense, Sadism, or Incongruity," which appeared in Volume LV: 19, pages 819–833, of the Journal. My thanks are also due to the Public Trustee and the Society of Authors, London, for extracts from Bernard Shaw's *Major Barbara.* Miss D. E. Collins has kindly granted permission to quote from the writings of G. K. Chesterton.

February 1961   M. C. S.

Contents

CHAPTER I

Language and Concepts

TREATMENT of comic laughter is rendered difficult from the outset both by the widely divergent theories found among specialists and by the medley of meanings attached in common usage to terms like wit, humor, the comic, mirth, and the amusing. The great variety of opinions expressed by writers on the ludicrous springs perhaps from variations in their approach: some consider it predominantly from the psychological point of view, others from the biological or the sociological, and a few from a philosophical angle. Aside from this, obstacles are multiplied by the public's casual use of language, in which terms like funny, ridiculous, amusing, or laughable are employed not simply in a wider and a narrower sense, but often as so much worn, interchangeable currency denoting nothing distinctively ludicrous, but merely something attention-attracting, slightly bizarre, pleasant, or contemptible, exciting along with some vocal resonance a certain facial contraction. Surely if a more definite, unambiguous usage of terms could be established and adhered to, understanding of the subject might be greatly improved.

Of course, in dictionaries the nomenclature of the behavioral side of the topic is settled to a degree. Thus in Webster "to laugh" is said to be "to express merriment by convulsive sounds accompanied by opening of the mouth and wrinkling of the face." But such a description, while excluding such things as

the mirthless laugh, the smile, or the grimace, does not in its
phrasing clearly indicate distinctively comic enjoyment. For
merriment is defined in the same dictionary as fun or gaiety,
by synonyms like jollity, joviality, glee, terms indicating high
spirits along with a possible variety of moods not necessarily
denoting appreciation of the ludicrous.

Indeed, dictionaries list numerically so many different meanings of the basic terms that it seems often simply a matter of
individual choice or of the context of discourse which is preferred. Besides including the wider and narrower usage of
words, they list synonyms and alternative phrases embracing
many different factors commonly associated with the risible
experience. Furthermore, in the dictionaries primary concern
is with usage and current frequency in the employment of
words, rather than with unambiguous analysis of their referents; so that if the locution of ordinary discourse abounds in
vague expressions, understandably dictionaries will do the
same. To repeat, dictionaries deal with verbal use and verbal
significance rather than with the analysis of the meaning of
referents of the distinctively comic experience.

In this essay an attempt is made, imperfect though it be, to
arrive, not at a psychological, physiological, or sociological
understanding of laughter, but to gain some modicum of
philosophic truth in regard to the comic, and to adhere to
some slightly more precise designation of terms with regard to
it. Here interest centers not so much in the existential features
and accompaniments of the experience itself, nor in the vocabulary employed to describe it, but rather in the import of the
experience and the ludicrous referent. As is often remarked,
there are many kinds of laughter, and a man may be known
both by what he laughs at and the tone of it. There is the
dry, mocking laugh, the vacant one, the nervous cackle, the
hysterical screech, the suppressed giggle, the uncontrollable
guffaw, the soulless roar, as well as the sympathetic echo, the
jovial, the ruminative, the wholehearted or genuinely appreciative laugh, to mention only a few.

Unlike the experience of beauty, perception of the comic tends to shake the frame and to involve labored breathing. Though induced by a relationship of ideas, it gives rise to feeling and marked bodily reactions. While intellection is necessary to determine what is laughable, full appreciation includes affective and motor response. But only when these latter ensue from mentation are they genuinely to be labelled as comic. A good jest, like Will Rogers' saying that "Our foreign policy is an open book—usually a check book" induces a laugh, a shift of emotion (here from national pride to self-criticism) and a considerable train of reflection. What induces the laugh of comic appreciation is that the remark awakens the mind to a perception of contrariety and absurdity. It is only when the image of the "open book" (suggesting frank, above-board diplomacy) is supplanted by that of the "check book" (suggesting eleemosynary prodigality—not a trade but a give-away), only when the figure of the honest broker is replaced by that of rich Uncle Sam with a touch of the simpleton, that we become aware of the equivocation by which the promise of a laudatory phrase is converted into a jibe at our wasteful openhandedness.

In the same way, though without the same ruminative and emotional resonance, the cigar-smoker's quip, "Anyone can give up smoking; I have done it myself a thousand times," turns on a glimpse of contradiction. Here the nub lies in the inconceivability of one's being simultaneously both a smoker and a non-smoker and the necessity of being one or the other, while the implied vacillation or seesaw between the two, which is the secondary meaning, obviously contradicts the primary import of the assertion. In both jests it is the sense of contrariety that makes you laugh; and if you laugh from other causes or do not know what you are laughing at, your laughter fails to be comic. Without penetration of a confused state of affairs and its transcendence, there is no relish of the ludicrous.

The most general terms we shall use to describe our subject

are the synonyms, the ludicrous or the comic. While the ludicrous tends to indicate simply the referent (i.e. we refer to "experience of the ludicrous" rather than to "the ludicrous experience"), the comic may designate either the experience, the referent, or both. Aside from this, they may be taken as interchangeable key notions constituting both the widest and most accurate designations of the field. Broadly, the ludicrous, or the comic, signifies that which is worthy of exciting laughter because of a certain inconsistency or absurdity in its referent. Though both terms cover the field as a whole, the comic (our preferred term), unlike the ludicrous, has both a wider and a narrower designation.

In addition to its meaning as a comprehensive genus, the comic is often distinguished as a species which stands in contrast to other species (such as humor, satire, or wit). But unlike satire or wit, the comic in the narrower sense does not always

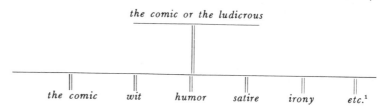

<hr>

[1] In addition to the chief varieties of the ludicrous, other minor subdivisions might be added, such as the whimsical, the grotesque, and the ridiculous. These, however, hardly warrant separate treatment. The whimsical, for instance, indicates something evanescently fanciful with a slight comic twist; the grotesque something stimulating exaggerated fancy, but bizarre and odd more than simply incongruous. Indeed, the grotesque is not unrelated to the weird, in which the gruesome, horrible, or ghastly appears in association with the fantastic as almost, if not quite, eclipsing the sense of comic incongruity. For that matter, in the so-called amusement arts today, a fairy tale, a horror or ghost story is often passed off as an imaginative expression of the ludicrous, even when the connection with laughter is entirely lost. On the other hand, the bond with the comic is not wholly erased in those imitative products in which an original work is subjected to undignified mimicry as in the parody, travesty, or burlesque. The ridiculous serves to indicate something incongruous that is worthy of ridicule or contemptuous laughter.

require verbal or symbolic expression, although the comic in words is a familiar type. That is to say, while wit lives in witticisms and satire in satirical works or remarks, the comic may inhere in characters, situations, or events, and be appreciated even though beyond linguistic reach. Again, experience of the comic in the narrow sense (unlike humor or satire) does not involve a strong emotional slant, either sympathetic or antipathetic. Nor does it like wit demand intellectual activity of a high order. Rather, comic insight in a restricted sense has more to do with ordinary minds, the dissonances or incongruities of everyday life that are not too exigent or weighty. Unlike satire or irony, moreover, it yields a spontaneous satisfaction largely unmixed with pain and free of derogatory intent.

A word of explanation should be added in regard to the term humor, which is frequently employed in everyday speech as broadly equivalent to the ludicrous. In the interest of clarity we have tried in what follows to restrict its usage to that of a particular variety of the comic that is contrasted with wit, satire, etc. Occasionally, however, we find ourselves forced to employ the term "humorist" in a loose, general sense to indicate simply a person given to comic insight and expression, as the alternative terms "comedian" or "jester" seem less adequate.

It is regrettable that the terms indicating the chief varieties of the ludicrous are not entirely parallel, since satire on first thought suggests simply a literary form, irony a figure of speech, wit and humor natural capacities apart from their expression, while the comic perhaps most often suggests some rather obvious aspect of appearances or behavior. Nevertheless, despite this variance in reference, these terms designate different divisions of the ludicrous, each with its distinctive characters. Indeed, without stretching things too far, traces of a hierarchical order may be looked for in the comic, humor, and wit, in which the comic in the narrower sense refers to the more super-

ficial incongruities manifest in action, speech, and sensuous
appearances; humor to the sympathetic stimulation and report
of deeper processes; while wit refers to the dryest, most intellectual expression of the three. However, admittedly in pro-
fundity of reach humor not infrequently surpasses the others.
At one side, at a high intellectual level, stand satire and irony
as two distinctive forms concerned with the fun of disapproval
and criticism. But enough of preliminaries.

The Comic as Nonsense, Sadism, or Incongruity

THE NATURE of the comic in general is not, I venture to think, the insoluble problem it is sometimes taken to be. Rather, a main difficulty with the subject has turned on the failure to distinguish normative from factual considerations, logical from naturalistic components of the field. To be sure, the search for common characters among the things that actually make us laugh seems almost hopeless; for anything and everything may upon occasion appear to do so: tickling, nervousness, relief from tension, nitrous oxide, a feeling of spite or one of exuberant health, or again mere social convention. In brief, any number of bodily conditions, psychological and social circumstances may act as stimuli to effect the response. If the question is simply as to the causes of laughter and its empirical consequences, the inquiry has no limits because by the operation of the laws of association or conditioning a correlation can be established between almost any datum serving as trigger-action and the mechanism of risibility. Yet where all emphasis is placed upon what sets off laughter and the ensuing factual reactions, *what it is about* becomes irrelevant and the comic as such turns into a species of nonsense. So viewed the comic may include the laughter of the baby, the drunkard, the hysteric or the idiot, the derision of pugnacity or aggression, the erotic, often obscene, jocosity due to the sexual urge, jollity expressive of the play impulse, the ambivalence of conflicting emotions, not to mention the limitless realm of habit formation and reflexes.

If the problem for aesthetic criticism is simply *what makes us laugh,* the origin and utility of laughter—and not, on the contrary, *what is worth laughing at,* what states of affairs are essentially ludicrous or deserving of mirth (a question of *value* not of *fact*)—then the subject covers merely information regarding the laughter behavior of various societies together with a study of our constitutional make-up, and is undertaken only as a descriptive record for science and social control. Here the sensory-affective-motor life of man is what is important, and there need be no *point* of a joke to be seen, no issue of validity to be grasped, no insight into essential values to be made plain. This is often the view of naturalism and empiricism, a group including the logical positivists, instrumentalists, cultural relativists, and those whose outlook is bounded by that of the physical and social sciences of the day. For them the causes and methods of making men laugh are all-engrossing, whereas the content of what is laughed at is accepted as endlessly variable, while the question of its logical pattern or inherent value is held of no account.

Typical in many ways of the naturalistic approach is that of the logical positivists. Although they have little or nothing to say of the comic directly, their attitude toward values and aesthetic values in particular is well known. To their forthright radicalism (especially in its earlier phases) philosophy is indebted for considerable clarification regarding the distinction between evaluative expression and assertions of fact. Writers like Carnap, Ayer, or Schlick placed great emphasis upon the empirical verification principle, and even where their views have undergone subsequent modification continue to deny that value judgments should be called propositions, since in their opinion there is no procedure for examining the value of the facts involved as distinct from the facts themselves.

"Every statement is either empirically verifiable, . . . analytic, or self-contradictory,"[1] declared Carnap in a famous dictum, thereby relegating valuations of every sort to the status of pseudo-propositions (nonsense) or analytic sentences (verbal conventions) explicative of the meaning of their terms. "Actually," said Carnap, in another context, "a value statement is nothing else than a command in a misleading grammatical form,"[2] the expression of an emotional attitude, neither true nor false. This means that the experience of the comic and its object can only be correctly described in a factual language, in terms akin to those of the sciences, capable of observation and experimental check. Otherwise we speak tautologically or simply give vent to our feelings in pseudo-propositions which are nonsense. Thus, if I say "Ordinary domestic ducks are white," my statement has literal, objective significance because I have available scientific means by which to verify it; but if I say "Ducks are comical," meaning that they are inherently so, my assertion is unverifiable, since I can point to no instruments of observation or measurement that would certify it.

But against this demand for strictly factual knowledge and an emotive theory of values, a rationalist might protest. Unlike the positivist, who in the interests of sensation reduces the laws of logic to mere tautological conventions, a rationalist acknowledges the primordial ontological validity of these laws as determinants of experience. Again, unlike the positivist for whom knowledge is rooted in sensation which is implicitly exclusive, particular, organic, he allows its grounding in reason which is general, inclusive, supersomatic.[3] When he says "Ducks

---

[1] Rudolf Carnap, *The Unity of Science* (London, Kegan, Paul, Trench, Trubner, & Co., Ltd., 1934), p. 28.

[2] Carnap, *Philosophy and Logical Syntax* (London, Kegan, Paul, Trench, Trubner, 1935), p. 24.

[3] Whereas to the rationalist there is no contradiction in adopting a transcendent point of view, in conceiving the world with Dante as a divine comedy, for the naturalist, on the contrary, to whom knowledge centers in an immediate confrontation by a particular percipient occupying a specific locus in a space-time matrix, such an assertion is nonsense. He

are comical" what he means to call attention to is an imbalance in them, an incongruity. This incongruity he finds between the duck's air-borne structure as a bird of flight and its aquatic structure as a swimmer, in the contrast between its flat bill, web feet, dumpiness, ungainly waddle on the one hand, and its wingedness, glossy feathers, far-sighted restless eyes on the other, a contrast culminating in its voice, that crowning absurdity, the quack.

Undeniably today, with the growth of naturalism, the interpretation of the comic has increasingly lost its connection with rational insight. Today the most popular theories of laughter explain it almost wholly in subjective or organic terms, such as ambivalent emotions, sexual desire, aggressiveness, the feeling of superiority (even Bergson's theory of "the mechanical encrusted upon the living" being but a variant of the superiority theory). Yet it should not be forgotten that Kant, on the contrary, held to the intellectual origin of the comic in "something absurd" and that it was "excited by ideas," accepting (as Schopenhauer did later) an incongruity theory. In this main contention Kant would seem to us to be right, as well as in maintaining that laughter conveys a sense of health or bodily well-being; yet he would seem to be mistaken in his further point that that which arouses laughter affords no satisfaction to the understanding and is merely a "*play* with aesthetical ideas or of representations of the under standing through which ultimately *nothing is thought.*"[4] Surely

cannot, like the rationalist, by carrying the notion of his experience to the limit grasp the idea of omnipresence, omniscience, omnisentience. He can admit no universal experience in itself, no perception-in-general. Nevertheless, the positivist is forced to admit verifiability in principle— and that "there is nothing in an *experience considered by itself* . . . to make it form part of one person's history rather than another's" (Ayer) —which to a rationalist seems tacit admission of the point at issue, that is, of perception-in-general as a thing in itself as transcendent as the God of theology.

[4]Kant, *Critique of Judgment*, trans. J. H. Bernard (New York, Hafner Publishing Co., 1951), p. 176. Italics mine.

Kant is wrong in holding that nothing is gained or thought in the perception of the incongruous, since at the very least there is negative learning, the discovery of what is finally excluded as contradictory from the structure of things; while on the positive side our acquaintance is enriched with regard to the possibilities of actuality.

Logical thinking and not mere animal sufferance is required for apprehension of contradictions. By exposing fallacies in thought, language, and ways of living, minds alert to the ludicrous may contribute not a little to human progress. Bad habits may be laughed to death. By uncovering neglected hypocrisies, illusions, vanities, and deceptions in the behavior of persons and societies, avoidance of error is promoted as well as knowledge of the truth. Neat presentations by the humorist of instances of men's vain conceit of their appearance, wealth, or wisdom, their pretensions to be what they are not, their illusions of grandeur, good looks, sagacity (as caught in various colloquialisms labeling the poseur, the pretty boy, the wind-bag, the know-it-all, the fourflusher), while making us laugh, also remove in part our blindness with regard to certain factual and moral weaknesses in mankind. Similarly the sudden grasp of cases of contradiction between word and deed, of men not practicing what they preach, of talking one way and acting another, in tickling our sense of the ludicrous may enlighten us as to sources of wrongdoing in ourselves and others. As suggested, succinct portrayal of the patterns of warring traits that comprise such different types as the quack, the bore, the gossip, the snob, the busybody, the fop, the egotist, the miser, the lady-killer, and the siren may help us to recognize and to be on our guard against certain deleterious tendencies of human nature. Acquisition of such knowledge, like the ability to classify diseases and to recognize their symptoms, is both of theoretical and practical advantage. But the deepest source of knowledge involved in the perception of the ludicrous we would venture to call metaphysical, as having to do with the structure of truth and reality. The standpoint of the comic raises itself, as it were, above the world, seeking to elude error by adopting an implicitly universal outlook and to survey events with an impartial eye. Through his effort to put himself in others' place and to see himself as others see him, the man with an eye to the ludicrous is able to reflect on even the most absurdly incongruous character, "There but for the Grace of God go I." What we are suggesting is that in the perception of the comic there is a transcendental element of cosmic perspective. For the moment at least, the humorist is a laughing philosopher out of this world, who sees bits of nonsense in a world that somehow makes sense, who grasps incongruities in a more comprehensive congruity, and finds contradictory sub-systems resolved in a non-contradictory entirety. In brief, he takes the world both from an over-all view and from a slant, both locally, empirically, and as a logician and metaphysician.

Metaphysically, we would suggest, the very presupposition of the possibility of taking an impartial, objective attitude in judging the ludicrous involves an ontological argument as to the genuineness of the universe as a rational structure—by a reaffirmation in denial similar to that used by Descartes and others to prove the reality of truth and of the self. For to maintain that the comic judgment has objective insight into the irrelevant requires assuming the logical integrity of the universe in which thought has the cogency to show forth such irrelevance with relevance. On the other hand, to deny that thought has the power to grasp irrelevance objectively is to operate on the assumption that thought has the capacity to disprove its own pertinence, which power is only possible on the presupposition of thought's ability to grasp objective irrelevancy owing to the logical structure of things. In other words, in our opinion the naturalists in aesthetics who maintain that the field of the comic is finally under the constraint of non-rational processes do so only by tacitly taking for granted that the soundness of their demonstration is confirmed by the logic of the cosmic scheme supporting it.

If we are right, the perception of the comic, besides involving emotional and physiological responses, requires logical and
metaphysical comprehension, a normative intellectual insight
which grasps what is worthy of laughter, what in a state of
affairs is laugh*able* and not merely what makes us as organic
creatures laugh. Just as logic when compared with psychology
is normative, in that the ways in which we often actually think
are very different from the valid ways in which we ought to
think, just as the rules of arithmetic differ from our blundering
additions and subtractions, just as the moral law or golden rule
serves to contrast how we ought to act with how we often do,
so what is comical (i.e. deserving of mirth) is often very
different from what upon occasion we actually laugh at. By
means of humor, as Kant says, through a certain originality of
spirit one is able to put oneself into a mental disposition in
which everything is judged quite differently than ordinarily,
though still in accordance with rational principles.[5] While this
transition to a novel standpoint, in our view, involves an
exhilaration arising from an intellectual insight, it has also its
animal side involving relaxation of tension and a feeling of
health. Yet, as we see it, at the lees of comic laughter lies not
simply the pleasure of bodily equilibrium or health but a sense
of total well-being or harmony. But when Kant describes
laughter as arising from a suddenly disappointed expectation
ending in nothing, he is regarding it from an organic point
of view not from the intellectual point of view of incongruity,
since he remarks that the enjoyment of it is not due to the
understanding but is caused by the influence of the representation upon the body with only a reflex effect on the mind.[6]
To us, on the contrary, it is the perception of a local incongruity as incapable of truth or reality against the normative
background of a universal relevance that affords the basic
satisfaction of the comic perception. Thus, in our view, a
comic mistake is possible, as when we laugh at what we take

---

[5] Kant, p. 181.
[6] Kant, p. 177.

to be a contradiction in the object which is not really present in it but arises from our faulty understanding, as when the farmer on first seeing a giraffe exclaimed "There ain't no such animal." Here the comic mistake is itself comic. In a sense most jokes involve logical fallacies, although not all logical fallacies are jokes (i.e. not all logical fallacies have to do with subjects closely related to human affairs or treated in a spirit not gravely serious or important).

Of course, since the comic is a referent of human discourse—since we are not dealing with the laughter of the gods—what is laughable cannot be entirely irrelevant to human health and experience; its content (like that of the beautiful) cannot be wholly unhealthy or vitally destructive. As is often said, the comic involves an affirmation of life. Thus murders, wars of extermination, the progress of an epidemic or mortal disease, starvation and death are not ordinarily chosen as comic subjects. Against this statement may, of course, be cited the current fashion of gruesome mysteries, tales of violence and homicide, in which involved schemes of treachery and mayhem are treated not only as of paramount interest but often as laughing matters. In these stories the worst catastrophes are taken as affording a grim humor, the meanest revenges are used to wring sardonic smiles from the audience, while the characters themselves converse in explosive wisecracks (presumed to be funny) suggestive of the "balloons" of "horror comics." But perhaps instead of being really funny, the so-called "comedies" of the genre of *Arsenic and Old Lace,* of child murderers, besotted drunkards, and mechanical supermen, are rather signs of aesthetic confusion.

At any rate, there is a long tradition sanctifying a distinction between tragedy and comedy. Comedy, it is held, faces the sudden reversals of fortune and vital threats to its characters with a lightness, a buoyancy suffused with a sense of jovial well-being far removed from the mood of pity and terror excited by tragedy. Whereas comedy turns on awareness of absurdities provoking laughter, in which adversity is gaily treated and the values of life are not finally threatened, tragedy provides its audience with a sense of fear and pity at the spectacle of human existence. Man suddenly perceives a gulf opening at his feet, a chasm of insecurity; he quakes at his own insignificance, feeling like a cliff-hanger facing imminent doom; yet in the greatest tragedies he gains somehow from the spectacle of his creature annihilation a sense of moral law akin to the sublime. That is, in tragedy, along with the perception of the gravity and mystery of man's destiny there is a cloudy sense of justice amid the pain. In comedy also, although the treatment is not solemn or important, there is at bottom an intimation of an evening-up, a balance in the nature of things. Yet while in comedy the zest for living is furthered without the total scheme of life and values being endangered, in tragedy both are at stake and the revelation of enduring values comes only with the destruction of life after everything has been cast into jeopardy.

Since experience of the comic centers in the perception of a contradiction or absurdity, it is rooted in the principles of consistency according to which everything is either a or non-a and not both, at the same time in the same respect. Thus if the comic lies in an incongruity that makes sense (a), then that which is exhaustively excluded is that which is non-sense $(non$-$a)$. But the term "non-sense" is often loosely used, sometimes only as a contrary or relative opposite (exclusive but not exhaustive), sometimes as a real contradictory. For instance, the distinction of non-a from a in the case of non-red from red covers under the genus "non-red" the colors green, blue, yellow as well as that which has no color. Similarly the term non-sense $(non$-$a)$ as opposed to sense (a) may refer not only to fallacies of all sorts and confusions of universes of discourse, but nonsense in the extreme form of the wholly meaningless. Still, the comic character who plays the fool does not masquerade as an imbecile but as one whose speech and actions are marked by frequent non-sequiturs, ambiguities, and contradictions, yet not by total incoherence. Nonsense in this last form of the completely meaningless, the alogical, is barred, in our opinion, from the range of the comic altogether.

Since the ludicrous involves perception of an absurdity, it excludes utter foolishness, pure silliness, senselessness. The ludicrous encounter must yield not blindness but an insight. Awareness of the comic requires an intellectual process, not mere confrontation of a blank wall but perception of a point. It must be about something, not about nothing; it must have some specific pertinence, gist, nub, import, drift; one must be able to get the hang or pattern of it. *Pure nonsense* as signifying utter meaningless or absence of rationality is not funny; for this one needs a play of thought, not its extinction, the detection of an incongruence canceled by an underlying congruence. Put otherwise, this is to say that the comic has always a method in its madness, a logic, and that it can never involve a total violation of logical laws.

Considering the extreme fashions in "nonsense humor" today, bizarre efforts to win the game by kicking over the table and disregarding all the rules of reason and discourse, the point is not without importance. Indeed, as it appears to me, the two outstanding effects of the naturalism of our times upon comic discourse are, on one side, the attempt to appeal to nonsense of an entirely senseless sort, and, on the other, to appeal to cruelty, brutality, to what can only in principle be called sadism. The first arises apparently from the current preoccupation with the organic stimulus-response mechanism of laughter to the disregard of its meaning; and the second from stress upon the natural egotism of the human animal, which gains a feeling of superiority from spiteful criticism and the infliction of pain with anaesthesia of the heart increasing proportionately. This last raises the question whether progress is currently to be found in the realm of the comic, whether we have really outgrown the brutal jibes of an earlier day at the cripple, the dwarf, the hunchback, the idiot, as well as the cut-throat ribaldry of political satire once used to crucify public men.

To come to the point boldly: in our opinion, if experience is not to dissolve into a welter without distinctive meaning, reference, or definition of terms, both logical laws and moral standards must remain effective in the realm of the comic. Let us begin with the logical requirements. Admittedly the discovery and creation of the comical is like inventing and taking part in a game. Participation in it involves a kind of sport, a contest of skill, acceptance of a set of rules or what is called today more abstractly a postulational system. Success with such a system involves committing oneself both to a freely chosen, local set of conventions and to the necessary, inclusive principles of rationality. Whether the content of the game be that of Boolean algebra, a non-Euclidean geometry, a Disney cartoon, or the Brobdingnagian world of Swift, the very criteria of the system, the meaningful integrity of the exercise of wit involved require not only abiding by the stipulations chosen, operating according to the elected scheme of rules, but also adhering to the laws of thought and inference. Everywhere in thinking there are two sets of requirements: those involving the postulates from which we reason and those involving the principles in accordance with which we reason: (1) the first, free assumptions of a point of view, optional conveniences, differing from one scheme of thought to another, and (2) the second, a group of comprehensive regulations necessary to all systems, the basic logic of sanity and rationality. These latter are the principles of consistency and inference. As such they are not factual (psychical or physical) laws but canons of validity, constituting the comprehensive framework of both thought and things, principles whose certification is discursive in that they are reaffirmed in their very denial. For since all thinking and intelligent action require referents of a certain scope, rules of procedure involving cases and their inclusion or exclusion, together with notions of negation and totality, all thinking and intelligent action presupposes the laws of thought (identity, contradiction, excluded middle) as well as the rule-case-result of inference and sufficient reason. That these principles are not mere optional conveniences for ordering discourse and behavior but constitutive necessities is shown by their universal acceptance as criteria even in the attempt to refute them. Throughout our changing world, theoretical knowledge, practical success, and predictiveness remain possible only on the assumption of the determinate constitution, unchanging relations, and relevancies of things.. Interwoven with these logical canons are standards of truth and morality: of *truth* in the requisites of integrity, consistency, systematic harmony in the game and its playing; and of *morality* in the obligation of promise-keeping, of uniformity in conforming to the code laid down, doing what you agreed to do, or otherwise being guilty of a breach of contract.

Needless to say, both sets of assumptions operate throughout the realm of the comic, even though awareness of comic incongruity arises from an attempt to violate either or both of them. Because the universe is *one in many* realms of being and discourse, it harbors within it one comprehensive, necessary set of operations as well as many alternative schemes of procedure. The incongruity which is comic may arise either from (*1*) a transgression of our local commitments, as where we deviate suddenly from our accepted code of conventions, or where two or more of our adopted codes collide, or (*2*) when we become aware of an infringement in the content of our thought of the basic inclusive logic—whereby we are guilty of the formal incongruity of *reductio ad absurdum* or presupposition in denial.

(*1*) Variants of the first type of incongruity are almost endless. Sometimes the contradiction occurs through a lapse in operating in accordance with the postulates of a particular field: as in a slip of behavior (gaucherie) or in a slip of the tongue. Again, the humorist may purposely deviate from his accepted rules of language, syntax, rhyme, meaning of terms, or realm of discourse. For instance, a poet like Ogden Nash introduces false or weakened rhymes and nonsense words into poems seemingly committed to a conventional language and rhyme scheme with decided comic effect.

> A girl who is bespectacled
> She may not get her nectacled
> But safety pins and basinets
> Await the girl who fascinets.[7]

Or again nonsense ideas and words may be used in a poem apparently committed to the categories of the everyday world, as in Edward Lear's *Nonsense Songs.*

> The lands where the jumblies live
> Their heads are green and their hands are blue
> And they went to sea in a sieve.

Countless material fallacies (e.g. equivocation or ambiguity) are laughable for the same reason (as in the orator's opening statement, "Aristotle said that all men are rational. Nothing was said about women."). The same comic result may be achieved by introducing some object deviant from common sense into a common sense world, e.g. an imp, or as in a late Broadway play, an hallucinatory man-sized rabbit. Or laughable incongruities may be obtained by viewing the same objects from two or more opposing standpoints at the same time with a consequent collision of categories. For instance, Carl Sandburg ("The People, Yes") tells yarns

> Of a skyscraper so tall they had to put hinges
> On the two top stories so as to let the moon go by.

---

[7] "Lines Written to Console Ladies Distressed by the Lines 'Men seldom make passes at girls who wear glasses,'" *The Face is Familiar* (Garden City Publishing Co., 1941), p. 134. (Quoted by permission of Little, Brown & Co.)

Here the discrepancy between the distances involved in astronomy and those involved in human architecture constitutes the absurdity. Indeed, much of the stock in trade of theatrical and literary drollery is to be found in contradictions between different universes of discourse employed in narration; as in the incompatibilities between *seems* and *is*, polite conventions and raw human nature, men's thoughts and behavior, the customs of different societies, or between the postulates of different worlds, as in the talking animals of *Alice in Wonderland*, Lear, Disney, Thurber, and others who have scrambled the rules of the human scene hilariously with those of the animal kingdom.

(2) There is another class of comic incongruities which arise not from conflicts due to the peculiarities of alternative fields but from a contradiction between the content of a thought and its form in an unrestricted sense as involving the basic logic common to all worlds. Such contradictions differ from the contrarieties arising within the subject matter of optionally chosen fields in that the content, by conflicting with the most general principles, is seen to be self-refuting on formal logical grounds. As instances, we may cite the man on the gallows whose last words were "This will certainly be a lesson to me," or Sandburg's yarn of "the man so tall he had to climb a ladder to shave himself," or of the man who looked into the window to see if he was home, or of the one who, in answer to the question whether he was married or unmarried replied, "Neither, I'm just experimenting." Again, there is Mark Twain's famous account of his interview with the cub reporter, to whom he disclosed that he was born one of identical twins known apart only by pink and blue ribbons, the story culminating in the statement, "We were twins, defunct and I. One of us was drowned in the bathtub. That was I." In such jokes the contradiction between the content of thought and the basic logic turns on a *reductio ad absurdum* or reaffirmation in denial which is self-refuting.

To repeat, if experience is not to dissipate into a fog without distinctive meanings, reason must remain reason and values values. Despite allowance for the widest choice of stipulations, all universes of discourse must conform to the basic logic of consistency and inference which involves canons of truth and morality: of truth in the requirements of rational probity and systematic harmony; and of morality in the obligation to conform to the assumptions accepted, recitude in keeping one's pledges in practice. Our answer to the question why the comic cannot be totally freed from moral and rational canons is that a completely hodge-podge world would have no discriminable qualities or meanings sufficient to denote the comic. A limit is reached in siphoning off rationality and value from the world, in treating lightly as of no moment the weightiest matters of life, a limit found in the comic with the discovery that certain values like formal truth, the obligation to operational integrity, and a kind of law of compensation are built into the very structure of experience itself.

Let us begin with the relation of the comic to morality. Those who defend the complete freedom of art and expression maintain that the jokesmith, the comedian, the literary humorist must not only have unrestricted liberty in his choice of subject matter (which may include unlimited immorality, crime, madness, neuroses, and pessimism) but also may treat it as he pleases—with a heart of stone, if his mood inclines him, and complete scorn of moral standards. To this, the reply already given by a rationalist is that jests will have no point, the comic will not be comic, unless respect for rational man and the rules of rationality are included. These remain supreme even when the comic incongruity turns on the tacit acceptance of conflicting codes and the ensuing clash of their postulates. To be sure, a slight deviation from the rules (if not serious enough to threaten the meaning of the game) may constitute a comic incongruity. But at the same time it constitutes a moral fault. For any inconsistency in thought is

cheating, a breach of obligation in not keeping the conventions of the code. The very meaning of the game requires in-
variance, regularity in the handling of cases, dealing with
persons and events *one as another*, admitting no favorites or
exceptions. (Even if inconsistent treatment should be the
rule agreed on, it must be consistently applied if the scheme
is to have significance on its own terms.) Because reason is
universal and thinking operates through the universal, the
comic cannot be freed from moral categories. In comic thinking as in other thinking, the operator like the operand, the
author no less than his characters, must be subject to the
same basic rules. Since self-reference is involved in universal
reference,[8] if total amoralism be the postulate of the comic
the same irresponsible, unscrupulous treatment meted out to
the puppets may be allotted to the puppeteer. There is the
rub. If uniformity implies that in destroying respect for the
subject matter, respect is also destroyed for its proponent,
the game becomes suicidal, self-refuting. Once the ridiculer
finds himself subject to the same ridicule he heaps on those
he makes ridiculous, and finds others dealing him the same
unbounded contempt he dealt them, he cries no play and
quits the game.

Because the brackets of abstraction placed around the field
of the comic will not stay bracketed, but the same logic inevitably extends from object to subject, from make-believe to
first person actual, a rationalist must deny the independence

---

[8] To those who deny this, and who hold that statements about the
fields of logic and morals are not themselves logical and moral statements (by taking refuge in so-called metalanguage of a "higher order"),
it may be replied that, if this were so, such statements would lose their
force and exhaustiveness and no longer mean what they purport to mean.
The attempt to claim that the totality one thinks about and refers to in
language is never the genuinely inclusive totality of the field involves
contradiction, since at the least one must think about and designate this
unrestricted totality in order to reach the positivist's conclusion that it is
undesignatable linguistically. (Cf. Marie C. Swabey, *Logic and Nature,*
2nd ed. New York University Press, 1955, p. 65.)

of the comic from morals and protest preoccuptaion with battle, murder, and sudden death in the media of light entertainment, in channels professedly meant to convey jollity and good humor. There is, for example, the modern fashion of the weird and the gruesome in magazines devoted to jesting and the so-called "horror comics," where the ruthless, inconsequential treatment of violence may be an index of moral and aesthetic decay. Such things occur in all manner of instances from the current (supposedly jocose) sally "Drop dead!" to popular cartoons like that representing the ghoulish owners of a mansion waiting in fiendish glee upon the roof to drop boiling oil and boulders upon the Christmas carolers before their door. Admittedly, many violations of the moral code, hypocrisies, and stupidities, if not involving vital threats to human values and existence, yield comic incongruity; but in the case of heartless brutality and widespread destruction, the logic of such a world becomes self-refuting, since it would destroy respect for life, character, and codes altogether. A rationalist's objection to amoral jesting is that it is finally self-stultifying. The principles of amoralism which such a jester blithely applies to others and to an imaginary world in his script, drawings, or game of wit ultimately return to his own world and himself. In the long run the logic of a realm in which vice is treated like virtue, inhumanity like humanity, the fiendish like the friendly, the decent like the depraved must finally, by evading all responsibility to law and order, drown itself in a chaos of nonsense.

But a large share of the generally recognized comic, it may be said in reply, has to do with a world of fancy in which the ordinary rules of life do not hold. Not only do animals, and even chairs, stones, and pokers talk and act like human beings, but characters pass through locked doors and even keyholes; they sustain mortal blows and eat deadly concoctions without apparent injury. Everywhere the impossible takes the place of the possible. Once the operative canons of our world be changed, it may be said, why may not such fates as boiling in oil, drawing and quartering, impaling on spears, hammering to pulp, shredding in machinery, and tortures of all sorts be meted out as comic fare to unpopular characters. Even in Edward Lear, Lewis Carroll, and so-called nonsense humor, a certain anaesthesia of the heart is clearly present. Hearing the shrill cry of the queen "Off with her head!" or gazing at the chill, gorgonlike visages of various eggheads and other droll characters in the illustrations of Tenniel and Lear, the spectator has a sense of his veins turning to ice water. Even the attempt, as was said earlier, to elude all responsibility by equating the comic with sheer nonsense or foolishness cannot suffice. In the very attempt to kick over the table, to deny all rules, the operator is driven back at least upon the rule that there shall be no rules, that the meaningless shall appear in a frame of boundary meanings, that the stipulations he applies to others apply to himself; that instead of anything following anything indifferently, there shall be a method in the madness, a consistency in its inconsistency, an intelligible logic that makes comic nonsense distinct from nonsense pure and simple.

The latent rationality and morality at the base of the comic, we may conclude, is something like that involved in gambling. In either case, rigid suppression destroys free reflection, action, and choice. Yet where there is no control of gambling (and no rational norms of the comic), where notions of the improbable receive unlimited encouragement from society in the form of lotteries and games of chance, the emotional powers of imagination get out of hand, leading to senseless extravagance in thought and behavior. The mind, through dwelling upon the potentiality of certain rare frequencies, comes to confuse the unlikely with the likely, to take what is not impossible as not merely possible but probable, to believe that since the lightning must strike somewhere it will strike here. In short, recklessness and heedlessness lead

it to disregard consideration of the enormous number of alternative chances at stake, as well as their weight in the premises,
and to focus on some particular outcome. Believers in luck or
the goddess Fortuna tend to deny that the preponderance of
evidence should govern conclusions and balance accounts
between grounds and consequents, holding instead to their
wishful hope of a rare chance in which the idle reap, the
thoughtless thrive, and fools sit in the seats of wise men. Instead of the logic of measure for measure, an evened score
between evidence and outcome, desert and reward, they hold
that absurdities and improbabilities rule the world. Nor is it
difficult to see how, in a universe so conceived, moral principles decline, since in a world in which logic has lost its supremacy, things are not repaid in kind, those worth least may
properly be exalted; reciprocity and equivalence being jetti-
soned as normative principles and the idea discarded of a
universe in which "with what measure you mete it shall be
measured to you again" and of a way of life in which one
should do as he would be done by.

CHAPTER 3

The Comic in the Wider and the Narrower Sense

OFTEN we use the term comic as referring simply to a quality of nature or art that provokes merriment or laughter. Indeed, this appears to be the loosest, perhaps the commonest, use of the term. Yet laughter, we have seen, is produced by many different causes and the mere power to elicit jollity accompanied by a respiratory spasm is hardly sufficient to distinguish the comic. Without attempting to deny that these are generally ingredients of comic experience, one must nevertheless allow the frequent expression of gaiety without any perception of the ludicrous. Nor does the admission of sportiveness or playful amusement suffice to repair the omission. To be truly comical a state of affairs must be seen to be funny, droll, exciting some ludicrous reflection. Again, pleasure or hedonic satisfaction may admittedly accompany all manner of experiences: eating, drinking, love-making, listening to music, and what not; yet even though such feelings may be granted as practically invariable attendants of comic perception, they are not what makes it essentially what it is. The same may be said of elements like release from tension, vital zest or high spirits so prevalent in its enjoyment; all of these being especially notable in the skylarking of children and young animals, yet without, so far as one can see, involving discrimination on their part of the distinctively ludicrous. Attempts to find the essence of the comic in a malicious relish or sense of superiority to others fall under the same criticism.

But since the comic appears to be the basic, generic category covering the various forms of the ludicrous, we must try to delineate its nature more exactly. As soon as we proceed beyond the loose usage of everyday speech in which the comic is spoken of as whatever is mirth-provoking and turn to that of more technical students of the subject, we find the meaning narrowed by the addition of an intellectual predicate. "The test of true comedy," says Meredith, "is that it shall awaken thoughtful laughter";[1] while similarly, according to Bergson, the comic, although indefinable, involves a play with ideas and the excitation of intelligence. Again, Freud describes the pleasure of the comic as arising from our economy of expenditure in thought in trying to understand another person. In comparing the psychic processes of another with our own, if we find that he employs more muscular exertion to accomplish the same mental task, we laugh and say that he should use his head to save his heels, or something of that sort. If, on the other hand, he appears to exert more mental effort to accomplish the same physical task in contrast to ourselves, we likewise laugh expending our surplus energy in comic pleasure.

In this more specific sense, then, the term comic is used, it appears, to designate the mirth-provoking that has some intellectual appeal—although when we go beyond this individual differences of usage may enter into its description. Thus, for Bergson, the comic enlists our intelligence pure and simple but is incompatible with emotion, for instance, is incompatible with pity, sympathy, fear; whereas for Freud in the act of comparison that discloses the comic, feeling of some sort is plainly involved. But more of this later. Here the point worthy of notice is that when the term comic is used in this more limited sense as involving an appeal to intelligence, it readily comes into contrast with humor and other forms of the ludi-

---

[1] George Meredith, "An Essay on Comedy," in *Comedy,* ed. Wylie Sypher (Garden City, N. Y., Doubleday & Co., 1956), p. 47.

crous. For the comic in this second sense is often employed
not simply as a genus but as a species coordinate with other
species of the ludicrous. Thus Meredith says, for instance,
that Molière's Alceste, Tartuffe, Célimène, and Philaminte
are purely *comic* characters but have no *humor* in them;[2]
while on the reverse side, recognizing that in *humor* feeling is
strong, he contrasts both *irony* as "the humor of satire" and
satire as the expression of moral passion, with the intellectual-
ism of the *comic*. In the same way, *wit*, as involving still more
highly charged cerebration, is distinguished by many writers
from the *comic*.

But before turning to the different species of the ludicrous
let us take note of a final generic designation of the comic in
which analysis of its import has been pushed furthest in pre-
cision and accuracy. This usage of the term as the *summum
genus* of the field covers in its meaning all such subsidiary
forms as wit, irony, satire, humor, and the comic in its narrower sense as a coordinate, contrasting species. In our opinion, as
suggested earlier, the most adequate generic definition of the
comic is: the presence of an incongruity, contradiction, or
absurdity that is humanly relevant without being oppressive-
ly grave or momentous. It is in this strictest sense that we use
the word as a synonym for the ludicrous as our most inclusive
category.

Usually in ordinary discourse the distinction between the
comic as such and the appreciation of the comic is not made
explicit, and for the most part we shall follow this practice.
However, in the preceding paragraph an implicit difference is
allowed for between the comic as referent and the experience
of it as limited to the sphere of human relevance and what
does not threaten the annihilation of values and existence. In
our view, comic perception is rooted in intellectual insight,
with conative feeling as an intermediary, and an ensuing tend-

---

[2] Meredith, p. 43.

ency to laughter. Thus, Mark Twain's saying that reports of
his death had been greatly exaggerated is a joke precisely
because it involves an objective contradiction. What makes it
a jest is that a man, no matter how old he may be, cannot be
both dead and not-dead at once, but must be one or the other,
there being no degrees in the matter. Furthermore a lifeless
man is speechless, hence he cannot comment on reports of his
own death. Without penetration of the absurdity as false and
consequent revelation of the truth as non-contradictory, there
can be no comic relish of the speech. If you do not see the
contradiction and that it must be rejected in favor of non-
contradiction but just laugh without knowing why, it fails
to be comic laughter. The pleasure arising from the insight
into the rout of unreason by reason, as well as the organic
impulse to laughter, both follow as effects. In fact, the extent
to which you laugh and have a marked feeling of pleasure
differs with different individuals.

To repeat, relish of the ludicrous is more than an imaginative, affective attitude of a subject in response to a representation. Its determining ground is logical and objective, only
secondarily involving taste and feeling. When we say, for instance, that the naïveté of children is comic, we do not mean
simply that their behavior in adult society appears to us by
contrast laughable. The meaning is rather that comicality is
genuinely inherent in their actions, as something on which
everyone capable of discrimination of the ingenuous from the
disingenuous, the artless from the artful, the unsophisticated
from the sophisticated, would agree. Any claim that appreciation of the ludicrous contains no significant thought and imports nothing as to the world outside is, in our view, quite
misleading.

But we also employ the term comic in a specialized sense
as the designation of a subclass distinguished from other species
of the genus. In fact, the present chapter will be mainly concerned with an attempt to elucidate the peculiarities that

differentiate the comic as a species from coordinate forms like wit and humor. While it takes the presence of incongruity in a state of affairs to determine what is comic generically, elements in the response (such as degree of mental activity, of emotionality, or dependence on symbolic expression) distinguish different varieties of the comic. Although at their core distinct and exclusive, it cannot be denied that these coordinate species frequently overlap and combine. For instance, there may be a witty satire, yet such a composition in so far as it is satirical is satire and in so far as it is witty is wit. Although in a witty satire we should judge the satire predominant, it is equally possible to have a work of satirical wit. Again characters may be both comical and humorous or like Alceste be one without the other.

In considering the comic as a specific type of the ludicrous on the level with wit, humor, irony, and satire, it is necessary to labor certain distinctions at the outset. To begin with, even though all terms descriptive of the ludicrous presuppose an objective incongruity, there is a difference of meaning among them as to their imputed relation to experience and symbolic expression. For instance, we customarily assume that comic or humorous objects may be *discovered*, and that consequently such comic or humorous states of affairs are genuinely *there* prior to, and independently of, their actual appreciation in experience. At the same time, this is not to deny that in addition to those discovered humorous and comical objects are constantly being *created* as human artifacts or linguistic combinations. But over against them there are other varieties of the ludicrous which in their essence require actualization in some form of linguistic or symbolic expression. Wit and satire are examples. Not only would they seem to have their chief locus in their overt expression (thus wit must be embodied in witticisms, satire in the satiric composition), but they would also seem to demand as part of their essence *communication*. That is to say, satire and wit appear in their natures to require a "triad of interpretation" involving a community of three persons: first, the wit or satirist himself; second, the butt of his jest; and last, an onlooker or detached spectator to whom appeal is made to render judgment upon it.

While satire and wit in adjectival form are occasionally ascribed to persons as traits, their primary reference is affixed to forms of expression, usually verbal but sometimes pictorial, as in caricature. Humor and the comic, on the other hand, as noun or adjective may be applied to anything (object, situation, even character) that appeals to our sense of the ludicrous in a certain way, quite distinct from any requirement of its verbal embodiment or other symbolic representation. While wit and satire are chiefly descriptive of modes of linguistic expression implying *mental ingenuity and art*, the terms comic and humorous are often used to refer directly to properties *in nature*, and not merely to human artifacts. Thus humorous situations and the comical behavior of animals are familiar to us all. That the comical and the humorous also play an enormous part in the arts cannot be questioned, though how far their presence extends to arts not employing verbal utterance (as the dance, dumb show or pantomime) is another matter. If they are present at all in the arts of music, painting, sculpture, and architecture, their role is a very minor one.

Although it is agreed that the comic is possessed of some intellectual appeal, as compared with wit its intellectuality is limited. In contrast, wit requires at once mental sharpness, intellectual abridgment, and linguistic embodiment. Whether the comic essentially appeals to emotion is a question usually answered in the affirmative—with at least one exception. Bergson holds that it induces anaesthesia of the heart so that only that side of human personality devoid of appeal to feeling and sensibility is capable of becoming comic. However, the general opinion appears to be that pleasure is a feature of the experience of the comic, while upon occasion pity and love as well as a modicum of pride or disdain may be ingredients of it. Nevertheless enjoyment of the comic is commonly regarded as definitely less emotional than humor, in which feeling plays a large, sometimes predominant, part. A certain moderation characterizes the comic both mentally and emotionally, but with the intellectual factor more pronounced. Chortles, hilarity, unbridled explosions of glee are more likely to be indices of humor. Satire also bespeaks a stronger emotional element than the comic, although much mental ingenuity may be employed to mask its hostile feeling.

The comic, it is allowed, deals primarily with man and human personality. Certainly the greatest amount of its appreciative attention is expended upon the actions of our own species together with the circumstances involving them. Nevertheless it seems to be going too far to say that there is nothing comic except man. Granted that man and his adventures are the main butt of jests, even the extreme humanist in regard to the comic admits that laughter may attach to impersonal situation, mere movements, or to an independent phrase. This appears enough to decide the matter. It is not necessary to consider how perception of the comic comes about, whether Freud's suggestion is correct that it originated in the comparison of another with myself, thence extending to the behavior and characters of many people, thence to the personification of animals and inanimate things, and finally to situations.[3]

The point to be made is that, while owing to what may be called the psychocentric predicament, it is impossible to consider the comic without employing the human mind, nevertheless its objects need not always be taken anthropomorphically. To us it appears false to say that we construe non-human events—such as the puncturing of a balloon, the bobbing of apples in a barrel under a flowing water tap, or the juxtaposition of an elephant and a mouse—as comical merely because

---

[3] Sigmund Freud, *Wit and Its Relation to the Unconscious,* trans. A. A. Brill (New York, Moffat, Yard & Co., 1916), pp. 302–03.

they provide human analogues or are inseparable from a human framework. The elephant and the mouse may appear funny by contrast as exhibiting the inconceivable variety of forms possible in existence. The spectacle of a giraffe and a spider monkey side by side may excite comic laughter not simply because of their extreme opposition in size and shape but through suggesting by their facial expressions their possession of contrary psychic characters or incongruous types of individuality. That they seem to us to possess psyches of their own does not necessarily imply that we regard them as people or construe them in human categories. Recognition of organizations of psychic experience in other species than man represents an objective discovery or encounter rather than a mere projection of the human ego. (However, exception may be made to the antics of animals in comic strips, since the human analogue often dominates in these creations.) As for the punctured balloon and the bobbing apples, the comic suggestion here depends upon perception of an incongruous analogy between the animate and inanimate.

That the comic as a specific term has reference to the general mind of society, to the aggregate of men in interaction, rather than to distinctive individuals is widely recognized. Whereas in contrast wit is contributed by persons of unusual powers, perception of the comic has its source in everyday men and the group, and is directed to them collectively in its appraisals. Its appeal, while not to dullards or fools, is to that average mentality of men in conjunction known as *common sense*, to obvious perceptions of the obvious in everyday sanity, something quite distinct from meditative sagacity, singular wit, or elaborate intellection. The comic in the narrow sense is discerned or created by the mundane wisdom of the herd in the market place. Presupposed in it is a certain rough realism, a knowledge of the uses and wonts of society that does not expect too much of mankind. Its concern is for the most part with the claims of the world upon the individual and its in-

fluence upon men's behavior rather than with human nature
in itself. Conventions and their effect upon men living together
in accentuating their likeness and repressing their separatist
tendencies is a favorite theme. Because those with a sense for
the comic see not so much with their own eyes as with those
of the group, they tend to deal with stock figures, particularly
with vexatious types (like the drunkard, the boor, or the im-
postor) who scotch accepted rules and threaten the welfare
of society. Simplified generalities are much easier to grasp and
"rib" than individuals in their rich complexity. That stereotypes dominate rural or street-corner jesting, rough-and-ready
horseplay, vaudeville, and lower forms of the comic may be
admitted without prejudice to our view that appreciation of
the variety of human nature appears at its higher levels.

But even if it be granted that the comic tends to reflect the
categories of the group mind, this is a very different thing
from maintaining that its actual operation is primarily as an
instrument of collective control, of practical discipline in the
interests of society. Yet certain evolutionary thinkers treat
comic perception as a critical overseer that obliges members
of a group through chiding and correction to conform to its
code of behavior. Being bent upon self-preservation, it is held,
society is hostile toward those who neglect its rules, greeting
with caustic laughter those who infringe upon them. Whenever through absent-mindedness or intent an individual dis-
regards the accepted modes of speech, dress, or behavior of
his community, he becomes, it is said, comical in its eyes—even
though, as in the case of men like Socrates, Voltaire, Dr.
Johnson, Byron, or William Blake, he may be learned, intelligent, possesseed of rare imagination or other talents. If, indeed, this be the predominant spirit of the comic, its effect
on men must be to encourage conformity, keeping one's ear
to the ground, adopting a protective coloring, and in general
avoiding independent thinking or such original enterprises as
put one out of line with the masses. From this standpoint,

with evolutionary advance such eccentric behavior with its threat to social cohesion would diminish, while comic laughter as expressing the need for correction would tend to disappear.

But, contrary to this view, there are other defenders of the comic who find in the prevalence of comic perception a chief mark of civilization and of society's advance. Comic insight, they hold, as expressing the common sense of the group, operates to refine men's characters through encouraging accommodation, politeness, consideration of others, and self-control. It makes for a spirit of fellowship, for uniting and pulling together, for discretion and good manners in social dealings. Communities with a strong sense of the comic show a lively give-and-take with all classes, a willingness to converse freely with women and servants, a social democracy which esteems sagacity from any quarter. Because it respects the sanity of public opinion (and not merely physical force), it is disposed to hearken to its voice from whatever source instead of always bowing to vested authority. A constantly widening scope in the appreciation of the comic and its more frequent incitement seem to mark the advance of civilization. For with each new invention in art, technology, or science, or changes in the fashions of daily life, fresh incongruities emerge and are called to human attention. In the twentieth century, for instance, with the development of gas, electric, and atomic power, a new world of jests has arisen in connection with automobiles, jet planes, electronic computers, Martians, flying saucers, Sputniks, and the age of space. Wherever striking originality declares itself successfully, society has to give ground and modify its rules. Instead of the innovator with his innovation being out of step, it may well be the group that is lagging and in need of correction. In such cases, the creators of novelties incongruous with the old, far from being greeted with suppressive guffaws, may be applauded with encouraging laughter as the promise of good things to come. Indeed, only by departing from the stereotypes of the past can we hope to achieve a better world in the future. Here relish of the comic, instead of serving merely as a negative discipline of the group, may function to give positive aid to general improvement.

This is not, of course, to deny the frequent employment of laughter as a social discipline, something already familiar to the ancient Greeks. In the *Philebus*, Plato discusses the relationship between the absence of self-knowledge and the comic.[4] The person who is ridiculous is he who is farthest from fulfilling the Delphic inscription "Know thyself." Such a one is ignorant of his own shortcomings, of his lack of personal attractiveness, of mental ability or of worldly goods, and is devoured by a lying conceit of himself which appears incongruous to others. There is an admixture of pleasure and displeasure in our perception of his folly, pleasure in our own shrewd detection of the true state of affairs and displeasure at the spectacle of ignorance and its consequent evils in another. While in his pretentious behavior the comic character seems often quite unaware of his own true nature, it is probably going too far to say, as do some moderns, that we are never ridiculous except in some point that remains hidden from our own consciousness, since the consequence would be that we could never see the comic in ourselves but only observe it in others. And such an assumption leads further to the view that, since we have first-hand acquaintance only with the ego, others' experience being impenetrable, the comic remains always on the surface, external, skin deep, never concerned with the truly individual.

This is not, however, always so. Nor is it true to say that once we become aware of what is laughed at in us by the world, we will set out to mend our ways, remove our faults, and in so doing cease to be comic. For often the contradictions or distortions inhere in our natures beyond redemption, irremovable—as with the medieval jester who was a dwarf, a

---

[4] *Philebus*, 47–50.

hunchback, or a fool, yet who knew and emphasized his deficiencies for professional purposes in his antics. It is not always the case that to know oneself as comic is to cease to be so. The professional simpleton may laugh at his assumed ignorance or distorted physiognomy. Rosalind may laugh at her dreamlike behavior in love, Sir Toby at his weakness for sponging and drink, Touchstone at his own jests, yet not lack the shrewdness to appreciate his own and the world's folly.

There is, indeed, a subtle difference between the view that regards the comic spirit as directed by free intelligence seeking truth and that which construes it as primarily guided by the interests of the group bent on survival. For the first, the comic spirit is humane, disinterested, expressive of common sense; whereas, for the second, it is practical, partial, inhumane upon occasion through concern for social solidarity. "We laugh," says Bergson, "every time a person gives us the impression of being a thing."[5] That is, the comic spirit, in his view, being directed above all to the continuance of human existence, excoriates with laughter every triumph of matter over consciousness and life. Thus the man who appears absent-minded, rigid, inelastic like an automaton suggests a dead man; he is laughed at as obliquely threatening the extinction of the species and the victory of inanimate mechanism. So it is that the man who is dull, awkward, says and does the wrong thing in company, who behaves like a jumping jack or wooden indian, is scored off with group hilarity. In being *perceived as a thing*, the comic character is trivialized, belittled, degraded, as having lost his *freedom as a person*. Instead of being directed by his own choice and mental purpose, he seems to be guided by a mere mechanism of associated ideas or manipulated by a physical clockwork of gears, wires, and springs.

With particular reference to clowns, buffoons, to the patter and gestures of stock funny men in the theater, this appears

---

[5] Henri Bergson, "Laughter," in *Comedy,* ed. Sypher, p. 97.

a brilliant suggestion. Yet while the mechanization of life undoubtedly covers many instances of the comic, there is more to the comic, we insist, than is covered by this theory. When we deal with the comic in character, for instance, the simple formula of the living behaving like the lifeless, the conscious like the unconscious, is far from being everywhere relevant to the field. A character like Falstaff is not mechanical in his behavior or mental processes; nor is Tom Sawyer, the "Duke," or Huckleberry Finn. Certainly the sly villians, gamblers, and con men of O. Henry show no lack of suppleness, nimbleness, or want of awareness of themselves or of life. Far from being dull, inert, repetitious stereotypes, these gentle grafters are alert, unpredictable, swift as lightning. What makes us laugh at them is their not letting their right hand know what their left hand doeth, the disparity between their lofty speeches and low behavior, their cockeyed views of the world.

In reply to the incongruity theory, the comic mechanists, as we may call them, contend that while some contradictions are comic they are not so in general. Laughable incongruities, they hold, are to be found only in characters that suggest an automaton: the sleepwalker absorbed in his dream, the predictable man of fixed ideas, robots who see what they want to see but fail to accommodate themselves to reality. Don Quixote, with his persistent inversion of common sense, seeing windmills as giants, furnishes to them the general type of comic absurdity. Thus the mechanist, wittingly or unwittingly, takes refuge in two "logics," the one the sound reasoning of waking reality and the other the counterfeit logic of dreams in which consistent meaning and rules fade away and ideas take on haphazard combinations. Actually, however, there is but one basic logic, sovereign over sleeping and waking. In consequence, we insist, incongruities, sophisms, rational mistakes, whether made by somnambulists or wide-awake thinkers, whether in the realm of illusion or of business at midday, are alike productive of comic laughter.

Admittedly as the role of machines expands in modern life, we come to live more and more through mechanisms. Yet the threat of automation that engulfs man hardly renders him more comical. On the contrary, it may well be urged that, judging by our current science fiction, the flood of supermen and supermice, and the mass productions of Disneyland, the comic spirit is almost dead. A picture in the *New Yorker* showing the interior of a giant plant in which steel mechanical men are manufacturing steel mechanical men, while in a corner one effete human says to another, "Sometimes I wonder where it will all end," perhaps best sums up the matter.

What started as analogy in many fields—man as like a machine—now threatens to be taken for identity. Among many casualties due to this faulty hypothesis, the comic is only one. In the view of cybernetics and other recent sciences, man himself is a machine. Human reflexes, the mechanical association of ideas, even rational substitutions and subsumptions are held to be reproducible by the blind clockwork of physical contraptions. The "mechanical brain," one of the great inventions of the age, can simulate, it is said, the self-regulatory processes of logical thinking. But, if true, is this indeed a supremely laughing matter? Can we laugh any longer (except in the hollowest way) at men whose mental operations turn out to be no more than the automatic action of self-made electronic computers? Surely in a world in which *homo sapiens* becomes a Frankenstein, a monstrous robot, we face the death of spirit, including the comic spirit.

Escape from this impasse, we insist, is possible only by repudiating man's subjection to the machine analogy and recognizing the roots of the comic in the autonomy of reason. For reason alone is able to deal with the world of logical issues behind and beyond the world of electric impulses, punch cards, magnetic tape, and lightning calculators. Questions of congruity and incongruity, as well as comic absurdity, depend on logical insight of a conscious subject into relations of con-

cepts, something presupposed by, but not included in, the
world of factual objects and machinery. In brief, the inventions
of physical science can never assess the logical laws upon which
the ludicrous turns, for the reason that science in attempting to
test such laws already grants their validity.

As suggested, the comic may be found everywhere, not only
in characters, actions, and situations but in or apart from
words. Here it differs from the predominant verbalism of wit
and satire, as well as from humor which occurs mainly in
action and character. Comic vision is direct, not requiring
an intermediary symbolism for its interpretation by others.
Thus I may divert myself at the beach by noting comic figures
among the bathers, the tall and short, the fat and lean; but
to ridicule them I must somehow simulate for another's benefit their shapes and gaits. This latter demands an activity
on my part of symbolic representation. Such a take-off may
be by means of my actual imitative behavior, by my drawing
a sketch, or by clever verbal description. Mockery makes
fun of its object through analogy and distortion, while the
laughable effect adheres primarily to the depiction, and only
secondarily to the original. Thus the fat man appears as a
balloon, the lean one as a stork in the caricature, though the
audience which laughs might hardly see for themselves these
likenesses in the objects.

Thus comic vision expresses fresh aperçus into the contradictions of the world, without necessarily involving (as in
satire, burlesque, or parody) a take-off fabricated through analogy and exaggeration. For all these latter forms suggest copies,
aping or mimicry at one remove from the original source
of the ludicrous and involving a triad of interpretation. All
indicate treatment (usually in the form of literary, dramatic,
or pictorial composition) of something or somebody by somebody for somebody to excite contemptuous laughter.

By contrast the comic is in large part free of the impulse
to imitate and degrade and does not require an echo. Nor does

it depend essentially on distorted reproduction. Still, in so far as the comic spirit fabricates its objects, exaggeration is usually brought into play. Overstatement, intensification, or depiction in excess of the facts, while not by and in itself funny, provides a favorite device for revealing the comic. In cartoons, for instance, overemphasis upon some idiosyncrasy in the appearance of a political leader, a jutting nose, jaw, or odd mustache, along with de-emphasis on other features, is a trick that often seems not merely derisive but comic. The comic effect inheres, however, not in the mere distortion (one hardly laughs at the distortions of El Greco or William Blake) but in the contradiction suggested between *what is* and *what isn't*; we laugh at the incongruous aperçu of what is at once true of the man's essence and false to his factuality.

Through the use of radio, television, motion pictures, and other media, the so-called amusement industries today employ exaggeration (and its inverse, diminution or understatement) in countless ways. The distorting mirror with its vertical and horizontal deformations, the camera with its "candid" shots catching the subject off balance or from odd angles, the visual and sound tracks that increase or diminish the speed, tempo, volume, or dimensions of phenomena all contribute to the art of exaggeration. What is often forgotten is that such exaggeration, though it may open the door to a mythical, offbeat world, is a means to the comic rather than in itself comic. Such oversight is especially common today when presentation by mechanical means of spectacles deviant from the mode, involving appearances and velocities out of line with everyday life, provides so much mass entertainment. As the fat man and the tall, the laggard and the speed demon are laughed at in daily life, so midgets and giants, supermen and brownies are laughed at in the show world of "comic" illusion. Brobding-agians, Lilliputians, and their kin have behind them a long tradition, and today in cartoons and "comic books" they continue as lively as ever.

Undoubtedly the doings in these fantastic realms are often worthy of laughter. But the comic, it should be remembered, inheres in pertinent incongruities, not in mere distortions and dissimilarities. What tends to be overlooked is that the portrayal of a mere wonderland of sensory exaggeration and fantastic dimensions, unless clearly brought into conflict with rational canons, cannot claim to be funny. A mere fairy-tale world of unfettered imagination, by being at variance with the expectations of ordinary perception, may of course serve as release from the tedium of everyday life. Admittedly, in the movie cartoon and the "comic book" men find momentary escape from the tensions and pressures of the contemporary scene; their diminutive folk, their creatures of forest and farm are often winningly mischievous. In them the puppeteer and ventriloquist of an earlier age find successors—though perhaps without the same freshness and individuality.

For who can deny that these productions, despite their frequent artistry and skill, are for the most part the work of draughtsmen and scientific mechanisms. This presence of the machine is shown not only in the relentless use of stereotypes and stock plots that have caught the popular taste but in the tendency to prodigality and too much of everything. Cheap, sensational, exciting, without the force of individuality or freshness, too many brands of "canned funnies" flood the market. The fact is that such dream worlds tend to stupefy the mind rather than to alert it to absurdities. Mere sensory exaggeration and roving fancy without a show of bedlam through pointed inconsistencies fail to arouse the perception of drollery. Only by being awakened to contradictions and their need of correction does the audience achieve true comic enjoyment.

Unlike satire, the spirit of the comic is untroubled, expressive of an easy frame of mind. Nor does it leave a disagreeable sting or bitter aftertaste, as is sometimes held. At the same time, there is a trace of truth in the saying that the comic tends to deprive the object of laughter of dignity while the humorous reinstates it. For humor with its stronger sympathy and wider view can reveal the treasures of the humble, the claims of the least of God's creatures. In any case, the comic is no respecter of persons, unabashedly twitting those in high places, though not so frequently perhaps as inferiors or the weaker members of society. Indeed, sometimes such free and easy treatment serves to disclose worth in unexpected quarters, to dispel mists of class and distance in a sudden warmth of democratic intimacy. In short, there is some reason to hope that through comic laughter men may improve in humanity and refinement.

But because it appeals to the common sense of the average mind the comic temper remains conservative. Even with radicals like Bernard Shaw it is the middle-of-the-road comic characters that have the sound, final word as against the witty social innovators with their sharply critical views. Yet as against the extremes of wit and satire the comic process, it is sometimes said, cannot withstand close scrutiny or the passage of time but evaporates like foam in our hands. Still against this it must be protested that characters like Eliza Doolittle's father and Aristophanes' sausage seller retain their comic vitality long after cleverer men have been forgotten. So long as the shrewd mundanity of common sense remains, its penetration of windy pretenses still seems laughable. Nevertheless a certain measure of justice must be granted to the contention. Certain comic types cease upon dissection to seem funny, and many comic stories when analysed or repeated lose their laughter-provoking power. This tends to be the case especially where the incongruities are relative to the peculiarities of a particular society, its nuances of speech and manners, or are dependent upon the conventions of the group. But against this the pithy insights of the plain man, the hard horse sense of those who bear the brunt of this world's labors, tend to persist through different periods and localities.

Lastly, but rarely, where the absurdity is formal (turning upon clear relations of self-contradiction) we may encounter the absolute comic, something which remains laughable despite repetition, which resists the destructive power of analysis and continues to be ludicrous wherever and as long as it is understood.

CHAPTER 4

Irony and Satire

PROBABLY the most philosophic species of expression of the comic spirit is irony, something peculiarly Greek in origin and associated with the name of Socrates as well as with that of Plato, to whom we are indebted for his portrayal in the *Dialogues*. Dictionaries describe irony (from the Greek word for dissimulation) as (1) simulated ignorance to confound an opponent or (2) a sort of drollery or light sarcasm which adopts a mode of speech the intended implication of which is the opposite of the literal sense of the words: as when an expression of praise is used when blame is meant, as in the colloquialism "A fine friend you are!" understood as a reproach. Or again as when one says during a heavy downpour, "Nice weather we are having." The distinguishing quality of irony is that the meaning intended is contrary to that seemingly expressed. Like satire it has a serious import beneath its jest but as an agent of correction is usually lighter in tone, with less warmth of reformatory zeal, less censorious, rather a challenge to others' pretensions in order to stimulate their thinking. But the term irony has a wide range of usage covering not merely a certain mode of expression (extending from an occasional remark to a method of inquiry) but also descriptive of the manner of occurrence of certain events (the irony of fate), or again as the mark of individuality of a char-

acter, like Socrates, or of a fundamental view of life, like that
of Anatole France.

Socrates, the father of irony, not only systematized it as a
method for philosophy but embodied it in his person. His dual
character, the paradoxical contrast between the exterior and
what lay within, the homely, barefoot, weather-beaten appearance and the nobility of the inner man, the wise fool, the jester
in deadly earnest, is perhaps a figure too complex for analysis.
Among the analogies describing him the most brilliant is that
of Alcibiades in the *Symposium* comparing Socrates to the toy
statues of the flute-playing Marsyas—a satyr outside yet when
opened containing little figures of the gods within. Elsewhere
he is compared to a long-legged wading bird stalking stiffly
about or to a torpedo fish with protruding eyes which gives
one a shock upon encounter. From these analogies we conclude that Socrates, like a satyr, had an unprepossessing, comic
appearance yet played his flute (or rather discoursed in
words) so enchantingly as to exert a fascination that was a
mixture of attraction and repulsion upon those with whom
he came in contact.[1] Irony as a method was employed by
Socrates for various different purposes: to frustrate and defeat
his opponents; as a means of discovering logical and moral
truth when combined with cross-questioning; as a stimulus to
others' thinking, the so-called maieutic method of bringing
men's thoughts to birth through interrogation; and lastly, as
a way of expressing his sense of his divine mission. For Socrates
wore a mask like the players in a comedy; he was at once
mischievous, roguish, sly, and profoundly in earnest; at once
a man of hard common sense and a kind of mystic; at once
unassuming, unpretentious yet possessed, as he believed, of a
voice within (his *daimon* he called it) indicating the true way
of life for men, which he was divinely appointed to show to
others. For the first two of these purposes Socrates often used

---

[1] J.A.K. Thomson, *Irony* (Harvard University Press, 1937), Ch. XI.

an indirect, dialectical method akin to that of the *reductio ad absurdum* favored by geometers. It was a procedure of cross-questioning often demanding the answer yes or no to a sequence of mutually exclusive and exhaustive alternatives. Step by step the assumptions of Socrates' opponents, which were the opposite of his own, were shown to be absurd (self-contradictory), thereby indirectly establishing his own thesis as alone left standing.

In the *Euthydemus,* one of the most amusing of the Platonic dialogues, Socrates uses this method to refute the Sophists and to show the necessity of presupposing in life and argument the principles of truth, rational knowledge, and the canon of logical contradiction. As professional teachers of wisdom and virtue, two sophists (Euthydemus and Dionysodorus) are preparing to instruct a new pupil in their art before an assembled company. At the outset the sophists inquire of the young man's sponsors whether the youth wishes to be wise. And, on receiving an affirmative answer, they elicit from them the further admission that in his present state the boy is not yet wise. To this, by a lightning change of front, the sophists suddenly retort, "Then you want him *to be what he is not,* and *no longer to be what he is,* which can only mean that you wish him to perish."[2] (Pretty friends you are!) Before long, by such protean tricks and irresponsible shiftiness in the use of language, the sophists have reduced their hearers to complete confusion. Besides maintaining that everything is in flux, and that there is no fixed meaning in thought or words, the sophists go the length of denying the logical principle of contradiction. That is, they deny the ultimate, exhaustive distinction of truth from untruth, reality from unreality, virtue from non-virtue, and knowledge from its opposite. At this point Socrates, unable to stand idly by hearing the law of contradiction denied, enters the argument against the sophists. To him it is plain

---

[2] *Euthydemus* (Jowett trans.), 283d.

that if, as they hold, one position is no better or truer than
another, and if *a* is not really distinct and exclusive of *non-a*,
then the sophists themselves can claim no foundation or special
merit for their own position. Piercing to the heart of the matter,
his words voice a ringing challenge. "If [says Socrates] there
is no such thing as error in deed, word, or thought, then what
. . . do you come hither to teach? And were you not just now
saying that you could teach virtue best of all men? . . . Perhaps I was right after all in saying that words have a sense . . .
If I was not in error, even you will not refute me . . . but if
I did fall into error, then again you are wrong in saying that
there is no error."[3] In exposing the self-stultifying character
of the sophists' position by showing how, through repudiating
truth and integrity, they repudiated their own pretensions as
teachers of virtue and knowledge, Socrates indirectly demonstrated by presupposition in denial and *reductio ad absurdum*
the basic principles of dialectic.

By laying bare the fallacies of the sophists, the verbal
quibbles by which they put words in place of things, Socrates
brings their methods to the bar of ridicule. Indirectly he is
offering a powerful defense of reliance on absolute truth and
noumenal reality against the Protagorean relativism of those
who hold that everything is a matter of opinion. Finally Socrates makes an ironic speech in praise of the sophists, lauding
precisely those qualities which he tacitly condemns, and thus,
while seemingly expressing his "approval" of their "kind and
public-spirited denial of all differences, whether of good and
evil, white or black, or any other," mockingly suggests the
absurd nihilism of the result—"the result . . . that every mouth
is sewn up, not excepting your own."[4] All of this is the height
of irony.

By asking rather than answering questions, and by keeping
his own position in the background, Socrates acted, as he said,

---

[3] *Euthydemus,* 287.
[4] *Euthydemus,* 303d.

as a midwife helping other men to bring their thoughts to birth. In place of merely battling with words, as the sophists did in the law courts, he sought with urbanity to develop a cooperative method for arriving at a common truth. Often his conduct of the argument built up, as it were, a strong electric charge throughout the company, while his questions touched off thoughts like showers of fiery sparks in different speakers. Through invoking participation his method left a more stimulating, lasting impression on his hearers than did that of the mere lecturer or rhetorician. Moreover, his irony, with its partly feigned humility, its understatement, and implied though silent counterstatements, carried a burden of deeper meaning. By suggesting his metaphysical intuitions, Socrates conveyed to many of his audience a sense of ultimate depths, unspoken imports, intimations about the nature of things beyond the snare of verbal quips and quiddities—of something imparted by an inner voice of almost mystical ruminative insight.

To the end of his life we find the same ironic spirit of raillery in a man at once unassuming yet dedicated and conscious of his powers, one of the greatest of teachers yet one who maintained that he knew nothing. In the *Apology,* addressing the jury which condemned him to death, Socrates begins and ends with irony, professing at the outset that the persuasiveness of his accusers has almost made him forget who he is so convincingly have they spoken, though hardly uttering a word of truth, and concluding with a plea to the citizens to punish his sons if ever in time to come they should think that they are something when they are nothing. Most curious of all, the same spirit pervades his words regarding his divine mission, when he claims that he has troubled the Athenians about truth and virtue only to test the credibility of the Delphic oracle in the vain hope of finding a man more sagacious than himself. For the oracle had said that no man was wiser than Socrates, and, since the god could not lie, he was puzzled that among all the poets, politicians, and others whom he had interrogated he alone was conscious of his lack of wisdom and his ignorance.

Unlike many other characters in ancient Greek literature, the Socrates of Plato, albeit ironic in person and method, does not protest the irony of fate. Indeed, he seems quite unaware of it. Unlike Oedipus, he does not complain of his doom. He does not bear witness to a mocking, contradictory outcome of events in his own life or in man's life in general in opposition to human desires, which is what is usually meant by the derisiveness of fate. Far from feeling that evil has befallen him, he finds fulfillment in his lot, well-being, a fitness in the nature of things, which makes him, as he says, sing like the swan in anticipation of death. Having been temperate and modest throughout his life, Socrates has not roused the jealousy of the gods; divine justice has not set nemesis upon his track; nor has he been plagued with visionary dreams of grandeur leading to a mocking sense of futility at the gulf between his longings and his attainments in life.

In the wake of Socrates have followed many skilled in the craft of irony, some in comic, some in tragic irony (though in a sense all irony is comic), some in that of plot or situation, some in "life's little ironies," and some in a universal irony. Passing over the Greeks, men like Horace, Lucian, Erasmus, Rabelais, Cervantes, Anatole France, to mention only a few, have been experts at it. Each practitioner is individual in its use. Each is oblique, circuitous, holding something back, disclosing his meaning by exciting reflection in others; yet none has been as successful as Socrates in conveying significances that reached far beyond the particular occasion or in using logic to uncover truth. Nothing is more important than to realize that, while irony lacks candor and is roundabout, it is never in its nature deceitful or dishonest. Innuendo appeals to partisan feelings by covert suggestion, insinuating prejudices and taking advantage of ingrained dislikes through the laws of association; but irony operates at the level of implication and reflective thought. Fundamentally it is neither misanthropic nor cynical, for the reason that it still trusts in the power of the human mind and the efficacy of truth.

Among philosophers, the one whose treatment of irony is most valuable after that of Socrates is Kierkegaard. To Socrates, Kierkegaard claims indebtedness for his use of the maieutic method and an ironic dialectic involving dissembling speech, doubt, questioning, concealment, assumed ignorance, procedure by an indirect path. "If you wish," he says in the *Journals,* "to be and remain enthusiastic, then draw the silk curtains of facetiousness (irony's), and so hide your enthusiasm."[5] In a serious age he asks nothing better than to be known as the only one who is not serious. And in an age which has sought to benefit mankind by making life easier by the invention of railways, steamships, telegraphs, and intellectual systems, he conceives it, on the contrary, as his duty to make things harder by providing people with the stimulation of difficulties. Hence his adoption of an antithetical dialectic as the best spur to spiritual advance. In this connection irony is invoked by him not only as a method and figure of speech but even more importantly as a level of human experience and as an outlook on life. To Kierkegaard, the comical is present at every stage of man's existence, appearing wherever there is a contradiction that is relatively painless or viewed as cancelled because it seems provided with a way out. For instance, a drunken man produces a comical impression because his movements contradict those of the normal man. Yet the contradiction is not serious, since we know that shortly he will be sober and able to get about readily. However, it is not the comical in general but two of its species, *irony* and *humor,* which interest Kierkegaard especially and which he treats as boundary zones of those levels of existence that mark the higher stages of human life: "There are thus three spheres of existence: the aesthetic, the ethical, the religious. Two boundary

---

[5] *A Kierkegaard Anthology,* ed. Robert Bretall (Princeton University Press, 1947), p. 134.

zones correspond to these three: *irony,* constituting the boundary between the aesthetic and the ethical; *humor,* as the
boundary that separates the ethical from the religious."[6]

To begin with, the individual lives in his immediacy, absorbed in enjoying the passing show, the sensuous appearances
of things. That is, he lives at the aesthetic level of existence.
At the aesthetic stage men fail to challenge appearances, to
ask whether things are really what they seem, or to distinguish
the inward from the outward. Such people see ideals in a
dreamy sort of way and are even aware of contradictions in
existence (like that between right and wrong) but remain
passive, indifferent, do nothing about them. In addition to the
aesthete proper, the aesthetic attitude toward life includes
that of the so-called common sense man, who takes at face
value the deliverances of his passing feelings and the hundred
and one conventions of daily life in all their triviality. Such
a one finds everything important but nothing really, absolutely
important. He lives in the relativities of the world but has
never felt the infinite requirement. Again there are the eudae-
monists, those absorbed in the pleasures of self-development,
in savoring to the full all the nuances and adventures of life
for what they contribute to enhance the fulfillment of one's
powers, one's self-sufficiency. Instead of taking a stand, committing themselves positively to existence, they dreamily pursue
pleasure, beauty, the development of their talents, until they
finally awaken to a sense of boredom, emptiness, and the
hollowness of life. With this comes the discovery of *irony,* of
which more anon. Lastly, to this class belongs the romantic
aesthete (like Don Juan), lost in self-enjoyment, who sports
with all the ordinary goals and ideals of existence, setting at
naught in his exhuberance of arbitrary freedom all accepted
bounds. Such romantic irony, Hegel suggested, turns on the

---

[6] Søren Kierkegaard, *Concluding Unscientific Postscript,* trans. David
F. Swenson; completed by Walter Lowrie (Princeton University Press,
1944), p. 448. Italics mine.

triumph of the artist's personality, which, given free reign over
the material, tends to dissolve away everything objective in
reality under the powerful solvent of his own fancies.[7] Yet
this untrammeled egoism of the aesthetic outlook is superseded,
in Kierkegaard's view, in the existential dialectic by the deeper
ironic insight as to the *vanity* of this world, which comes with
the artist's realization that the fusion of ideal and appearance
in beauty is but a transistory semblance as it were. Taken as
an end in itself the visible world harbors only emptiness and
vainglory; as he gets further the artist tends to construe it as
a symbol or index of something deeper, nobler, more ideal.

With irony as the sense of the vanity of existence, the individual becomes a subjective thinker, troubled with doubts,
questions, unable to enjoy life in the old unthinking, comfort-
able way of those who dwell in immediacy. With irony, the
contradiction between the hidden reality and outward show,
between the temporal and eternal, between the relative and
the absolute, appears. For instance, when Socrates says in the
Gorgias[8] that it is strange that the skipper who has brought
you in his vessel from Italy to Greece should accept pay on
arrival as if he had done you a good deed, although he does
not really know whether he has rendered his passengers a
service, or whether it would not have been better for them to
have been drowned at sea, his remark appears merely facetious,
a jest contrasting knowledge and ignorance. Actually it is irony
in which what appears to be said in jest is really said in earnest,
with a deeper meaning contrary to that speciously expressed.
A matter which others regard as a trifling joke he regards as
of the highest importance. For Socrates has executed the infinite movement and has established relationship with the
absolute Idea. Having discovered the disparity between the

---

[7] G. W. Hegel, *Philosophy of Fine Art,* trans. F. Osmaston (London, G.
Bell & Sons, Ltd., 1920), 2, 386.

[8] *Gorgias,* 511; referred to by Kierkegaard, *Concluding Unscientific
Postscript,* p. 77.

inward and the outward, he sets it forth in irony. By appealing
to his *daimon* (and by assuming that others can do the same)
Socrates, according to Kierkegaard, invokes the essentially subjective, inward side of life that can be communicated only
obliquely through maieutic artistry, and eludes any direct form
of expression. For that which has to do with the existing subject's relationship to the absolute and ideal is something hidden,
inward, private, *essentially secret,*—something quite different
from an *accidental secret,* such as the action taken by a cabinet
in politics but not yet publically revealed. Ideality is not loose
change which can be passed from one person to another; it is
something that I know by myself. To know that Caesar is
great I must have had experience of what greatness is through
actual living. "To believe an ideality on the word of another
is like laughing at a joke because someone has said that it was
funny, not because one has understood it."[9]

Irony is the mask which Socrates assumes to screen the
infinite within him, his incognito as an ethicist who acknowledges an absolute requirement and whose sense of transcendent
obligation tends toward the higher stage of the religious. With
him, irony is not simply verbal, a form of words or phrases,
but a fundamental expression of an attitude of spirit. Not all
users of ironic speech are in reality ethicists or have passed this
boundary. One has often to tease and trick a man to find out
whether his irony is merely a pose. Usually the best way to do
this is to try to find out whether he can speak about himself
as about a third party, or whether instead he retains certain
illusions of his existential superiority, as might a millionaire
among poor men or a university professor among rural school
teachers. Such a man, who cannot consider himself as merely
relative in the relativities of the world, and who cannot view
himself as a vanishing particularity in relation to the absolute
requirement, is not a true ironist. "Irony," says Kierkegaard,

---

[9] Kierkegaard, *Postscript,* p. 289.

"arises from the constant placing of the particularities of the finite together with the infinite ethical requirement, thus permitting the contradiction to come into being."[10]

   In *Either/Or* we are told how the aesthetic man is granted by the assembled gods the favor of a wish. After due thought the wish that he asks for is that *he may always have the laugh on his side*. At this the gods begin to laugh. They laugh presumably because this man who has hitherto lived for enjoyment has raised himself to a transcendent, ironic view, no longer demanding simply a life of self-gratification and merriment but assurance that his future course shall be grounded in the true nature of reality. Living no longer in immediacy, the ironic man has passed from the aesthetic stage to the boundary zone of the ethical. To him the given world appears full of flaws and absurdities; he has come to doubt its beliefs and culture; they have lost their authority. Nevertheless the ironic man only reaches a border area but does not really, according to Kierkegaard, penetrate the next stage. Though he has dethroned the aesthetic, he has not committed himself finally and completely to the ethical. Rather, he remains contemplative, polemical, standing on the brink; but he does not take the plunge as would a positive activist. The ironic man is too negative, pointing through veiled criticism to something better, instead of boldly unsheathing the sword of the crusader and embracing responsibility for the struggle of the moral life. At the ethical stage a man does not simply *look* at life's contradictions or contemplate the disproportion between the ideal and actuality; he acts, chooses, commits himself wholly to the conflict between good and evil, realizing his obligation to society through marriage and a family, laboring at a calling having social utility, and in all ways seeking by doing his duty to mankind to sound the depths of existence. But further discussion of the ethical, as well as of the religious stage, must be

---

[10] Kierkegaard, *Postscript,* p. 448.

postponed at this point until we come to the subject of humor in the next chapter.

It is enough to say that the ironic man purports to be not so much a teacher as a learner, one always inquiring, always striving for the light; yet in gaining it he turns his back to the Idea, as it were, letting its beam fall indirectly over his shoulder. Ruminative, bantering in tone, the ironist is not without some warmth of feeling. Deep sympathy with pain may be hidden under some droll disguise. Always a master of himself, however, he suppresses the intrusion of sympathetic feeling into his merriment by resorting to the quizzical use of reflection.[11] Mark Twain's remark regarding Helen Keller, "If I could have been deaf, dumb, and blind I also might have arrived at something," is a rare example of the way in which praise and dispraise, a mood of joy and sorrow may be suggested by irony.

Like satire, of which we shall speak presently, irony jests with serious intent, pricks bubbles, strips away false fronts, and frequently assumes the incognito of the ethicist—as in Mark Twain's story *The Man that Corrupted Hadleyburg*. Here the import of the title is the opposite of that seemingly expressed, since the story shows the person referred to not as corrupting the town but as purifying it through exposing the hypocrisy, rottenness, and hollow pretense of its leading citizens. With the ethicist, the ironist seems usually concerned with the fate of the human race and to take the point of view of humanity. But while irony borders on the ethical, it is less ethical than satire, being more intellectual and detached. As Kierkegaard suggests, following Aristotle, "the ironical man evokes the ludicrous for his own sake, the jester for the sake of others."[12] Always he remains something in his own eyes, aloof, retiring from the world to an independent stand, indifferent to the eyes upon him. Still in irony as against satire there tends

---

[11] Kierkegaard, *Postscript*, p. 401, note.
[12] Kierkegaard, *Postscript*, p. 464, note.

to be more kindliness or at least less indignation toward the object of criticism, in satire more hostility. Both wear masks, involve double meanings, but the meaning of satire usually requires less effort of thought to detect, is less deep in concealment. The ironic spirit has more moderation, restraint, less reformatory ardor. Its mood is lighter, more jocular, whereas satire tends to be abusive, intense in its ridicule, unrestrained in its eagerness to censure bad manners, moral corruption, and human follies. That the presence of this lightness of mood may be challenged in the case of tragic irony or the so-called irony of fate, in which the outcome of events contradicts creature hopes and the promise of things, seems hard to deny. Neither involves laughter unless by a kind of *as if* the laughter of the gods be assumed at things like the fate of Oedipus or the sudden disappearance of the dodo, the dinosaur, or the island of Atlantis from the world. In tragic irony and that of fate, the meaning of irony as a mode of thought and speech is analogously extended to include an art form and the cosmic pattern. But with certain differences. To say that irony is essentially comic signifies, of course, that the incongruity involved is viewed with a certain detachment or transcendence. But if tragic irony and the irony of fate are included in the ludicrous, then the ludicrous must be used in a sense that goes beyond the Aristotelian dictum of "a defect that is not painful or destructive,"[13] and that covers cases in which detachment is carried so far that events which from the creature's natural point of view are fatally ruinous may appear from a transcendental point of view comically incongruous, as to the dinosaurs' ballet which quipped

and winked

"It's kind of fun to be extinct."

In farewell to the subject of irony we may quote a contemporary instance of it, which is also a parody or burlesque

---

[13] Aristotle, *Poetics,* V. (Butcher trans.)

imitation of a serious composition, involving a kind of facetious light sarcasm in which the ironic effect is achieved by using undignified, absurdly censorious expressions in place of laudatory ones, whereby nonetheless a positive evaluation of conscience is implied. This parody by Ogden Nash upon Wordsworth's *Ode to Duty* is entitled *Kind of an Ode to Duty*.

> O Duty,
> Why hast thou not the visage of a sweetie or a cutie?
> Why glitter thy spectacles so ominously?
> Why art thou clad so abominously?
> Why art thou so different from Venus?
> And why do thou and I have so few interests
>   mutually in common between us?
> Why art thou fifty per cent martyr
> And fifty-one per cent Tartar?
>
> Why is it thy unfortunate wont
> To try to attract people by calling on them either
>   to leave undone the deeds they like, or to do
>   the deeds they don't?
> Why art thou so like an April post-mortem
> Or something that died in the ortumn?
> Above all, why dost thou continue to hound me?
> Why art thou always albatrossly hanging around me?
> Thou so ubiquitous,
> And I so iniquitous.
> I seem to be the one person in the world thou art
>   perpetually preaching at who or to who;
> Whatever looks like fun, there art thou standing
>   between me and it, calling yoo-hoo.
>
> O Duty, Duty!
> How noble a man should I be hadst thou the
>   visage of a sweetie or a cutie!

But as it is thou art so much forbiddinger than
    a Wodehouse hero's forbiddingest aunt
That in the words of the poet, When Duty whispers
    low, You must, this erst-while youth replies,
I just can't![14]

Closely related to irony is another variety of the comic involving adverse criticism known as satire. To ridicule the
vices and follies of mankind is the business of satire, a term
applied both to its spirit of moral condemnation and to the
genre of its literary expression. Like irony, satire often appears
to be saying something else than it genuinely intends, feigning
often a certain naïveté in its comments upon existent reality.
But whereas in irony the words are to be understood as meaning the opposite of what is expressed (as when Socrates' praise
of the wisdom of the sophists is to be understood as covert
affirmation of their foolishness), in satire instead of a reversal
of meaning there is often a shift of reference to another object
than that purportedly dealt with. While seeming to talk about
the fanciful world of Gulliver, Swift is really censuring his
own generation and society. As a satirist he criticizes the state
of affairs through analogy, figuratively, symbolically, presenting contemporary life under the image of the abominable
Yahoos, and the British legal system under the pretended
likeness of that of the Lilliputians.

Though irony may be construed as a method of adopting
in pretense a view to which we are opposed in order to expose
its falsity, and though it is often combined with satire, nevertheless it is a mistake, in our opinion, to classify irony as a
species of satire. Despite resemblances, the two differ in important respects. As already suggested, whereas satire censures
culpable wrongs and injustices, irony more often uncovers
ignorance and stupidity, being less interested in social reform
than in the love of truth. By contrast, irony stands smiling with

---

[14] Ogden Nash, *The Face is Familiar*, pp. 175–76. (Quoted by permission of Little, Brown & Co.)

its fingers on its lips letting reason into dark corners, whereas satire by its imaginative eloquence excites anger at human misdeeds and cruelties. While a writer like Dickens does not create an outright world of fantasy as the analogue for his satire, nevertheless through exaggeration and distortion in the treatment of his subjects he suggests their resemblance to monsters in a monstrous world. As might be expected, the cautious understatements of irony are often in marked contrast with the overstatements and sharp emotional intensity of satirical comment. Indeed, the laughter of satire appears more spiteful, contemptuous, scoring the badness of actuality, as against that of irony, which appears more concerned with the ought to be, deploring the defects of what is in comparison with ideality. As against the ironist's use of inversion to encourage thinking for oneself, the satirist employs rhetoric, analogy, imagery, and invective. While irony persuades us through our own mental exertions, satire tries by tricks of literary suggestion to convince us that its opponents are wicked and depraved. Appealing to negative feeling through eloquence, the satirist seeks to instill an attitude of condemnation in his audience rather than to arouse them to independent reflection leading to logical rebuttal.

Sometimes, however, satire is considered so broadly as to be indistinguishable from irony, as when G. K. Chesterton describes it as "taunting reasonableness," declaring its "essence" to be "that it perceives some absurdity inherent in the logic of some position, and . . . draws the absurdity out and isolates it so that all can see it." "True satire," in his opinion, "is always, so to speak, a variation or fantasia upon the air of pure logic,"[15] yielding some critical insight as when we say, "The trouble with politicians is that they have no politics." In epigrams like this the satiric element resides not in analogy but in duplicity with words, which makes them appear to

---

[15] Quoted in Edgar Johnson, *A Treasury of Satire* (New York, Simon & Schuster, 1945), p. 19.

assert both the *A-ness and the non-A-ness of A*. And whether such words voice the calmness of the judge or the fierceness of the prosecutor must be left to the decision of those best acquainted with politicians.

That is, whether the abusive temper of satire is due to the antagonistic self-feeling of the satirist or to his appreciation of objective evils, whether it is rooted in moral indignation or merely in personal disappointment that the world is not shaped nearer to his heart's desire, is not always clear. Certainly many satirists have drawn their swords in great causes, protesting mortal and not merely venial offenses, attacking not simply individuals but reigning social institutions for their absurdity, corruption, and brutality. Thus Voltaire satirized the religious superstition, the political injustice, and chicanery of his time; Mark Twain defended human rights in all ages by attacking the ignorance, tyranny, and cruelty of medieval chivalry in his *Connecticut Yankee at King Arthur's Court*; while Dickens provided a biting exposure of Britain's poor houses, orphanages, schools, debtors' prisons, and the inequities of the legal system in the nineteenth century. On the other hand, a mixture of motives is no doubt often present, so that we are led to wonder in the case of satirists like Alexander Pope or Bernard Shaw how far a desire for fame and a favorable regard of their own talents, combined with a Hobbesian sense of superiority, led them to express their harsh opinions of others.

In satire, wrath, derision, an impulse to degrade the object is present, unlike the mellow good nature of humor, for instance, so conducive to putting us in an easy frame of mind. Indeed, it seems hardly too much to say that the satirist, tied to this world and with his indignant undertone, never reaches the freest ranges or loftiest heights of the artistic imagination. To him is allowed a certain understanding of evil and error, of the darker side of human nature, but he is denied appreciation of man's greatest achievements, the high-hearted gaieties, the luminous harmonies seen by others at the heart of things.

His task is to rail at the iniquitous faults of the actual, which never fulfills the rosiness of dream, to excoriate the existing order for its blemishes, for disappointing human hopes and being less than ideal in fact. Nevertheless satire is probably the most socially effective form of the comic, with the greatest utility as a practical instrument for the destruction of evils. And this is precisely because it combines anger with laughter in attacking its subject, although its rough, exaggerated sweep may cut down many flowers of innocence in its path and defeat some good as well.

Among the greatest satirists stands Voltaire, whose life despite its flaws was largely directed to battling intolerance and the cruel social contradictions of his time. In this crusade his pen was his weapon, although he supported his literary assaults with bold actions often at great risk to himself. Among his satirical works attacking the hollow pretenses of an age in which the upper classes hid their eyes from the rank injustices and superstitions surrounding them, none is more deadly than the tale of *Candide* (1759). Despite familiarity, the story merits a word. Its shafts, as is well known, were aimed at Pope's *Essay on Man*, Leibniz' *Theodicy,* and Rousseau's *Public Letter* of August 1756; but above all at the shallow complacency of churchmen, politicians, and intellectuals who in the face of war, starvation, corruption still maintained that all was well in this best of possible worlds. To attack this philosophy of "all chance, direction which thou canst not see—all partial evil, universal good,"*Candide* was written. Its story is that of a youth reared in this all-for-the-best view of life, who finds on going out into the world that the very opposite is the case. Instead of everything tending toward the good, he suffers continuous indignity and calamity, being confronted with the spectacle of unceasing slaughter, pillage, deception, and outrage. The lesson to be learned from our experience, Voltaire seems to suggest, is that while life is a sorry affair we may still make the best of it if we work hard, cultivate our garden, and refrain from considering metaphysical problems about the destiny of the world. On putting the book down we scarcely know, as Tallentyre says, whether to laugh at the absurdities of the immortal Dr. Pangloss, the incurable teleological optimist, who argues that " 'noses have been made to carry spectacles, therefore we have spectacles; legs have been made for stockings, therefore we have stockings; pigs were made to be eaten, therefore we have pork all the year round'—or to weep over the wretchedness of a humanity which perforce consoles itself with lies and, too miserable to face its misery, pretends that all is well."[16] In passing, it is worth remarking that while in satire—as in humor—we may have the impulse both to laughter and to tears, they are not combined in the same way. For in satire we generally remain aloof, at once mocking and deploring man's weaknesses, yet *looking at him from the outside*, whereas in humor we delight and sorrow *with* him, sharing, sympathizing, comprehending his frailty and tribulations.

On this account presumably much reading of satire (e.g. of the works of Voltaire) tends to produce a spiritual dryness; the world shrivels to the reader, its concerns seem petty (an ant under a microscope still appears but an ant!). Too dark a picture is painted of human life; at the same time the remedy for its evils is little considered in detail or else largely ignored. Issues are oversimplified, while the means of reform are cursorily treated, perhaps because the cure for man's social troubles still eludes us and is not at hand. In many ways the lesson of *Candide* is repeated for our own day in Aldous Huxley's *Brave New World*. But in place of the teleology and theology of the eighteenth century, mechanism and science have now become the accepted framework of thought and provide the butt of the satiric attack. Since Voltaire, the wheel has almost turned full circle, and the goals of secularism, scientific progress, and material comfort that served as the beacons of

---

[16] S. G. Tallentyre, *Life of Voltaire* (New York, Loring & Mussey, n.d.), p. 372.

an earlier age have become to Huxley pungent sources of disenchantment.

Brave New World is a picture of Utopia in reverse, a cold farcical projection of the course of our present society in terms that grip our sense of reality, although at first sight they seem fantastically unreal. In his satiric portrayal Huxley shows us our world revolutionized by current scientific tendencies carried to their extreme. Present patterns of life have been disrupted and new ones improvised through discoveries in the physical sciences and engineering, through economic changes introduced by mass production into industry, and especially by developments in the sciences of life (biology, physiology, psychology), which have transformed human beings body and soul. The brave new world is one geared to creature happiness, security, peace, and painlessness, in which comfort replaces God, conditioning replaces morals, and truth is replaced by drugs and propaganda. To obtain these ends, governments have become completely totalitarian, in other words, they have become welfare tyrannies of scientists, in which nature is lost in artificial controls, individualism is eclipsed by communism, and "everyone belongs to everyone else."

For these purposes, highly effective techniques of suggestion have been provided, including infant conditioning, sleep teaching (hypnopaedia), regimented schooling, and drugs (like scopolamine), so that the citizens, without any feeling of being coerced, come to love their chains. Even more important, a foolproof system of eugenics has been designed to "standardize the human product" so as to insure the right man for the right place. A scientific caste system (analogous to ant societies), involving the specialization of the creature to its task and the production of masses of stereotyped "workers," facilitates the job of the managers. To keep their subjects happy, the bosses encourage them in the use of drugs, mechanical amusements, and in sexual promiscuity. Sexual freedom, they find, does much to reconcile the people to their servitude, while anesthetics remove pain, and narcotic substitutes for alcohol (soma), along with movies, canned music, television permit them to daydream away their leisure hours. Although at first sight this world of sleep-teaching, bottled babies, and standardized semi-moronic workers may appear far in the future, closer inspection, Huxley assures us, of our life of city apartments, skyscrapers, heliocopters, rockets, and sexual license shows it well on its way. In many respects the welfare-tyranny of Utopia appears near at hand. In the end, the reader's horrified reaction to the new order echoes that of the "noble Savage" or stranger in the book, who when brought to view it cries in revulsion, "But I don't want comfort. I want God, I want poetry, I want real danger, I want freedom, I want goodness, I want sin."[17]

As often happens in modern satire, the virulence of the attack almost eclipses the comic spirit. Scorn and contempt of "man, proud man" who

> like an angry ape,
> Plays such fantastic tricks before high heaven
> As makes the angels weep[18]

drives out the jollity essential to the ludicrous. Just as in Shakespeare the analogy of man to the ape, which might be expected to excite laughter, is drowned in bitterness, so in *Brave New World* the loss of belief in eternal values and of depth in human relations robs the book of most of its chuckles at the picture of man's mechanized future of the soft life.

Many literary devices may be employed for satiric effect: from artistry in name-calling and epithets (unsurpassed in Rabelais) through various kinds of mimetic misrepresentation to elaborate parallels and projections, like Huxley's, in which

---

[17] Aldous Huxley, *Brave New World* (New York, Harper & Bros., 1946), p. 288.
[18] Shakespeare, *Measure for Measure*, II.2.121–23. (The Yale Shakespeare, rev. ed. 1954).

the audience through applying the analogy gains the impression of arriving at the unfavorable judgment for itself. All are take-offs of a secondary, imitative nature relying upon fanciful exaggeration, such as the burlesque, the grotesque, the parody, travesty, or caricature. All tend to degrade their subject, while the effect of the grotesque, for instance, in stressing the bizarre, often horrifying aspects of the theme, is far removed from common sense jocosity. Indeed, the grotesque often in association with the weird, in which the gruesome and ghastly are offered as purportedly "funny," appears increasingly in modern presentations. But when satire loses its lightness and comic effect it ceases to be satire and becomes mere reprimand or criticism.

Occasionally with the passage of time, as the original men and institutions adversely criticized are forgotten, a satire loses its force. Today *Gulliver's Travels,* deprived of its sting, is read mainly by children as a diverting fairy tale of imaginary journeys. But too often in satire there is a basic negativity, a failure to grasp positive values, in pointing always to the defects of the actual. Besides a sharp eye to faults of fact, besides attacking the imperfect realization of men's dreams, the satirist seems to make fun of the ideals behind the dreams, at things longed for by the spirit that can neither perhaps be proved nor disproved, but will not be denied. Unlike freer minds, the satirist fails to comprehend that life requires acceptance of shadowy indications, hints, nuances of translunary things as just that—benisons and beacons that remain always disparate and unattainable as compared with our imperfect approximations of the everyday world. Intent upon criticizing the actual under allegorical disguises, the satirist falls short in his appreciation of the ideal. But such is not always the case, as we shall try to show.

While satire usually lacks the tolerance and larger comprehension of humor, sometimes as in, for instance, *The History of the Famous Don Quixote de la Mancha* (1605), the two

are combined. Beginning as a satirical attack upon the ro-
mances of chivalry, the work is suffused as it proceeds with a
humor at once charitable and profound, embracing the whole
of life in its contemplation. In the preface, Cervantes declares
through a friend that his aim has been no more than an invective against books of knighthood, to "diminish the authority
and acceptance that books of chivalry have in the world, and
to urge the melancholy to laughter"; but as his writing progressed the possibilities of his subject widened and deepened
into an interpretation of the entire human spectacle. At a
deeper level, what had seemed but an extravagant burlesque
became the story of the conflict between man's realism and
idealism, his preoccupation on the one hand with the facts of
everyday sensible existence, and on the other with the nobler
nonsensuous realm of values, with the standards and goals of
aspiration.

The don and his squire, Don Quixote and Sancho Panza,
madman and bumpkin, come to symbolize two fundamental
attitudes toward life, the world as it ought to be and as it is.
The don is mad basically because he refuses to admit the distinction and unbridgeable gulf between the objects of selfless
aspiration and those of everyday life; whereas the clown is a
clown, despite his shrewd practical wisdom, because of his
blindness to the presence of a higher invisible world. The weakness of the don, like that of the heroes of his romantic tales,
is that he attempts to play Providence to man—unprovided
save with good intentions. Without reflecting that he has no
adequate resources, no sufficient knowledge of method or conditions at his disposal, he launches upon his mad enterprise to
save the world. Life to him is a dream, and he follows imagination and faith, as against reason and the senses, ignoring
the gulf between means and goal, vision and practice. Noble,
upright, fearless, he clings to the ideal. But the ideal obscured
by daydreams becomes a mere mirage, an air castle. In consequence his undertaking is robbed of success. Through the

pages of *Don Quixote* the reflective reader may come to find
the great Crusades and other heroic adventures of chivalry
largely shorn of their dignity and turned into pursuits of illusion. Imagination and romantic tales make attainment of the
heart's desire seem cheap and easy, but the quest in actuality,
Cervantes suggests, often follows an *ignis fatuus* leading to
heartbreak.

But to the patient reader comes deeper insight. While at first
we laugh unfeelingly at the absurd misadventures of Don
Quixote, attacking windmills perceived as giants and flocks of
sheep as armies, mistaking innkeepers for knights and peasant
girls for great ladies of the court, after a time our laughter
changes its key and we find latent tragedy in the comedy. For
the don's gaunt nobility, his unbending probity of spirit, we
come to feel an increasing warmth of regard. We come to
recognize that despite his unfailing, painful defeats, though
he loses yet he wins, since the reward of his integrity lies in
that inviolable integrity itself, something in a sense more valuable than the gross profits of the material world. Seldom has
the humor of incongruity and contrast, together with the
metaphysical suggestions of the ludicrous, been conveyed in
more picturesque terms. Here we have the two sides of human
nature represented against a background of striking verisimilitude to the life of sixteenth-century Spain; on the one hand,
the romantic idealist, a figure of ruthless consistency pursuing
an impossible goal, inspired by dreams and intimations of a
higher supersensible destiny, and, on the other, the practical
man engaged in the never-ending battle for the necessaries of
existence. This picture of man's nature as both worldly and
unworldly, conquerable and unconquerable, pursuing both
the finite and the infinite, the obtainable and the unobtainable,
provides a satirical tale yielding gradually the deeper wisdom
that somehow both in the nature of things must always be
found together.

CHAPTER 5

Wit and Humor

WHILE wit, like humor, is a term subject to widely various usage in relation to the comic, its meaning generally refers to a ludicrous quality of speech or writing marked by unusual mental sharpness and originality. Occasionally, as when someone is described as a "wit" or "witty," its use is extended to the person or trait exhibiting this quality. But, unlike humor, the meaning of wit (like that of satire) attaches primarily to its *expression*, and cannot be attached to objects, happenings, or situations apart from it. It is sometimes said that, while humor is found, wit is made. As compared with humor, wit seems more coldly intellectual, intentional, creative, using condensation in words and needing to be imparted; whereas humor is warmer, more sentimental, and may be enjoyed alone and unverbalized. While it may not heighten our sympathy, wit widens our horizons by its flashes, revealing remote hidden affiliations and drawing laughter from far afield; humor, in contrast, strikes up fellow feeling, and though it does not leap so much across time and space, enriches our insight into the universal in familiar things, lending it a local habitation and a name.

Yet this description of wit (as against the discovery of a felt quality of a situation, object, or character in humor) has not told us in what precisely the ingenuity or creativeness of the witty expression consists. To say that logical trenchancy is its

outstanding feature would, in our opinion, not be far wrong.
Take as a familiar example Benjamin Franklin's pithy warning to the Continental Congress that "We must all hang together or else, most assuredly, we shall all hang separately."
Here the pith of the condensed truth propounded turns on the
pun in the word "hang," which may mean either "work together" or "die by strangulation." The gist of the argument,
for it is an argument, is: Either cooperate or die. (Stated
hypothetically, this becomes the proposition, If you do not
cooperate you will die. And since death is assumed to be a
closed option, the necessity of the alternative conclusion—
denying the antecedent—follows.) "United we stand, divided
we fall" is the age-old counsel of the group against individualism. Franklin's jest summarizes the political situation in a
pun indicating the two possible but contradictory courses open,
one of which appears fatal, leaving only the other to be
adopted; the whole achieving an acme of compression. The
point of the witticism lies precisely in its sense in nonsense, in
the cogency which we grasp at the end of what appeared to
be inconsistency at the beginning. For the use of one and the
same word, "hang," identical in sound and spelling, for two
opposing meanings at first sight seems to indicate a breach
of rules but on reflection is found to express a forceful, valid
argument.

Before proceeding further, it is worth pausing to point out
that the view of wit presented here differs basically from that
of Freud. To us wit turns upon the intellect's recognition of
sense in apparent nonsense and rejection of an absurdity in the
light of consistency as a standard. The wit of the Irishman's
bull, for instance, about his having visited a desert island
where the hand of man had never set foot, turns finally upon
the hearer's grasp and rejection of the contradiction in the
mixed metaphor. It is in the victory of systematic thinking
over muddled, inconsistent expression that the comicality con-

sists. In short, wit is a game in which logic sends illogic flying, and reason rails at unreason. As Shakespeare says,

A jest's prosperity lies in the ear
Of him that hears it, never in the tongue
Of him that makes it.[1]

That is, completion of the witticism lies in the insight of the auditor, who, being a sound thinker, detects the inconsistency in the speech and finds it worthy of laughter. In Freud, on the contrary, wit, though using certain intellectual techniques, is essentially a weapon *against logic,* stemming from the irrational unconscious, and being in fact a device to gain pleasure by eluding reason through substituting the infantile for the adult state of mind.[2] The child's fondness for pure play with words, for nonsense and unrestrained expression find an outlet in "harmless wit" enjoyed for its own sake and not yet subdued by reason. Besides the harmless variety, there is a second kind, so-called "tendency wit," which indirectly satisfies the basic impulses of pugnacity and sex through disguised expressions of hostility and obscenity that elude the social censor. The libido of the primitive unconscious, repressed by the critical intellect in higher societies, finds an outlet through witticisms with aggressive or indecent suggestions. Pleasure in such matters, which would not be allowed direct expression, gains public tolerance through wearing the mask of witty absurdity as satirical invective or as an intriguing shady story. A mild instance of the latter is the anecdote regarding the famous walks taken by President Theodore Roosevelt and Jules Jusserand, the French ambassador. On one of these rambles, the story has it, the two came to a flooded creek too deep to wade across. Accordingly, the President stripped off his clothes and plunged in. And the ambassador, after carefully folding his

---

[1] Shakespeare, *Love's Labour's Lost,* V.2.869–71.
[2] Freud, *Wit and Its Relation to the Unconscious,* p. 196.

attire and placing it under a tree, followed his example. Continuing their walk on the other side, Roosevelt turned to Jusserand with the surprised remark "But you still have on your kid gloves, Mr. Ambassador!"—to which Jusserand replied, "Ah, but we might meet some ladies!" Here the forbidden topic of nudity between the sexes, so pleasing to the unconscious, is introduced behind the façade of a laughable contradiction between absent-mindedness and the niceties of etiquette.

Both wit and dreams, according to Freud, spring from the amoral, alogical unconscious (i.e., from the primitive, submerged, unknown area of mind which is nonetheless capable of becoming conscious); and both assist in the liberation of repressed emotions. They differ, however, in that while wit centers in verbal technique and the pleasure of play, dreams are wishes whose imaginary satisfaction is predominantly through an escape from pain. Again, whereas dreams are private, asocial, and usually incomprehensible to the person who has them, the skylarking of wit is verbal, social, and decipherable both to the author and to a second and third party. Its technique involves mixed words, displacement, condensation, allusion, indirect expression, *double entendre,* and the replacing of object associations by word associations. The pleasure of wit for Freud lies in the playful liberation of the unconscious disguised as nonsense, thereby escaping the censor. A nonsense witticism may turn upon advancing something apparently nonsensical, which nevertheless contains enough subliminal sense to reveal some other absurdity. Thus to the saying "Never to be born would be best for mortal man," the *Fliegende Blätter* adds "But hardly one man in a hundred thousand has this luck."[3] Here the patent absurdity of the second statement (assuming that a man may have the choice not to be born) exposes the absurdity of the first (since for the

---

[3] Freud, p. 74.

unborn there can be no values like "best"). Or again the
pseudo-sense in wit may turn on word-play, as when Heine
on noting that Rothschild, despite his great wealth, treated
him as an equal, remarked that the banker had treated him
"quite famillionaire." Here a hybrid combination of syllables,
quite nonsensical from one point of view, nevertheless affords
a residue of agreeable meaning from another. But a mere apt
phrase or *mot just* does not suffice to constitute wit without
a keen penetration of contradictions and a valid sense of logical
relations. Against Freud's interpretation of wit as the triumph
of unreason over critical judgment and the struggle of the
unconscious to regain biological sources of pleasure, we shall
continue to maintain on the contrary that wit involves an
intellectual victory and the rejection of illogicality. With this
goes our further repudiation of his view of wit as an entirely
different category from the comic, the first as springing from
the unconscious, the second from the foreconscious; on the
contrary, we regard them either as correlative species, or the
comic in a wider sense as the genus of the other.

While flashes of wit abound in books, the real home of wit
is the witty exchange in conversation. For its fulfillment, as
already suggested, three persons seem necessary: the speaker
who launches the barb, the recipient or one spoken to (who
seeks to return as good as he got by countering with some
clever repartee), and the listener or third party who serves
as judge or arbiter. The aim of the contestants is each to produce laughter in this third party, to win, as it were, a victory
of comic persuasion by "getting the laugh on his side." This
is not the same as winning victory in an argument by producing a convincing preponderance of evidence in demon-
strative order but rather consists in skill in handling verbal
and logical techniques imaginatively, so as often indeed to
make the worse appear the better reason. At the same time,
the wit himself by his keen insight knows his way around and
is not unaware of the absurdities he utters. Falstaff in *Henry*

IV generally has the laugh on his side even though the weight
of the argument is against him. A victory of wit is an aesthetic
victory, in which concern is not with demonstrating the real
factual truth of the matter but with ingenuity in verbal and
rational devices in presenting a skillful pattern of appearances
for consideration. Often the battle of wits is largely through
phrase-making, in a celebrated instance of which Winston
Churchill beat Bernard Shaw to the verbal draw. Shortly
before the opening of one of his plays, Shaw, it is reported,
sent Churchill a pair of tickets with a note saying, "Come to
my play and bring a friend, if you have a friend." Churchill
sent back the tickets with the message, "I'm busy for the
opening, but I'll come on the second night, if there is a second night." Here the cleverness of the mock insults exchanged
lies in the contradiction suggested in the assumption, on the
one hand, that one of the most successful politicians of England
should not have a friend (not being by implication a true
statesman), and on the other, that a play by her most famous
playwright (not really being a good one) might not excite
sufficient interest to have a second performance—since, if any-
body had friends, Churchill, the great popular leader had, and
if any living playwright's play was likely to have a long run, it
would be Shaw's. The wit here is ironic, an expression of
meaning through the opposite, and the victory is Churchill's
since he was able to turn aside Shaw's thrust by an exactly
parallel, apparently casual, stab in rejoinder.

Wit, more than any other form of the comic, is like a game,
an intellectual play with words in which, as Sully puts it, a
subject is tossed out like a ball and each side tries to strike it in
turn to keep the game going.[4] Shakespeare, a master in
dialogue at this tennis or shuttlecock kind of wit, speaks in
Love's Labour's Lost of "a set of wit well play'd."[5] It is like

---

[4] James Sully, *An Essay on Laughter* (New York, Longmans, Green,
1902), p. 355.
[5] *Love's Labour's Lost*, V.2.29.

a sport in which a challenging theme or expression is flung out
by some one and others join in trying to toss it back and forth,
scoring hits and keeping the play going as long as possible.
The motives of the participants are often varied; besides the
desire to shine by showing one's skill, to be victorious in the
contest, as well as to relieve hostility and gratify one's social
impulses, there is the love of the game itself coupled perhaps
with a desire to gain new ideas, *aperçus,* stimulation. In a way
the exchange of wit resembles the medieval tournament or
mock battle of chivalry, but with swords and lances replaced
by words, ingenious fancies, and logical quibbles. While there
are no practical rewards or prizes, and concern is as much with
the process itself as with the outcome, there is great interest
in imaginative originality, the expertness with which connections are developed between widely disparate ideas, as well as
in the feints and turns by which overthrow is brought to an
opponent. Coolness, swiftness, surprise, self-restraint, and control are demanded together with conformity in operation to a
complex code of conditions. These limiting conditions, as well
as the wit achieved within them, differ often with the subject
matter dealt with in the jest. For example, there is legal wit,
political, scientific, commercial, theological, urban, and rural
wit, not to mention that peculiar to different times and geo-
graphical locations. Wit may be difficult to share with out-
siders, with those unacquainted with the ways of life and
thought peculiar to these different fields.

In addition, there are rules governing the logical and linguistic limits of wit not to mention those of manners, morals,
and decency. Undeniably we have an imaginative impulse to
defy these rules, to exhibit incongruity by departing from them,
to secure a laugh from far afield by drawing it from the depths
of the totally unexpected or forbidden—as from linguistic
gibberish, ferocious manners, or obscenity. Nevertheless only
if these departures are subordinated to certain ultimate requirements that mark the canons of the comic can they be

accounted true witticisms. Pure nonsensical chatter, inco-
herent barbarisms, and indecency are not wit. It is only when
such things are clothed with a certain aesthetic and logical
form (as appropriate to contemplation not action, with a
congruity behind their incongruity and respect for a standard
in the background despite the foreground violations) that they
qualify as jests. Implied in wit is a deeper code behind the
codes laughed at. Even in the wildest license of the plays of
Aristophanes standards are appealed to. Canons guide the
satiric laughter of the audience at the feigned exposure of the
pandemonium of Athenian life. Although his public of the
fifth century B.C. seemed to tolerate the most outrageous gibes,
respecting no decencies divine or human, and allowing the
representation of its world as greedy, treacherous, chaotic,
full of self-abuse and dissoluteness, there is still awareness of
aesthetic distance in its laughter (that this is only pretense!)
—along with recognition that the treatment of men *in actuality*
as ignoble vermin violates certain basic principles of human
dignity, tending thereby to the extinction of the individual and
the social system as well.

In its aesthetic distance and creative skill wit is a kind of
art and like art depends upon special talents limited to a few.
Like the artist the wit is often himself surprised at what he
creates, since in its rightness it seems more than an accidental
shuffling of materials yet exceeds his conscious prevision and
effort. In consequence not a few ascribe both wit and art to a
source in the unconscious, regarding its impetus and roots
as fundamentally irrational. With Freud the unconscious is
viewed as an undifferentiated psychic process (the source of
all others), which is at once blind, automatic, and governed
by our organic drives to satisfy creature needs according to the
pain-pleasure principle. Wit's function is to discharge psychic
energy in such a way as to free emotional forces from repression.

But if wit arises as the lily from the mud, and is controlled
by its roots in the alogical and irrational, the question is how

to account for the striking aptness and intelligibility of its product, the witticism, which stands the test of revealing sense in
nonsense, some pithy insight as its core. Just as it seems to
us inconceivable that a totally alogical world should generate
a logical one, so, we should say, the idea that we can have
a kind of awareness of an existent mental world within ourselves of which we are nevertheless unaware, a consciousness of
a *terra incognita* of the unconscious, seems absurd. Those who
hanker for a limbo of the unconscious should restrict its locus,
in our opinion, to physiology, should derive their conceptions
of wit from biology and relinquish such scientifically unverified
quantities as psychic energy, subliminal thought and perception.

Admittedly there are vast differences of clarity discernible
between the focus and fringe of consciousness, between foreground and background, attentive and inattentive awareness.
Still, admission of these distinctions appears preferable to accepting such contradictory notions as thoughtless thought,
senseless sense, or illogical logicality. Descartes was right, in
our opinion, in defining the psyche through self-consciousness
and implicitly derogating any psychic unconscious to the status
of self-contradictory nonsense. Undeniably in the creativity of
wit the formation of a new pattern of meaning in words where
previously there was none has a mysterious quality, assignable
by some to inspiration or to Platonic mania (madness) or
again to intuitive reason.[6] The latter especially seems to touch
the heart of the matter. For reason has a life, a power of illumination sometimes so swift, so deep as to seem without articulation or movement from premise to conclusion. Called intuition
or immediate inference, its light may be so bright as to hide
the source of its radiance. "It is intuitive reason that grasps
first principles," as Aristotle says;[7] and the wise man ought
to comprehend both their truth and the inferences from them.

---

[6] Jacques Maritain, *Creative Intuition in Art and Poetry* (New York,
Pantheon Books, 1953), p. 95.

[7] *Nicomachean Ethics* (Welldon trans.), 1141a-2-8.

Yet these first principles from which knowledge proceeds are
not so much discursively demonstrated as *seen,* for, like reason,
they cannot themselves be subjects of scientific empirical verification. Unlike the unconscious, which is conceived as an
adjunct of the body and its needs, as often pathological and
as always precritical and prelogical, intuitive reason shines in
its own light, carrying its canons in itself in self-confirmatory
insights involving reaffirmation in denial and *reductio ad*
absurdum of the opposite. Recognizing grounds as its basis,
reason is directed to ends that gratify intelligence, while the
body with its pleasures is treated as an instrument, not as a
first and final cause.

For all its fantastic levity, wit makes sense combining, as
we have said, insight into logical relations and the correction
of contradiction with a *mot just* or apt expression. Accordingly,
we must reject the view of wit as centered in uncovering "unconscious modes of thinking" derived from childish playing
with words or from thoughts prohibited by social criticism.
The Cartesian view is right in defining mind through self-consciousness, which through the operation of intelligence has
developed the realm of natural science with its tools of pre-
cision, as well as directing man's inner life to spiritual reflection and ideals. To conceive the mind, on the contrary, as an
iceberg for the most part hidden in the depths beyond penetration by consciousness, is to challenge not only our traditional conception of ourselves and the world but our accepted
techniques of advancing knowledge. Such a view represents
man as unable to understand himself merely by taking
thought, as largely blind hitherto as to the motivations and
psychic forces that move him, and hence unable to direct
his behavior by the logic of his conscious efforts. For to Freudians the greater portion of psychic life is hidden in the depths
of the unconscious concerning which most men have no knowledge. While admitting that the unconscious is capable of being
brought to awareness, Freudians regard it as beyond the reach

of ordinary self-analysis or introspection. Rather it is said to have its existence indicated through dreams and experiments in post-hypnotic suggestion. Divided by depth psychologists into the realms of the individual or *personal unconscious* and the *collective unconscious,* the subliminal mind is regarded as especially the seat of impulse, feeling, and emotion. Even though it is claimed to have the power to build up within itself an inner monitor (censor, superego) as a guide to principles and ideals, nevertheless the laws of its own nature are held devoid of the power of rational criticism, morality, or logic. Operating through associated imagery rather than grounds, leaping across time and space, without distinguishing between fantasies and facts, the unconscious self follows its feelings without regard to consistency so that opposing attitudes like love and hate, attraction and repulsion are not excluded from each other.

The aim of psychiatry, it is said, is to remove the human personality from control by the unconscious or subliminal forces of mind of which it is ignorant. Yet only a specialist in psychoneurosis, one skilled in the peculiar laws and behavior of this nether region, can present it to the understanding of consciousness. Precisely because the unconscious is beyond direct exploration by the intellect, beyond reach of the scrutiny of introspection, the first person subject possessing the unconscious mentation cannot bring it to light himself. His rational thought operating as interrogator, critic, censor, and policeman of his psychic life can never achieve full comprehension of his frustrations, repressions, fantasies, and motivations. If it could, he would have no unconscious left. In the end it would appear to be precisely because psychoanalysis claims to be an intellectual, scientific technique that it claims that no man can psychoanalyse himself, not even the psychoanalyst. That one cannot trust one's rational analysis of his consciousness to fathom the secrets of psychic life is, according to depth psychology, the great negative lesson learned since Descartes. To understand the unconscious, one must be analysed by another, and that other by still another, and so on in an indefinite regress. However, as in theology, a first cause or source of the series must be finally assumed. In depth psychology it is Freud, the founder of the system, who acts as God the Father, for whom alone initially the unconscious was not beyond the reach of introspection and intellectual exploration. He it was, according to the faithful, who deciphered the laws of the unconscious, and who alone by plumbing the abyss achieved true self-knowledge. His was the ascendancy of knowing the unknown.

But to use the Freudian thesis with its claims to discovery appears largely beyond proof or disproof, a *petitio* by which such psychiatry assumes the point at issue. The fact often noted that in many cases witticisms cannot withstand attention, so that to explain a joke destroys it, is due in the view of those who put the source of wit in the unconscious, to the blindness of the ordinary world to the subliminal, that is to the killing effect of a dissecting technique which moving wholly within the limits of conscious intelligence is cut off from understanding the fantasies and emotive symbols that emerge from a nether region beyond conscious control. But to those of us who question the existence of the unconscious as a part of mind with its own set of psychic processes this tendency of wit to evaporate when analysed applies especially to jokes that are not formally, intrinsically laughable to a marked degree but rather derive their incongruity from local peculiarities of custom, time, place, dialect, or other verbal idiosyncrasies. Thus the force of the witticism concerning a famous French beauty (I believe Manon Lescaut) that "She had every virtue but virtue," since it resides in the pun and is mainly verbal, may be destroyed on analysis or translation into certain other languages. On the other hand, Mark Twain's reply to the reporter, already cited, that "Reports of my death are greatly exaggerated" remains ludicrous despite analysis (and may be increased by it), since in any natural language or thought system a man must be either dead or not dead; it cannot really be a matter of degree nor can the deceased confirm his own death without flagrant self-contradiction.

As a kind of art, we have suggested, wit involves techniques of some refinement. On the logical side this ranges from clear invocation of formal laws to tricks or sophisms extending from simple ambiguity to implication of the opposite, paradox, and absurdity. While wit is said to thrive on faulty thinking, this is not the full essence of the matter, since detection of the error is required both by the wit himself and by his audience, which must be competent to relish its exposure. In short, blunders or fallacies are the material rather than the substance of wit, which demands for its appreciation high intelligence. Impossible as it is on the verbal side to enumerate all the linguistic devices used in wit (though Freud has attempted it) —which include besides word mixtures, substitutions, alterations in verbal order, usage of the same word for different images, and allusions—one device at least must be dwelt on: *condensation.*

In a very real sense, brevity is the soul of wit. Such brevity, which bespeaks both a verbal and a logical impulse, is rooted in the principle of simplicity or parsimony, familiar to science and known to scholastic logic as Occam's razor (entities should not be multiplied beyond necessity.) In large part the cleverness of wit consists in the originality combined with adroitness with which shortcuts and epitomizations of thought are expressed in pithy form. Slang, especially American slang, is often credited with witty additions to locution on this ground. Although slang is often rather the stuff from which witticisms may be made more than wit itself, H. L. Mencken in his work *The American Language*[8] has clearly shown how slang has provided ingenious minds an important way to make the

---

[8] H. L. Mencken, *The American Language* (4th ed. New York, Alfred A. Knopf, 1938).

language more terse, pungent, striking, picturesque, and to
give expression to new shades of insight. Expressions like
pussyfoot, wisecrack, bluff, debunk; compounds like hot-spot,
sob-sister, wind-bag, high-brow, sky-scraper, brain-trust, spell-
binder, fat-cat, do-gooder, kill-joy, lame-duck summarize
trains of thought in succinct epithets and images which convey
more than many words. In the speed-up of our modern mechanized world, such additions to the vocabulary recommend
themselves by their bare directness, their time and space sav-
ing quality as shortcuts. Mere brevity in itself, however, is not
enough to make them expressions of wit. For this they must
also possess some logical superiority—of relevance, clarity,
truth, especially some advantage of "least means" (of deriving
more from less, more meaning from less verbal outlay by by-
passing circumlocutions in argument), any one of which con-
tributes to the victory of parsimony. While the language of
previous "good English" may appear to be more polite, culti-
vated, elegant, and genteel—in short, the language of the
classes rather than the masses—slang by contrast seems less
banal, convention-ridden, roundabout, less given to pretense
and euphemisms.[9] It is fresher, more vivid, democratic, forceful, and blunt in facing facts; it is taut, well-knit, pertinent,
hitting the nail on the head, grasping the nub of the matter,
uncovering shams and hidden interconnections.

Moreover, far from being the product of the "unconscious
genius" of the race for language-making or of the natural

---

[9] Regarding the intrusion of slang into the British House of Commons, Mencken quotes from the English paper *Echo* for 1934: "Every
time the House of Commons meets things are said in a phraseology that
would shock and baffle Mr. Gladstone . . . Even Mr. Baldwin, one of
the few authorities on the King's English in the House, used in his
speech yesterday the expressions *backslide, best-seller,* and *party dog-
fight.* I have heard him use *to deliver the goods.* The House is undoubtedly Americanized in some of its phrases. I have heard *whoopee*
and *debunked* in the debating chamber, and *oh yeah* and *you're telling
me* in the lobby. *To pass the buck* is a well-known House expression and
it is often used." (*The American Language,* p. 228.)

drollery of the people as a whole, slang is found upon inquiry
to be the product of the intellectual ingenuity of a small
minority, the creation of special talent. "College slang," it
is said (and from its currency comes some of the best), "is
actually made by the campus wits, just as general slang is
made by the wits of the newspapers and theaters."[10] The
chief coiners today of the pregnant, dramatic words and
phrases called slang are found to be popular journalists, head-
line writers for the press, comic strip artists, college and
theatrical wits, telecasters, and other specialists in the so-called
arts of communication. All of these are bent upon capturing
a wider audience by devices of abbreviation, pungent phrasing,
graphic picturization, a feat largely accomplished through
the invention of a type of speech with power and punch
enough to waylay even a jaded, apathetic, uncultivated public. The avidity of press, publishers, and broadcasters to reap
the profits to be got by commanding the attention of millions
of citizens ordinarily engrossed in their personal affairs is im-
mense; and the extremes to which they will go to arouse interest, by fitting their message into the contracted dimensions of
the screen or press headlines, as well as into the limited reading, viewing, and listening time available to busy men, is
amazing. Yet these are the factors which in large part account
today in America for the increasing use of wrenched, com-
pacted, and compounded words in public speech, in what to
purists seems the most barbarous way. In some quarters the
new jargon or lingo has been scornfully referred to as "head-
line English." "This," said G. K. Chesterton, "is one of the
evils produced by that *passion for compression* and compact
information which possesses so many ingenious minds in
America. Everybody can see how an entirely new system of
grammar, syntax, and even language has been invented to fit
the brevity of the headlines. Such brevity, so *far from being the*

---

[10] Mencken, p. 559.

soul of wit, is even the death of meaning; and certainly the death of logic."[11]

But whether this modification of the language through the intrusion of slang does indeed mark the death of wit, meaning, and logic may be questioned. Admittedly, in so far as the increase of slang marks a rise of irresponsible exaggeration and emotionalism, a preference for the melodramatic and violent, it is seriously disturbing. Many deep social causes (quite distinct from the "passion for compression"), including the growth of democracy, mechanization, and the new technologies of communication, have contributed to such tendencies. On the other hand, as already conceded, mere brevity is far from being identical with wit or intelligence. On occasion truncated utterance may very well be a mark of feeble-mindedness or lack of meaning. Still it is otherwise with succinct, pregnant expression. In so far as society comes to prefer this to more verbose, vague, roundabout locution, in so far as a few words can be made to do the work of many without loss of relevance, clearness, and consistency, we have an advance in logical parsimony. In this sense witticisms represent a victory for rational method, that is for "least means," the shortest route in speech, the minimum outlay of terms. Epigrams, witty thoughts tersely expressed in proverbs, are a widely popular form of wit (not dissimilar to slang) found in most cultures, from *Poor Richard's Almanac* ("Experience keeps a dear school, but fools will learn in no other") to *Don Quixote's* "He who is covered with honey will never lack flies," or again to such Chinese proverbs as "A dragon stranded in shallow water furnishes bait for the shrimp" or "He who rides the tiger finds it difficult to dismount." In all of these the principle of least means is utilized to expose amusingly the incongruity in a situation in the most condensed, vividly provocative form.

The aim is not, as Freudians suggest, to achieve an economy

---

[11] *G. K.'s Weekly,* May 2, 1931. Italics mine. Quoted from Mencken, p. 185.

of biological energy, by avoiding thought and taking the easiest way *psychologically*, but to minimize the outlay in argument while enriching and clarifying the interconnections. In other words, the impulse is to bring out the relation between seemingly remote ideas and to epitomize them in apposite expression, as in the proverb that likens the great man to a dragon and the crowd of small ones to shrimp. This tendency to derive much from little, to achieve the shortest distance between premise and conclusion, suppressing intervening stages of reflection, appears constantly in Shakespeare: for instance, in Hamlet's ironical censure of his mother's hasty remarriage, "Thrift, thrift, Horatio! The funeral baked meats did coldly furnish forth the marriage tables." By a concise image Hamlet reveals in these incongruous events the source of his distress. Far from indicating thoughtlessness or irrelevance, wit turns on the versatility of mind to find fresh affiliations and applications, to double on its tracks, as it were, linking items far afield in new integrations which suggest the ultimacy of system.[12] The same effect is produced by Voltaire's epigrams, such as "You cannot tell the truth without singeing somebody's beard," or "Burn a good book and the cinders will fly up and strike your face." Here the unexpected image of fire suggests the uncontrollable power of truth and the dangers of censorship in an incomparably succinct way.

Of Voltaire's wit in repartee many tales are told, particularly of his trials at Fernay with persistent and often self-invited guests. One, the Abbé Goyer, on his arrival calmly announced that he had come to stay six weeks. "In what respect, my dear Abbé," said Voltaire, "are you unlike Don Quixote? He took inns for châteaux, and you take châteaux for inns?" The Abbé left the next day. To avoid such guests, Voltaire sometimes went to bed and said that he was dying. One caller who had received this message returned the next day. "Tell him

---

[12] M. C. Swabey, *Logic and Nature*, pp. 77–78.

I am dying again," said Voltaire, "and if he comes any more, say I am dead." But his visitor, a doctor, shrewdly replied, "Then I will bury him. In my profession I am used to burying people." This wit appealed to Voltaire and the caller was admitted. "You seem to take me for some curious animal," said Voltaire. "Yes, Monsieur," was the rejoinder, "for the phoenix."[13]

Wit, particularly in repartee, is not long sustained but lives in flights and perchings, in challenge and rejoinder. Often it turns on logical or verbal quibbles (as, in the Voltaire example, in the impossibility of the same man dying or being dead several times) accompanied by an unmasking of double dealing or hidden motives. Of especial interest is the suppression of any sign of sympathetic feeling in the witty locution, although compassion with the appearance of unjust suffering may have been the motive in certain cases for the resort to barbed witticisms. Still, one of the marked differences of wit from humor is the predominant intellectuality of the former accompanied by a chill aloofness, a standoffishness toward its object, the frequent proclivity to exhibit a cutting edge suggesting definite hostility or intended cruelty in its effect. In humor, on the contrary, we laugh not merely *at* but *with* the person or situation that is the occasion of the joke; our convivial fellow-feeling at once stimulates our humorous perception and enters into its expression, so that our emotional attitude is positive and expansive rather than negative and contractive as is so often the case with witticisms. Nevertheless the *playfulness* of wit in both thought and words is at least equal to that of humor. Perhaps indeed, as has been suggested, wit excels other types of the comic in its resemblance to a game, a form of sport or frolicsome action carried on in a lively, recreative spirit. To be both fun and funny, it must admit of restraint by rules, which are fairly, honestly obeyed as in other

---

[13] S. G. Tallentyre, *Life of Voltaire*, p. 365.

gay, light-hearted contests, one of the chief of which is *to lose without whining.*

To repeat by way of summary, although wit appears often unstudied, swift, unpredictable, drawn from more remote, secret corners of the mental background than other expressions of the comic, its source is not attributable to the murky depths of an irrational, illogical unconscious. In substance, wit calls attention to some congruity in incongruity of the scene in a light, playful way, which is nonetheless compact with reflection and conveys an intellectual insight. To construe its brevity of locution as simply economy of expenditure of psychic energy is altogether a mistake, since the wittiness of wit consists not so much in its psycho-physical peculiarities as in its logical adroitness, crispness, aptness, or concinnity at the level of conscious understanding.

As opposed to wit, which we have seen lives largely in language asd is predominantly intellectual, humor signifies a quality that pertains to actions, happenings, situations, or upon occasion to the verbal expression of ideas, which appeals markedly to sympathetic emotion for the appreciation of incongruity. As noted at the outset (Ch. 1), we have sought to avoid the use of the term humor in a generic sense in this essay, as a synonym for the ludicrous. For instance, we have not employed the phrase "the sense of humor," which seems to indicate a mental faculty or disposition to grasp the whole range of the ludicrous, our objection being not only that such an expression encourages confusion as to the meaning of the term "sense" (restricted in exact usage to a capacity possessing a specific end organ for receiving impressions of the outside world—as sight or smell—whereas humor has no such specialized end organ), but also because of the difficulty induced by the phrase of distinguishing humor from wit, irony, satire, etc. as a species among other species of the ludicrous. Although wit and humor cannot always be distinguished as different varieties of the comic, the humorous situation, insight, or remark is noteworthy as stimulating man's genial, sympathetic sensibilities as much as, if not more than, his reflective acuity.

Lincoln is remembered not so much for his wit as for his humor. A typical instance is his advice to Grant on the capture of Jefferson Davis. As so often, he began with a leisurely, seemingly purposeless story about a town drunkard who took the pledge. The next day, said Lincoln, the drunkard became terribly thirsty, so he went to a neighboring saloon and ordered a lemonade. As the barkeeper was mixing it, he said to him "Can't you just unbeknownst to me put a shot of whisky into that lemonade?" "Just so, you Grant," said Lincoln, fixing his eyes on the general, "having captured Jefferson Davis, might unbeknownst to ourselves let him escape." To which singular order the general replied, "I will do my best, Mr. President." Here the nub of the joke lies of course in the impossibility of the command's both knowing and not knowing of the prisoner's being afforded a means of escape, as in the analogical absurdity of ordering without ordering an alcoholic lemonade.

That the deliverances of humor allow more room for sentiment and geniality of feeling, that they are characterized more by a fund of wisdom from experience than by the intellectual brilliance of strokes of wit, seems generally admitted. Whereas wit is dry, tense, compressed in expression, humor tends to be loose, easy-going, meandering, often seemingly oblivious of the absurdity at its base. While some (like Sully) describe humor as "the quieter enjoyment of things laughable," this appears to us as by no means always the case. On the contrary, the deliverances of humor are often turbulent, unsubdued, and uproarious. That this is so may be owing to its wider range of expression which, unlike the verbalism of wit, may be found frequently in occasions beyond the reach of words. Humor may show itself in pranks, horseplay, practical jokes, in the odd appearance or erratic behavior of clowns, freaks, and fools, in things which excite strong reactions.

Nevertheless, if not quieter, humor is more contented, usually lasts longer, is more sustained in attitude and expression than wit—perhaps because its demands are not so exacting. Because it makes less demand on intellect and allows free play to feeling, humor is more liberating, expansive, less inhibiting and restrictive than wit. The humorist has often a deep understanding of life with its problems, an imaginative sympathy with the objects of his jests. He has sagacity rather than cleverness and a sentiment of kindness toward things as they are. Indeed, this relish of things as they are with all their defects occupies the foreground; there is not much stress upon the normative or what ought to be, either as a positive goal to be sought or as a negative standard by which (as in wit) human shortcomings are singled out for cutting emphasis. The perceptions of humor are warm and good natured, not biting and cold. Its mood is less corrective than tolerant, even compassionate, toward the imperfections of the world. The humorous man has known sorrow; his own experiences of inadequacy and failure help him to share the feelings of others. Savoring both the laughter and the tears of things, his spirit is at once grave and gay. It is this acceptance and appropriation of suffering that especially characterizes the humorous insight, and that brings it sometimes within hailing distance of the religious outlook. However, discussion of the relation of humor to the religious attitude must be postponed till later in the chapter.

While wit is admittedly akin to art, there is more difference of opinion as regards humor. According to Kant, for instance, humor, while involving a certain gratifying exhilaration of originality, lacks the talent requisite for high art.[14] Humorous expression, in his eyes, though exhibiting the capacity voluntarily to assume a frame of mind the reverse of the ordinary in order by contrast to excite a laugh, nevertheless hardly

---

[14] Kant, *Critique of Judgment*, p. 181.

suggests more than a pleasurable pastime demanding skill. But since the object of humor requires no seriousness and need have no worth in itself, its presentation cannot be properly included in fine (or beautiful) art.

The great champion of humor as art—particularly *humorous* exposition as opposed to the *comic* or the *witty* narration—is Mark Twain. His chief concern, as in the case of Kant, is with the funny story told by word of mouth. The comic and the witty story are credited by Mark Twain to the English and the French respectively, but the humorous one is held to be distinctively American. While the comic and the witty anecdote seem to demand a crowning contradiction, being brief and to the point they can be told by *anyone* without special gifts or talent. In contrast, the humorous story is held to depend mainly on the *manner* of the telling rather than the content, and its narration is a work of art. Often the humorous presentation is rambling, disjointed, spun out to great lengths, seemingly arriving nowhere. "To string incongruities and absurdities together in a wandering and sometimes purposeless way, and seem innocently unaware that they are absurdities, is the basis of the . . . Art."[15] Even when occasionally the story does lead up to a "snapper," the nub is often slurred, something never done by the teller of the comic story, who likes to prepare his audience in advance (by saying perhaps that this is the funniest story he has ever heard), who tends to bear down upon and shout the climax, or even to explain it afterward—a thing so "depressing," says Twain, as to make one want to "renounce joking and lead a better life."

Besides slurring the nub and the rambling presentation, two other features of the humorous story are the dropping of a studied remark innocently as if one were thinking aloud and the use of the *pause*. In the last, exact timing is all-important. For if the pause before the climax is too short the interval will

---

[15] Mark Twain, "How to Tell a Story," Vol. 22, Author's National Edition (Hartford, Conn., 1901).

not suffice for the audience to build up a strained expectation
for what is coming, so that they will not appreciate it on arrival; while if the pause is too long they will be led to expect
too much, and the climax will not come off. From all this
emphasis upon technique we gather that dramatic ability to
produce a certain psychological effect upon an audience is the
chief requirement of the humorist, who may succeed with
almost nothing to tell just as a good comedian may get by with
some very poor jokes. Indeed, the humorist may be applauded
for a story which has no intellectual point, no central contradiction of plot or dialogue at all. Rather his success may depend upon his peculiarities of manner as a raconteur: his
semblance of innocent foolishness, his tricks of dialect, local
color, exaggeration, small absurdities by the way, repetition,
and timing. By his guileless inadvertence of manner the humorist gives his auditor the pleasant illusion of discovering
these drolleries for himself, while the confidential tone of the
telling awakens the hearer's sympathetic rapport.

By way of illustration two stories are offered, one described
as comic, the other as humorous. The comic story, said to have
been popular throughout the world for a thousand years, is
called "The Wounded Soldier." It relates how in the thick of
a battle a soldier whose leg had been shot off appealed to a
comrade to carry him to the rear. Just after the Samaritan
had shouldered his burden, a cannon ball, without his being
aware of it, took off the wounded man's head as well. On
reaching the rear, the burden-bearer was accosted by an officer
who called out "Where are you going with that headless
carcass?" At this, the Samaritan put down his burden, and
looking around at it in surprise exclaimed, "Why he told me it
was his leg!" Here the culminating contradiction is so obvious,
that, as Mark Twain says, "a *machine* could tell the story."
However when a humorist such as James Whitcomb Riley told
it, impersonating a dull-witted old farmer, his characterization,
according to Twain, so enriched the telling as to make it *a*

humorous story many times funnier than the comic one. In short, the difference between the two is between a logical effect produced by a narration centering in a contradiction in the content and a psychological or theatrical effect produced by the narrator through his artistry.

This contrast is brought out even more strikingly in the second tale offered to illustrate the strictly humorous as opposed to the comic. This is a negro ghost story told with great success by Mark Twain to large audiences, but which set down in cold print without the charm of his drawling characterization amounts to little. The story (called "The Golden Arm") concerns the death and burial of a colored woman possessed of a golden arm and its retrieval from the grave at midnight by her husband for mercenary motives. As he returns to the house with the precious object, he is pursued by his wife's spectre asking "Who's got my arm?" Suspense mounts with each repetition of the question till the climax, when just as the culprit regains his bed and cowers beneath the covers he is seized by the ghost with the triumphant yell "You've got it!" Here the only pattern discernible is the psychological one of strained expectation ending in nothing, and unless we are prepared to admit that nervous laughter giving vent to surprise is the mark of humor, and that the dramatic manner of the telling, rather than the form or matter, is all, we must in our opinion give up the claim that this is a truly humorous story. For although as in most ghost stories there is some contradiction of natural laws, there is no intellectual incongruity to give point to the content, no warmth or pathos in the characters to arouse our sympathy, both of which, as we see it, are necessary to the humorous anecdote.

Curiously enough a view somewhat akin to this of humor as ultimately turning upon an expectation ending in nothing is offered by Stephen Leacock. Indeed, when viewed with detachment, life itself as tending to annihilation becomes a joke. The best examples of humor cited by Leacock as expressing the confrontation of nothingness and unanswered hopes have a metaphysical slant: Huck Finn and Nigger Jim floating down the Mississippi on their raft discussing the mysteries of the universe, or the spectacle of Dickens' debtors. "Thus does life," Leacock assures us, "if we look at it from sufficient distance, dissolve itself into 'humor.' "[16] But in its highest form humor no longer excites laughter; rather it represents an "inner absorption of the mind in something utterly unconnected with the pains, the pleasures, the profit, and the work of life" (p. 263). Its standpoint is outside the vital process, "a retrospect, as it were, in which the fever and fret of our earthly lot is contrasted with its short-comings, its lost illusions and its inevitable end" (261). At bottom humor harbors a metaphysical contrast that remains unresolved, an insight that "nothing matters" since nullity, nonentity puts a term to it all. Like scientific naturalism Leacock looks forward to the finis of things, when life, mind, matter, together with the framework of space and time, shall be destroyed. At that date, everything dissolves into humor. "All ends with a cancellation of forces and comes to nothing; and our universe ends thus with one vast, silent, unappreciated joke" (268).

For our part, on the contrary, while agreeing that humor is metaphysical, we are far from finding its upshot in the cosmic irony of extinction or an atheism of spirit. Instead of exploding like a blank cartridge, humor in its highest reaches, as in Shakespeare or Cervantes, appears to us to express an outlook that resolves the incongruities of the world into an enveloping harmony. The mood it excites is genial, compassionate, and inclusive. And whether regarded as a mode of appreciation or as the quality of a state of affairs, humor centers in a timeless pattern akin to value and mind.

Mention of the metaphysical intimations of humor brings us back to the point touched on earlier of its relation to the re-

---

[16] Stephen Leacock, *Humor: Its Theory and Technique* (New York, Dodd, Mead & Co., 1935), p. 268.

ligious attitude. Here philosophy owes to Kierkegaard its most
penetrating treatment of the subject. "I am not," says Kierkegaard self-depreciatingly, "a religious individual, but solely a
humorist."[17] Yet to humor he attaches the greatest importance
as the border zone, the incognito of the religious life. Existence,
as we saw in the last chapter, is divided by him into three
stages: first, the *aesthetic* phase having irony as the border
area separating it from the *ethical* or second stage; following
this comes humor as the *confinium* between the ethical and
the highest or *religious* phase. Humor has this close kinship
with the religious outlook, not simply because it achieves (like
irony) a transcendental standpoint, but because it includes
awareness of what Kierkegaard calls human guilt—of man's
responsibility yet inadequacy to measure up to the absolute
Idea—so that in consequence *suffering* is of the very nature
of his existence.

Once the individual has passed beyond the *aesthetic* stage on
life's way, has outgrown merely dreaming over and enjoying
life (or even making ironic comments upon it), he plunges
into the midst of things, he commits himself and becomes
involved (*engagé*) at the *ethical* level. This means that he no
longer stands on the sidelines viewing the contradictions and
fusions of the ideal and the real. But he leaps resolutely into
the welter of actuality, accepting for himself the obligations
of the moral life. He takes sides in the great struggle between
right and wrong, assuming his burden as a finite being who
submits to an infinite requirement. He becomes aware of his
duty to marry, to raise a family, to cultivate friends, to adopt
a calling, and to relate himself to the problems of the public
world, as a means by which to reach union with humanity and
to sound the depths of existence.

Thus the ethical stage is essentially struggle, a struggle
through which a man comes to himself as a member of society

---

[17] Kierkegaard, *Concluding Unscientific Postscript*, p. 448.

and the human world. Yet in the process of this striving the individual becomes increasingly aware of his own and others' failures in comparison with what ought to be, the perfect, the infinite demand. Painful awareness grows of how far he and mankind in general fall short of the ideal. The individual acquires a deepening sense of wrongdoing, weakness, distress, and a desire for repentance. At the close of this second stage, a man comes to know himself as a *guilty* being; he *despairs* with his whole personality, whereas the *ironic* doubt which plagued him at the close of the aesthetic level was more superficial and intellectual. Yet although a man acknowledges *guilt* at the ethical stage, he does not, according to Kierkegaard, completely experience the consciousness of *sin,* the full sense of individual responsibility for his failure, until he attains the religious level.

However, the ethical stage culminates in repentance, in recognition of one's failure to find fulfillment in human relations and social life, in an emptiness at the core. There is a yearning for something further that shall lead us beyond the world of natural existence. Such an attitude of despondency at not finding what we sought, at a lack of bed rock within the human scheme, leads to transition to the third level of the *religious,* with its awareness of an eternal power permeating existence. This level, although distinctively marked by suffering, brings with it a sense of fulfillment. Its dialectical or quasi-contradictory character *unites the suffering of repentance* (which comes through breaking the tie with existence by realizing that the relativities of this world should be taken relatively) *with the leap of faith,* by which, though aware of one's nothingness in the face of the infinite, one feels related to an eternal blessedness and knows an absolute joy. "Humor," says Kierkegaard, "is the last stage of existential inwardness before faith."[18] It is familiar with suffering, rooted in seriousness,

---

[18] Kierkegaard, *Postscript,* p. 259.

aware of the difference between a relation to the relative and
a relation to the absolute *telos*. But though cognizant of the difference between the finite and the infinite, the temporal and the
eternal, the humorist does not sustain a living relation to God.
"The humorist," says Kierkegaard, "constantly . . . sets the
God-idea into conjunction with other things and evokes the
contradiction—but he does not maintain a relationship to
God in terms of religious passion *stricte sic dictus,* he trans-
forms himself instead into a jesting and yet profound exchange-
center for all these transactions, but he does not himself stand
related to God. The religious man does the same, he sets the
God-idea into juxtaposition with everything and sees the contradiction, but in his inmost consciousness he is related to
God."[19]

While the humorist as such *knows about* the religious attitude, he lacks the decisive commitment to it which bespeaks
the inwardness of faith. Yet because he has known reflectively
the suffering, the moral conflict, and deep disappointments of
life, existence has lost its authority over him; in contemplating
its pretenses and pathos, the posturing of the finite in the face
of the infinite, he grasps the abysmal absurdity of the spectacle.
The humorous outlook, having acquiesced in sorrow as part
of the secret of life in place of vainly trying to escape it, tries
to transcend it. Kierkegaard remarks in his *Journals,* July 9,
1837, "I am a Janus *bifrons;* I laugh with one face, I weep
with the other. But *humor is also the joy which has overcome
the world.*"[20]

In grasping suffering as essential to life the humorous man
distinguishes it from misfortune. He comprehends existence as
one thing, and fortune and misfortune as something else hap-
pening more or less accidentally to the individual. The mere
removal of misfortune, he understands, cannot change the
nature of human life which is a process of growth, conflict,

---

[19] Kierkegaard, *Postscript,* p. 451.
[20] *A Kierkegaard Anthology,* ed. Bretall, p. 8. Italics mine.

inner and outward striving. Existence cannot stand still; we must go forward or backward, expand or contract so long as we live—which means that we must undergo toil, trouble, distress—since an eternal happiness cannot be had in the temporal process. So when someone undergoes a misfortune and cries out in despair, thinking himself undone by this one mishap, and that if he were only free from this how perfectly happy his life would be, then the humorist, who has learned to reconcile himself to pain, ascends his higher standpoint and makes a jest. His jest may take some such homely form as saying "Aye, what poor wretches we human beings are, involved in all these manifold miseries of life, we all suffer; now if I could only live to see the day when my landlord installs a new bellpull . . . I would count myself the happiest of men."[21]

Such a pleasantry has varied implications. In noting that "we all suffer" the humorist swings away from concern with the individual to the species, calling attention to the common lot of misery in human life. He hints that life itself being a process of change in its nature involves distress, adversity, and disappointment, hence the condition is irremovable. Elsewhere he admits that "we are all debtors" apparently allowing misfortune as a payment for guilt. In any case, standing as nothing before the absolute, we are all offenders, transgressors, deserving neither happiness nor good luck. Seen against the absolute as a background there is an absurdity in taking the relativities of this world, the accidental differences of weal and woe as between man and man, as ultimately significant. Hence the humorist parries the complaints of the sufferer with a jest.

Even if we do not entirely agree with this account, we must recognize that it touches upon a profound point, that of the metaphysical, supermundane quality of humor, particularly of the higher humor. Sex, politics, the manners of society, the existent world of here and now are for the most part the theme

---

[21] Kierkegaard, *Postscript,* p. 401.

of wit and of the comic in its narrower connotation. Such things as beginnings and ends, anxieties of the soul, death, spiritual destiny, and divine law are largely beyond these latter —though not entirely beyond the reach of humor. For humor has a speculative, a poetic range whereby the feelings, intuition, and intellect, being in union, sometimes reach out and touch translunary things.

In the picture of Falstaff's death (*Henry V*, II. 3) is the pathos and illimitable humor of all human frailty. On the dark side is the verdict that "the king has killed his heart" (inducing thereby chills and a burning fever); we hear how in his delirium Falstaff, mistaking a flea on Bardolph's nose for a black soul burning in hell fire, cried out of his sins to God three or four times; and how the kind heart of Mistress Quickly, yearning with the ancient sophistry of death-bed manners, urged him to good cheer saying there was no need to trouble with such thoughts yet. What unfathomable humor and pathos in the hostess' account of his passing—how, striving to speak well of the dead, she attempts to gloss over his references to his besetting sin about women, until contradicted by the innocent voice of youth, when the boy cries out that he said they were "devils incarnate," to which she equivocates with the priceless rejoinder "A' could never abide carnation. 'Twas a color he never lik'd," and seeks to cloak as scriptural learning the knight's talk of whores and "the whore of Babylon." On the bright side, we have her compassionate assurance that "A' made a finer end, and went away an it had been any christome child," while among his companions grieving for him, Bardolph exclaims "Would I were with him, wheresome'er he is, either in heaven or in hell!"—a wish bespeaking a pitch of devotion such as few better men have awakened in their friends. To which the hostess retorts in pure genius "Nay, sure, he's not in hell. He's in Arthur's bosom, if ever man went to Arthur's bosom."

Instantly we feel the appropriateness of this, the impropriety

of sending him either to heaven or hell. We love the old hum-
bug; he must evade our moral judgment and be sent back to
some happy hunting ground. This great child of nature with
his inextinguishable joy in life must be consigned to some
near-pagan, kindly, mythical realm fit for men of abounding
vigor, for hardy heroes of the race, in short, to Arthur's bosom.

For although comedy, as well as tragedy, has its nemesis, its
penalties are of this world and may (if the comedy is humorous) be softened by pity and kindliness. In a fashion the fat
knight has paid the debt for his sins: for his idleness, coward-
ice, lies, drunkeness, gluttony, and lechery, through the diseases
and low estate that these indulgences brought upon him, and
worst of all through his being cast off by the prince. For he
had loved the prince, not merely as the potential giver of all
good gifts but as the sole kindred spirit worthy of him in wit
and fantasy. Then came the cold shoulder to all his dreams of
bibulous revelry at court; and he found himself instead left
lonely, ailing, and pining to his death in a mean hostelry. True,
this old white-bearded satan is the author of his own undoing,
the agent of his proper woe. He is, to mix metaphors, hoisted
on his own petard, his chickens come home to roost, and his
sins carry their punishment with them. In him we sense the
self-destruction of evil through its own inconsistency.

Yet for all his vices Falstaff is no villain; in him one discovers none of the chillness of heart, sour temper, ill will,
malice, envy, vengefulness, vaulting ambition, and deadly
hypocrisy of Shakespeare's great villains. Presumably his vices
mainly injure himself; perhaps indeed the appetite for socia-
bility has been his downfall ("Company, villainous company
hath been the spoil of me"). "If to be old and merry be a sin,
... if to be fat is to be hated," then only shall we hate Falstaff.
Rather we forgive him his sins for his enormous gusto, amia-
bility, his exuberance toward life. As has been said many times,
in him we find our other selves; we gain release for our impulses, for our bodily appetites that are conventionally held

in restraint, and from our cautious, prudential, rather petty selves, tethered to thrift yet longing for rashness. We laugh both with him and at him for, as he says, he is both witty in himself and the cause of wit in others. Without serious thinking, he comprehends both the world and himself. One cannot imagine him grave, solemn, sedate for a moment. Always on his mettle, he comments on his own dwindling decline ("withered like an old apple-john") and his need for repentance in the same jaunty vein as he chafes Justice Shallow. Somehow he reconciles us to the universe; unfailingly at home in the world, he makes us feel at home also. Here humor, instead of simply economizing the feelings as Freud suggests,[22] provides in the picture of his life and death a catharsis of them or liberating effect.

As with other men, the comicality of Falstaff's character stems from his contradictions: his pretended bravery, patriotism, industry, and sense of honor, as against the reality of a boastful poltroon, deadbeat, thief, and rascal. Not only do his protestations quite gainsay his practice, not only is a knight, a member of the gentry, found consorting with cutpurses and the lowest scum, but we are fascinated by other conflicting facets of his personality. Here is old age with the spirit of youth, a nimble wit in a lumbering body, the slow motion of a corpulent frame coupled with mental resourcefulness and lightning ingenuity.

Especially in his joy in make-believe, in change of fronts, and juxtaposing opposites through masquerade, we have one of his distinctive traits. With Richard II, Falstaff may well say "Thus play I in one person many people." Yet in his love of disguises and protean forms Falstaff expresses his imaginative versatility, his delight in comic incongruity rather than any real taste for being an actor—that is, for mimicry and producing good imitations. On the contrary, so carried away is Falstaff by the ebullience of his comic imagination that he is hardly concerned

---

[22] Freud, *Wit and Its Relation to the Unconscious,* p. 384.

that his shams should deceive others—as when relating his prowess in the robbery at Gadshill he so enlarges on the number of the enemy, together with the circumstantial detail of their buckram suits of Kendall green seen in pitch darkness, that the story collapses of its own weight. As the prince says, "These lies are like the father that begets them: gross as a mountain, open, palpable." Indeed, anyone who has known in the course of his life some strikingly humorous character will recall their possession, similar to Falstaff's, of a love of tall tales, pranks, horseplay, tomfoolery, beguiling tricks, put-up jobs, and ingenious misrepresentations. As for Falstaff's impersonations of Prince Hal's father (Henry III) or of the Prince himself, not to mention his play at being dead on the field of battle, at being deaf before the Chief Justice, or his painting himself as reverend virtue—all this is the jest of *seeming* what you *aren't*, changing shapes, standing outside oneself, enjoying pretense, counterfeit as against reality.

Humor, as we have said, is metaphysically deeper than wit. Whereas wit stands above life's battles, crowing like chanticleer over some men's victories and others' defeats; whereas it stands apart from the turmoil like a Micromegas or a Gulliver scoffing at the pettiness of human affairs, humor surpasses wit in its capacity to be both immanent and transcendent in outlook, to enjoy both something like total perspective which reapportions the importance of things from an Olympian slant, and also humanly to share a vicarious intimacy with others. Humor introduces us to the hearts of our fellows, enabling us to compare others with ourselves, and ourselves with them. Sometimes bacchanalian, never puritanically censorious, it accepts man's nature, its fleshly and spiritual mystery, as beyond the shallows of mere fashion and convention. Where wit is dry, humor is freshening and enlivening. Though wit is more social, more public in its demands, usually requiring a trio in communication, humor is more an inner mood, yet always friendly in spirit even when appearing in the silent appreciation of a situation by oneself alone. As we have said, the secret of the

highest humor is generosity, broadmindedness, and beneficence; its concern is with the whole twisted, agonizing yet
somehow joyous process of living, with humanity and not
merely with a particular society or the manners of a day. It
takes us out of ourselves on a voyage of discovery, enabling us
to scrutinize the world at different levels: to observe its sensuous appearance, its accent, face, and gait, its clothes and
gestures; to grasp the underlying traits of characters and the
problems latent in situations; and finally to touch the hem of
the infinite through the contradictions of the finite in the
mortal yet immortal intimations of the whole human comedy.

As on the moor the fool with Lear "labors to outjest his
heartstruck injuries," as the quips and quibbles of the grave-
diggers mingle with Hamlet's soliloquy on the skull of Yorick,
as the unquenchable dignity amid indignities of Don Quixote
and his squire awaken us from satiric mirth to the pathos of
man's nobility, so the greatest humor haunts the caverns of
the soul, suggesting at once the petty scale of our doings and
the vastness of an unfathomable destiny. At its core humor
seems to point to a consonance of the comic and tragic, by
which the great and small incongruities of life are somehow
reconciled in a cosmic unity. One feels it in the spirit of bene-
diction hovering over the greatest tragedy and comedy. Indeed,
one may catch a hint of this ambivalent unity in the simplest,
crudest love story: the tale of a boy and a girl, of a pert miss
and a mere slip of a youth, without distinction of character,
talent, or good looks, yet in whom awakens a spark with its
claim to be an absolute passion, which arouses in us at once
an impulse to laugh and an intimation of the profound mystery
of the soul in its search for the infinite. In Kierkegaard, we
find this consciousness of the unity of the comic and tragic in
life, as when he says, "In poverty I see the tragedy that an
immortal soul suffers, and the comedy that it all turns on two
shillings."[23]

---

[23] Kierkegaard, *Stages on Life's Way,* trans. Walter Lowrie (Princeton
University Press, 1940), p. 418.

CHAPTER 6

Types of Comic Incongruity

HAVING traced the meaning of the comic, in the broad sense, to that quality of a character, action, situation, or expression of ideas which appears incongruous, we are led to pursue the matter further by seeking to discover the different uses and degrees of import of the term incongruous. Things are commonly said to be incongruous when "characterized by lack of harmony, consistency, or compatibility with one another," or when they "disagree" or are "misfits"; while fitness is described by such synonyms as appropriate, proper, suitable, adapted or qualified for a purpose. Although the basic terms here (harmony, consistency, compatibility) are obviously drawn from the sphere of logic and the fundamental principles of rationality, nonetheless in other phrases defining the incongruous as "lack of mutual fitness," "unsuitable," or "unadapted," the logical connotation is lost or rendered subservient to the teleological.

Here we come upon a puzzle concerning the ludicrous, one particularly connected with the name of Kant, as to whether the judgment of the comic is logical or teleological. At first sight, the very notion that perception of the comic requires ideation or mental activity seems to imply that it is primarily a logical judgment. But against this stands the Kantian contention that in the excitation of comic laughter there is no satisfaction of the understanding but a mere play of representations through which ultimately nothing is thought.[1] Consequently the comic judgment is not logical but aesthetical, by which is to be understood that whose determining ground can be *no other than subjective.*[2] That is to say, comic laughter, on the Kantian view, expresses no cognition of the object but refers through the imagination to the feeling of pleasure or pain in the subject as affected by the representation, and hence is called aesthetical. The aesthetic judgment is said to be teleological, moreover, because it ascribes to the imputed object a certain adaptiveness of its parts in the whole, a certain purposiveness without purpose, which is presumably only in us but not out there in the external world.

But in our view, as against Kant, the judgment arousing comic laughter contains an objective insight into the rational order of things, even though we should not deny its secondary involvement of sensibility or feeling. On the one hand, such awareness centers in a conflict of representations infringing on, but corrected by, objective logical laws; on the other, it is accompanied by a pleasing sense of fitness or appropriateness, which may be called teleological or aesthetic. For instance, we laugh at the naïveté of a child who, on receiving an unpleasing gift, frankly avows his distaste for it to the giver. Here the original simplicity of human nature, which does not understand how to dissemble, breaks out in contrast to the arts of polite dissimulation. Our expectancy of a "fair but false show" of feigned pleasure is "suddenly transformed into nothing"[3] on hearing the voice of unspoiled innocence. We laugh with delight at the refutation of the world's conventional hypocrisy by the frank deliverances of youth. Here, *grasping the contradiction along with its rectification* constitutes the core of the ludicrous insight in our opinion, rather than the *nullification of our anticipation* as Kant holds, since we may have suspected

---

[1] Kant, *Critique of Judgment,* p. 176.
[2] Kant, pp. 37–38.
[3] Kant, p. 180.

from the beginning that a child untrained in social pretense would openly report his feelings. At the same time we are aware of a vague perception of rightness in the child's gaucherie, an appropriateness in his spontaneity, a pleasing fitness in his unfitness, a welcome feeling of adaptation in the occurrence although it served no particular purpose. Often in the enjoyment of a joke, comic object, or situation there is a teleological sense of the parts being somehow *made for each other*, rendered all the stronger by the fact that it may involve a slightly painful absurdity. Yet despite this there is a kind of adroitness in its maladroitness, a cleverness in its stupidity, a concordance in its confusion.

As Kant allows, the judgment inducing comic laughter yields a disinterested, contemplative satisfaction. It reflects upon an imputed object with a certain detachment, free from the desire for possession and indifferent as to its existence in the world of fact. Its concern focuses mainly upon an incongruous pattern of appearances, upon the comic show before the mind of the subject. Thus we laugh with delight at the antics in a stage play, at some exaggerated tale of our own irresistible attractiveness, or at a hundred "funny stories" without the least concern that these are all patent fictions. We relish them for their *value* as ludicrous, not as matters of *existence* in fact. Moreover, we impute a similar satisfaction to others, assuming that all men should find worthy of laughter what we do, although actually such unanimity may be lacking.

Such failure of agreement in regard to the laughable is due, in our opinion, not to lack of an objective basis but rather to failure in reflecting development on the part of certain persons. Take, for instance, Will Rogers' jest on the huge appropriations passed by Congress for government expenditures. "I guess that's all right," said Will. "We are not paying our national debt anyhow, so it doesn't matter how much it is anyway." The American who finds no hint of the comic in the public acceptance of this idea of continued government

borrowing with no intention to repay is obviously one lacking
in the mental clarity to grasp both the logical contradiction
of a debt that is not owing (not a debt) and the absurdity of
an *open* conspiracy concerning it or *secret de Polichinelle*.

In Kant's opinion, aesthetic judgment finds expression in
different arts through what may be called the language of the
senses, affections, and imaginative ideas. Curiously enough, he
finds a peculiar parallel between music and the art of jesting.
Both, in his opinion, involve a play (*Spiel*) by the laws of
association with imaginative ideas, yielding no thought but a
brief, lively gratification. But because both provide merely
fleeting enjoyment rather than cultivation of the mind, they
cannot be ranged with the great civilizing arts whose effect is
serious and permanent in increasing the urbanity of the higher
cognitive powers. Instead, the gratification they afford is not
only transitory, but centered in the bodily processes whose
frequent excitation induces weariness. With music as in that
which produces laughter "we recognize pretty clearly that the
animation in both cases is merely bodily, although it is excited
by ideas of the mind . . . It is not the judging the harmony
in tones or sallies of wit . . . but the furtherance of the vital
bodily processes, the affection that moves the intestines and
the diaphragm—in a word, the feeling of health . . . that
makes up the gratification felt by us."[4]

Inadequate as Kant's treatment of music is generally recognized to be, most of us would admit that music and the comic
resemble each other in rather markedly involving bodily processes. At the same time, we must acknowledge that his view
of comic laughter as excited by the idea of something absurd,
which appears to be a version (albeit subjective) of the incongruity theory, gets badly confused with notions of the feeling
of health and disappointed expectation. In this latter connection Kant's error is two-fold: first, in denying that comic
laughter expresses an intellectual satisfaction; and, second, in

---

[4] Kant, pp. 176–77.

maintaining that a feeling of bodily well-being or health is induced by a disappointed expectation. Usually, thwarted anticipation gives rise to a sense of unpleasantness, bafflement, or frustration. It is ridiculous to claim, on the contrary, that just as after tossing a ball to and fro we feel pleasure on being freed from the alternate sensations of tension and relaxation, so in playing with ideas in jesting we enjoy a welcome relief on suddenly discovering that *there is nothing in them,* accompanied by a feeling of health or vital equilibrium. As Kant puts the matter, "In everything that is to excite a lively convulsive laugh there must be something absurd . . . *Laughter is an affection arising from the sudden transformation of a strained expectation into nothing.* This transformation, which is certainly not enjoyable to the understanding, yet indirectly gives it very active enjoyment for a moment. Therefore its cause must consist in the influence of the representation upon the body and the reflex effect of this upon the mind . . . bringing about an equilibrium of the vital powers in the body."[5]

But, as we have said, disappointed expectation would seem to produce not a feeling of pleasure or health but a sense of let-down, dis-ease, or frustration. While Kant very acutely suggests that comic laughter is occasioned by the subject's discovery of some self-deception on his part rather than in the lying report of others, he is wrong in describing the enjoyment of it in predominantly somatic or therapeutic terms as induced by nullified anticipation. It is far from being the case that the transformation of an anticipatory judgment into nothing gives pleasure because of a wholesome shock to the body. The fact is that the discovery of mistakes is painful, although the *correction* of an error by the understanding gives satisfaction as making for the victory of reason over unreason in the world. The enjoyment of comic laughter, far from arising from an anti-climactic release from psychological tension, turns on apprehension of a logical error, which, being fallen into and

---

[5] Kant, pp. 177–78.

then detected, gives us, as it were, a double intellectual satisfaction in the discovery of the error and its rectification through awareness of congruence as the standard.

Were disappointed expectation enough to explain the satisfaction of comic laughter, what have come to be called "shaggy dog stories" would be accepted as wholly adequate examples of the ludicrous, which they are not.[6] These are stories in which the raconteur, taking advantage of the listener's training through long experience to expect a funny story to work up to a point, presents him suddenly at the end with an entirely pointless one. The surprise at such a build-up to a psychological let-down may produce the laughter of annoyance or frustration in the hearer at being tricked, or that of malicious pleasure in his deception on the part of the narrator, but in neither case will it be truly comic laughter based on wholehearted enjoyment of the ludicrous.

For example, the raconteur—having remarked that his hearers will find it difficult to believe this story—may relate how a young woman, who went to Europe on her honeymoon, was standing by the shiprail one evening playing with her wedding ring, and suddenly dropped it overboard. Fifteen years later she and her husband made a second voyage to Europe. When on the first night out they were having dinner, she started to cut her fish—and struck something hard! "What was it?" . . . (pause) . . . "Fish bone!" Whereas a truly comic story affords some insight gratifying to the mind, this type is more in the nature of a practical joke (like the rubber marshmallow, the exploding cigar, the itching powder, the boutonniere that squirts water, the chair offered and suddenly withdrawn as you sit down). The purpose of the deception or disappointed expectation is to make you appear foolish and to get the better of you. It is a trick to belittle the hearer by entrapping him in a mistake, a stratagem to get a laugh at his

---

[6] See D. H. Monro, *Argument of Laughter* (Melbourne University Press, 1951), pp. 73–74.

expense rather than to give him something to laugh at. And that even the laughter of the so-called practical joke does not arise mainly from disappointed expectation is shown by the fact that the victim (whose anticipation is frustrated) laughs only very weakly if at all, whereas it is the perpetrator of the joke and those in on the outcome in advance who express real jubilation.

Kant illustrates his theory of laughter by three funny stories.[7] Yet the comic reaction to these tales centers, we maintain, not in the disappointed expectation by which the tension of the audience resolves itself into organic equilibrium but rather in their grasp of an absurdity or conflict with the laws of logic and phenomenal reality. According to the initial story, an Indian on first seeing a bottle of beer opened, stood in amazement at the quantity of frothy overflow, remarking that what he wondered at was not that it should flow out, but how they ever got it in. Here the Indian finds himself confronted with an apparent contradiction between a premise of his thinking and a sensible perception which seems to deny it. He assumes that only what is put in comes out; yet here more apparently comes out than was put in, so that something has come from nothing. But, to the bystanders familiar with the process of fermentation, the apparent contradiction is easily resolved with consequent laughter.

In the second story, the heir of a rich relative who sought to arrange an impressive funeral for his benefactor found his purpose defeated by the fact, as he said, that "The more money I paid the mourners to look sad, the more cheerful they looked." Here the nub of the joke is not in the sudden anti-climax or chagrin of the heir at the unfulfilled promise of the mourners but rather at the contradiction inherent in the idea of paid mourners, the absurdity of imagining that the expression of personal grief at the loss of a friend can be purchased by payment of a large sum of money.

[7] *Critique of Judgment*, pp. 178–79.

Lastly, comes the story of the merchant who, having embarked with his goods on a voyage, was forced by a violent storm to throw his merchandise overboard and whose consequent grief was so great that his wig turned gray in a single night. Here, to be sure, our expectation that the narrator would say that the merchant's hair turned gray in a single night is disappointed. Were frustrated anticipation the crux of the matter, this would hardly be more than another shaggy dog story. If, on the contrary, there is anything really comic here, it must turn upon a train of ideas harboring an inherent inconsistency. Extreme worry, we may reflect, often turns the hair gray very rapidly, and this was a case of extreme worry. But at this point we are brought up short by the contradiction that this was not the merchant's *hair* but a *wig*, hence the inference involves an absurdity. Yet on the whole, despite his fertile suggestions, Kant through his appeal to disappointed expectation and bodily feelings falls short of maintaining a complete incongruity theory.

At this point it may be well to consider further the range of usage of the term incongruous, here regarded as the key to the comic, since it is employed in such various ways. According to the view we are defending, the comic ultimately depends upon, and is referrable to, an element of logical contradiction suggested in the joke. However this is often admittedly difficult to maintain in the face of different degrees of strength or weakness attached to the meaning of incongruity. Thus—to mention only the most important—sometimes the notion that things are incongruous emphasizes chiefly that they are markedly dissimilar or in contrast to one another; sometimes that they are inappropriate or unsuited to their situation; again that there is a lack of relevance between them; again that there is clear-cut incompatibility or inconsistency between them (as indicating that they are mutually exclusive, without necessarily mutually exhausting all possibilities). And lastly, incongruity may plainly mean contradictory: that two propo-

sitions, properties, or states of affairs are opposites in the full
sense, so that the denial, absence, or falsity of one of them is
equivalent to the affirmation, presence, or truth of the other,
since between them they exhaust the range of possible alternatives.

In the weakest sense, things are offered as comically incongruous when they possess strikingly contrasting qualities at the
farthest extremes of the scale from one another, as in our
earlier examples of our laughter at the juxtaposition of the
elephant and the mouse, or the giraffe and the monkey. Here
a feeling of the ludicrous arises on being confronted with objects of the same genus widely variant in size, shape, and presumed psychic qualities. The suggestion of logical contradiction
(but it is only a suggestion!) appears in the conflict between
thought and perception of which we are aware in facing the
bizarre fertility of nature—as if we said, "Such different animals! How unimaginable and inconceivable! Yet here they
are!"

A slightly stronger sense of incongruity is that which construes it mainly in terms of unfitness or unsuitability to a
particular situation. Here "inappropriate" or "out of place"
seems to be the chief import of the incongruous. Illustrations
offered by Monro, who defends this view of the comic,[8] are:
the trick of mispronouncing words, the picture of a girl trying
to climb a mountain in high heeled shoes, or the cartoon of
a beaming housewife saying to her harassed husband shovel-
ing snow drifts outside their door, "Like fairyland, isn't it,
dear?" Inappropriateness, however, is an incomplete, equivocal conception of incongruity, since mere lack of fitness or
suitability in a particular case is not the same as logical transgression, in which, in our view, comic incongruity ultimately
consists. For us it is the illogicality of trying to combine the
characters of *climber* and *non-climber* that renders the girl
on the mountainside slightly comical, just as it is the contra-

[8] Monro, *Argument of Laughter*, Ch. 19.

diction between the outlooks of the *toiler* and *non-toiler* in the snow scene, and the categories of the *meaningful* and the *meaningless* in the mispronounced words.

Another weakened usage of incongruous is that of irrelevance, lack of relationship or implicative connection between things. Here, though want of aptness is indicated, at first sight there seems no outright clash of contrariety. The story of the fond mother, who remarks to her husband "Robert's teacher says he ought to have an encyclopaedia" and receives the grumbling reply "Encyclopaedia, fiddle sticks! Let him walk to school as I did!" illustrates irrelevance. But beside mere want of pertinence, we should point out, the germ of positive incompatibility is to be found here in the father's pretense of knowledge without knowledge, in his grossly mistaking a learned work covering all branches of information for a child's toy (a velocipede), clearly indicating thereby his son's need for a new source of knowledge.

Again incongruity is used as meaning incompatibility or inconsistency in so far as opposing subjects or attributes are recognized as incapable of both being present, real, or true at the same time in the same respect. But sometimes this is accompanied by the fallacy of wrongly identifying alternatives that are merely exclusive of each other for those that are exhaustive or contradictory. Many jokes turn upon *mistaking contraries for contradictories*, as when the Sunday school teacher, inquiring of the little boy whether he would rather go to heaven or hell, is startled by the answer, "I'd rather stay right here." Or again, as when in the *New Yorker* two steel riveters are pictured in conversation some twenty stories in the air on the skeleton of a skyscraper, with one saying to the other, "I figure what's it all matter? If cigarettes don't get us, radiation will." Here for the reader the incongruity of mistaking cigarettes and radiation for the exhaustive possibilities to the neglect of the far more imminent peril of falling off the girder is the point of the joke.

Lastly, incongruity may be understood in the full sense of contradictory. That is, two states of affairs or propositions are complete opposites when the presence or affirmation of the truth or reality of one is equivalent to the absence or denial of the other, since between them they exhaust the universe of discourse. This is the basic meaning of incongruity, which, in our opinion, serves as the standard of all genuine examples of the ludicrous. Sometimes, however, a comical effect is achieved by the attempted joint assertion of opposites, as when there is failure to recognize that affirmation of one contradictory amounts to denial of the other. Such an absurdity of supposing that one can have his cake and eat it too seems to be present in Hegel's "unity of opposites." It is the basic irrational absurdity of which the ideology of Marxian communism is accused in George Orwell's *Nineteen Eighty-four:*

> Top is bottom
> Black is white
> Far is near
> And day is night.
>
> Big is little
> High is low
> Cold is hot
> And yes is no.[9]

But though the incompatibility of contradictories is the ultimate meaning of incongruity which acts as the standard of the comic, its presence is often only indirectly suggested. Often, as we have seen, the comic incongruity appears in weakened form or in varying degrees: as a matter of contrast, a lack of relevance, an inappropriateness, or a contrariety rather than in the full sense of contradictory opposition.

---

[9] George Orwell, *Nineteen Eighty-four* (New York, Harcourt, Brace, 1948.)

Again, because of the complexity of the content in which it is imbedded, the comic incongruity may require a fund of special information for its detection, or quite a train of thought to unravel. Acquaintance with literary allusions, with the argot of a special group, familiarity with the fashions, politics, or historical landmarks of a certain field, may be the precondition of jokes whose appreciation depends upon knowing one's way around some special subject matter. Usually such a delayed reaction fuse, requiring of its audience both considerable logical intellection and being "in the know" regarding certain factual matters, is characteristic of the jokes of such sophisticated magazines as *Punch* and the *New Yorker*. The impact of cheap "comic books," on the other hand, tends to be direct, making minimal demands upon reflection and factual information. Such differences in immediate obviousness, in the amount of knowledge and cerebration required, also enter into what we have called degrees of incongruity. But in the end any genuine incongruity must lead to a contradiction. For since any inconsistency involves a denial of logical laws, upon which all thought and existence depend, their denial in a particular case undercuts the basic structure of the whole subject matter.

Inconsistency in the full sense involves the denial of implication, the rejection of the linkage between a general rule and the cases exemplifying it—a denial which appears in the conclusion. But to assert the premise and deny the conclusion in inference is to defy the law of contradiction. In the domain of the ludicrous this is like agreeing that, if a cat is a cat, it cannot grin, talk, fade away in the air—in short be a non-cat —yet at the same time to allow that the Cheshire cat does precisely this, apparently thereby defying the laws of thought, existence, and inference. Characteristic, however, of the ludicrous incident which seemingly admits that *S can be both P and non-P* is the fact that by its laughter comic insight allows its fanciful contradictions to be false and absurd. That is to say, comic insight stops short of full defiance of logical laws, admitting by its jocose reaction that its attitude is mere *feigning* and that it sees that such irrationalism would reduce to chimerical nonsense both itself and the articulate structure of the world. Thus indirectly comic insight authenticates itself, as it were, by appealing to rational principles as the criteria to render judgment upon its effort to infringe them. By our laughter we reject the non-feline cat, the talking quadruped, as impossible and so reaffirm the supremacy of the logical world and the cogency of thought to grasp it. In brief, perceptions of the comic turn upon insight into the falsity of any attempted denial of the laws of thought and inference, while insight into the failure of such attempts is what constitutes their comic self-contradiction.

As maintained in this essay, comic laughter is never resolvable into matters of mere empirical habit, custom, the association of ideas, or into simple feeling and sensation. Basically, perception of the comic requires the grasp of incongruities that are both logical (as regards the science of reasoning) and teleological (involving a fitness of the parts within the pattern of the whole)—a sense of consonance in dissonance, concord in discord, that is, congruence in incongruence. As has been suggested earlier comic incongruities may be divided into those which appeal strongly to our sense of rational form (*logical incongruities* proper) and those which appeal more obviously to our sense of incompatibilities in their matter (which may be called mainly *factual incongruities*). For the balance of this chapter our attention will be largely devoted to illustrations of this division.

Beginning with cases of formal incongruities leading to self-contradiction that are the most obvious, let us consider the instance of the small boy's essay on Lincoln which began "Lincoln was a great Kentuckian. He was born in a log cabin, which he built with his own hands." (Here Lincoln, in building his own birthplace, is assumed to exist before he came to

exist.) Similarly, in weaker, non-propositional form endless
comic situations are presented in which the tables are turned:
the robber is robbed, the villain victimized, the man in a
passion inveighs against passion, or the "deceased" attends
his own funeral. Again there are countless versions illustrating
the absurdity of the universal doubter, as when the sceptical
father says to his son, "My boy, never say you're certain of
anything. The wise man is always doubtful." "Are you sure of
that, father?" "Yes, I'm certain of it."

Sometimes such comic assertions are singular or *wholly self-
referent* in their contradiction; at other times they have an
extra-reference, that is, a general assertion is made which
covers many cases including that of the proponent but in
which the proponent's case also contradicts the general assertion rendering it self-contradictory. Of the first sort is
H. L. Mencken's remark of Gertrude Stein, "She has no
ideas and she can't express them." Or again the story of the
professor and the hold-up man, in which the thief says, "If
you move, you're a dead man!"—to which the precisionist *in
extremis* replies, "On the contrary, if I move it shows I'm
alive."

The second sort, involving the assertion of a whole contradicted by the case under it, is more familiar. One recalls
Groucho Marx's quip, "I wouldn't join a club that would
have me for a member." Perhaps better still is the story of
the minister who preached a sermon against hate, pointing
out that it was contrary to Scripture, degraded both the hater
and the hated, and many other aspects of the subject. At the
close he requested that if there was anyone present whose
heart was free of malice toward all mankind he should stand
up. After a long time an aged man arose. Applauding him
as an example for all to see, the minister finally inquired of
the old man how he had achieved this laudable state of not
having an enemy in the world—to which came the unexpected reply, "I've outlived all the dern skunks!"

This pattern of obvious self-contradiction appears in a variety of comic stories that, with incidental changes of setting, go round the world. Everybody knows of the householder who on hearing a cackling in his hen house in the dead of night, threw up the window calling "Who'se there?"—to which a dusky voice replied "Nobody but us chickens." Or of the professor hearing a noise under his bed who called out "Who is that?" and receiving the answer, "Nobody," turned comfortably on his side murmuring "Well, I thought I heard somebody." Similarly there is the Chinese version of the husband returning home at night who almost surprises his wife with a lover. The paramour has just time to take refuge in a large rice bag standing in the corner. When the husband, noticing a movement of the sack, suddenly calls out "What's in that sack?", a muffled voice replies "Only rice." Again there are slightly different patterns of self-contradiction like that of the misanthrope who maligns all men as false, forgetting that he himself is a man and hence cannot set himself up as a true standard in judgment of the race. There is Rosalind's banter, when in male disguise she slanders her sex to Orlando, and so falsely libels herself. And there is the pattern of Molière's Miser, who in his ecstacy of horror at being robbed of his strong-box, cries "Come quickly, magistrates, police-officers, executioners . . . Everyone seems to be a thief. I will have the whole world hanged, and if I do not recover my money, I will hang myself."[10] In all these examples the ludicrous effect of the assertions turns upon the inference: *Since P implies non-P, P is false.*

Sometimes comic self-refutation takes the form of a play upon the law of identity, as in Gertrude Stein's "A rose is a rose is a rose." Here the inconsistency rests in the claim to include some additional novel meaning in the reiteration *a is a,* which is really redundant. Equivocation of the same sort is found in the clerk's query to the customer in the Travel

---

[10] Molière, *The Miser,* end of Act IV.

Agency, "Just one more question. Can you give me a rough idea of how much you are prepared to spend over what you are prepared to spend?" Or again it is found in the liquor advertisement picturing a bottle labeled "The BIG JUMBO quart."

Comic incongruities of the predominantly formal sort often turn upon a violation of the law of excluded middle, in which mutually exclusive and exhaustive alternatives plainly neutralize or refute one another. Such is the case of the man sued on the charge of his dog's having bitten a neighbor, who defended himself in court by saying "In the first place, I have no dog. And I have eight other reasons just as good." (Here the defendant appears unaware that any addition to his first reason undercuts or refutes his case. A similar pattern of two contradictory alternatives excluding a possible third occurs in the well-worn story of the borrowed kettle which showed a hole on being returned. The borrower excused himself by saying that, in the first place, he had not borrowed the kettle and in the second place that it already had a hole when he borrowed it and, lastly, that he had returned it intact without a hole.

Resembling this is the account of the ancient sceptic who argued that: Nothing exists; if it did, it couldn't be known anyway; and even if it could be known, it couldn't be communicated. Here, somewhat less obviously, (1) the statement "Nothing exists" nullifies the existence of the sceptic and his statement; (2) the proposition "If something exists, it could not be known" contradicts the claim to know this; and (3) the assertion "If it could be known, it couldn't be communicated" is contradicted by the sceptic's communication. Also, as was seen earlier (p. 112), there are many cases in which the joke turns upon slipping between the horns of what seemed to be an excluded middle but in which the alternatives proved to be not mutually exhaustive after all—as when the small boy, faced with the dilemma of going to heaven or hell, expressed a natural preference to continue in this world.

But instead of dwelling further upon such instances of the ludicrous let us consider those in which the emphasis is mainly upon some factual incongruity in the content, and in which the formal weakness is only secondarily apparent upon analysis. Nevertheless, it must be remembered that a formal infirmity is always present, and that such things as mere psychological shock, disappointed expectation, release from bodily tension, emotional triumph, as well as jumbled content, are alike insufficient to constitute the comic.

Verbal jokes and those which turn chiefly upon scrambling the matter of the argument may be found to illustrate practically all of the so-called material fallacies. Equivocation or ambiguity, as is well known, is a type of fallacy playing a large part in the excitation of comic laughter, particularly at its lower levels. Usually the jest arises from the duplicity of using a term in two or more senses, thereby violating the laws of inference. When one of the Marx brothers says "I tried to pick up a little Hungarian, but she slapped my face," there is equivocation both on the term "Hungarian"—as meaning either (1) a language or (2) a person native to Hungary, and the term "pick up"—as meaning either (1) to acquire knowledge in an unsystematic way or (2) to force one's acquaintance upon another without introductions. The revelation in the conclusion of the use of the term in the premise in this secondary, slangy sense is what gives the unexpected comic effect. Similarly the old class room jest about all men being mortal but George Eliot not being so, since she was not a man, turns on the equivocal use of the term "man" to indicate in one case the *genus homo* and in the other as restricted to the male sex. In the field of action something very like this occurs when women appear disguised as men (or vice versa), or when the comic plot turns upon twins or mistaken identity, since in such cases invalid inferences are drawn from subjects wrongly judged to be the same. Sometimes, on the other hand, an erroneous identification of terms entirely different may provide the nub of the joke as in the confusion already cited between the terms encyclopaedia and velocipede, or again as when (in the *New Yorker*) a pompous lady informs her deaf companion with the cupped ear "I didn't say that my husband chewed all forms of tobacco. I said he eschewed all forms of tobacco." Like most verbal jokes, the fun usually evaporates upon translation to another language, and unlike clear formal contradictions does not preserve its flavor through many repetitions.

Fallacies of irrelevance or *non sequitur* provide the crux of many cases of the ludicrous. The comic effect consists in presenting widely separate or disconnected elements from different fields *as if* antecedents and consequents of one another. Consider, for instance, Mark Twain's homage at the tomb of Adam in *Innocents Abroad:* "The tomb of Adam! How touching it was here in a land of strangers, far from home . . . to discover the grave of a blood relation . . . I leaned upon a pillar and burst into tears . . . Noble old man—he did not live to see me." But nobody is less related to Mark Twain than Adam. The term kindred is usually reserved for those persons closely connected by ties of blood or marriage. If the first man, Adam, is a relative, all human beings are relatives, and the distinction between relative and nonrelative disappears. The second absurdity is to be found in the colossal egotism and reversal of logical order in the phrase "Noble old man, he did not live to see me." Certainly Adam's nobility, if he possessed it, was inherent in his own character and not attributable to his descendants, particularly not to this questionable specimen who sees the universe as centered in himself and pities Adam for having missed his acquaintance.

A prevalent type of comic factual incongruity deals with the disparities in subject matter, modes of operation, and conventions of two different worlds. Today perhaps scientific jokes, contrasting the highly technical, specialized outlook of the different sciences with the common sense categories of everyday life, are the most popular. For instance, there is the sketch representing the interior of a great observatory with two charwomen dusting the lens of the giant telescope, as one says to the other "And you should have heard him swear when I showed him it was only a fly speck." Concerning the theory of relativity there is the familiar limerick

> There was a young lady named Bright
> Whose speed was faster than light.
> She eloped one day
> In a relative way
> And returned on the previous night.

Here the fun springs from the contradiction between the conventional common sense conception of time computation and that of the new theory, including the equivocal use of the term "speed" in two senses, one borrowed from current slang and the other from physics. Again, there is the anecdote of the electronic computer competent to answer all questions, which on being asked "Is there a God?" returns the lightning typescript "There is one now." There is the plump lady pictured in the airways office gazing in bewilderment at the hands of the different timepieces labelled: London, Bombay, Sydney, Tokyo, etc., and exclaiming "My goodness, are all these clocks right?" Needless to say, such gibes run the gamut of the subject matter of the different sciences, but for the sake of brevity we may confine ourselves to one final example from medicine.

> I heard them speak of allergy
> I asked them to explain
> Which when they did, I asked them
> To please explain again.

I found the pith of allergy
In Bromides tried and true;
For instance, you like lobster,
But lobster don't like you.

Does aspirin cause your eyes to cross?
Do rose-leaves make you nervy?
Do old canaries give you boils?
Do kittens give you scurvy

. . . .

When Duty sounds her battlecry,
Say never that I shirk
It isn't laziness at all,
But allergy to work.[11]

Needless to say, contradictions between the data and categories of different worlds are to be found not merely between
science and common sense, but between the latter and Aeso-
pian fables, mythologies, fairy and adventure tales, science fictions, and other domains defying natural laws. To be truly
comic, however, such free-for-all realms built upon reversals
of the laws of nature must conform to at least one requirement: they must keep faith with their chosen rules and not
play fast and loose with them. What makes Mother Goose
comic when the cow jumps over the moon and the dish runs
away with the spoon is that its world, while incongruous
with the domain of fact, retains internal congruity with itself.
Granted that our chief amusement is in the disparity between
these two worlds, nonetheless this bizarre realm must have
a certain regularity of its own that can be counted on. Only
so is the contrast between the two sharply sustained enough
to be truly comic. If in the midst of a presentation a flip-flop

---

[11] Ogden Nash, *I'm a Stranger Here Myself* (Boston, Little, Brown
& Co., 1939), p. 125.

is executed without warning from the categories of one world to those of another, the effect tends to confusion and forfeits our interest. Instances of such flip-flops in abbreviated form occur occasionally in shaggy dog stories that achieve their shock of disappointed expectation by failing at the crucial point to stick to the logic of the field, and so fail to be really comic. There is, for example, the story (Monro) of the two young brothers who went fishing together to a neighboring pond. But each time they went the younger brother caught all the fish. Finally the older one decided to go by himself to see if he could not have better luck. After sitting on the bank for several hours, he had not had a single bite. As he rose dejectedly and prepared to go, a fish jumped out of the water and piped "Where is your brother today?" Here, since up to the final punch line the setting has been realistic and commonplace, the sudden violation of nature in the talking fish is startling rather than comic. "That's not fair!" sums up our reaction.

Another type of incongruity that fails to be comic is that which involves a strong inversion of values. Just as a story told in gibberish or the depiction of a nonsense realm without consistency is not ludicrous, so a world without values is not either. Presentation of the world turned upside down, in which crime, horror, and perfidy replace goodness, beauty, and truth, and in which respect for life and person is mocked, leaves no room for the comic. In a realm in which force supplants ideal worth, the spirit that denies is ascendant, artists sell their souls to the devil, and darkness reigns triumphant. Bereft of a sense of purposive fitness, of harmony, such a world travels the road to ruin, its articulate structure destroyed.

Today propensities of this sort are present in certain quarters in which the inversion of values is passed off as comic incongruity. The extent to which the "moral disarmament" of our society has progressed under the pretense of cultivating the comic spirit is brought out in such works as Frederick

Wertham's *Seduction of the Innocent*. Especially, in his opinion, through the circulation of so-called "comic books" (some
sixty million appearing each month) and to a lesser extent
through the "comic strips" of newspapers, this degradation
of values goes on. In many of them pictures of violence por-
traying lives of extreme license and vulgarity are presented
to the youth with a remorseless iteration that, besides tending
to weaken the moral standards of the community, is almost
totally devoid of humor. Even the Pacific Fleet Command
during the war, says Dr. Wertham, banned the sale of most
comic books in their ships' stores as too gory for the American
sailor.[12]

One needs only a cursory nodding acquaintance with such
material to feel that there must be real ground for concern.
Aside from the relatively innocent, puckish world of animal
pictures, there seems to be a garish, exaggerated world peopled
in large part by supermen, tough guys or hoods, who glory
in fast action, getting their man and never giving the other
fellow a break. Too often the women, if not horror types, tend
to be molls, prizes, or little spitfires, sexily drawn and scantily
clad. In contrast to leading male figures of magnificent prowess and physique, there are of course their foes and submen
made only to be vanquished and pushed around. Against
their enemies, the heroes are always triumphant, accomplish-
ing prodigious feats through muscular strength, "X-ray eyes,"
and incredible scientific powers. Needless to say, their representation as beings who solve all problems and conquer
all foes with the greatest ease falsifies the true picture of life
with its sweat, trials, defeats, and unending exertions. As for
the excuse of the publishers that in these "comics" justice
always triumphs and crime does not pay, such lame pretexts
are nullified by the fact that a "good ending" at the last mo-

---

[12] Frederick Wertham, *Seduction of the Innocent* (New York, Rinehart & Co., 1953), p. 393.

ment cannot erase from young people's memories the glaring impressions of violence that comprise so much of the fare.

Besides the aid furnished by such books to the erosion of morals and the comic spirit, other tendencies could be mentioned. There is the fashion of cruel greeting cards that make fun of things that are often far from funny. For instance, there is the card to be sent to a fat person with the legend "Want to lose ten ugly pounds? Cut off your head!"; the graduation card inscribed "For the man who is nothing going nowhere!"; and the greeting labelled "Happy Birthday!" above the picture of a sinister figure reading newspaper scareheads about H-bombs and enemy missile threats. As against these, the popularity of irreverent jokes (such as "It would have been a great blessing if, instead of the Pilgrims landing on Plymouth Rock, Plymouth Rock had landed on the Pilgrims") seems hardly worth mentioning. Of course, in support of such jests it may be said that the comic is only *feigning*. Yet in rejoinder it may be urged that whatever the circumstances good taste forbids aspersions on human dignity and making light of basic things that are no laughing matter.

In conclusion, the fact that feigning and pretense are essential to ludicrous representations brings us naturally to a consideration of the world of make-believe in stage plays and the subject of comedy and the comic.

CHAPTER 7

Comedy and the Comic

As an artistic form comedy in its treatment sometimes seems
to bear little relation to the perception of the comic. What is
called comedy is not even always drama, since narratives like
Dante's *Divine Comedy* and Balzac's *Comédie Humaine* go
by the name, historically perhaps because they are part of a
traditional genre of works using popular language, a certain
detachment of treatment, and characters that are to a large
extent commonplace.[1] In any event what goes by the name
of comedy is sometimes serious in tone as well as free of witticisms, jests, and quips. In the two works referred to, while
there is enough presentation of the contradictions of human
life to serve as the thematic material of comedy, there is also
enough regarding human failures and calamities to suffice
for innumerable tragedies. Still Dante's great poem has a
happy ending, ultimately resolved by the omnipotent love
that rules the sun and stars, while similarly in Balzac's work
as a whole the suffering in so far as retributive may be said
to be just, and (unlike tragedy) the basic values are not
placed in jeopardy.

However, if we limit comedy to the genuine dramatic form
and if we conceive drama for the moment as restricted to
comedy and tragedy, it must be allowed that these two may

---

[1] Dante, *The Divine Comedy*, trans. with an introduction by H. R.
Huse (New York, Rinehart & Co., 1954), Introduction, p. xi.

be combined and interfused so closely in a single work that it is sometimes difficult to determine which type is dominant. The result is that often nowadays nothing may be said to be left to distinguish comedy in the blanket sense, save that its chief function is apparently to amuse[2]—merely that and nothing more—even though the entertainment it provides may not always provoke laughter or invariably lead to a happy ending.

Accordingly, to us it seems wiser to allow that comedy and tragedy do not exhaust the possible types of dramatic form between them. Broadly, of course, what is called drama always comprises a certain structure articulated for the stage involving the action of a limited number of characters speaking in the first person, whose doings form a close-knit pattern divided into successive episodes, scenes or acts, and culminating in a climax and denouement. What is called comedy, if taken in the sense of the great classical examples of the field, may be said to be characterized, as it seems to us, by three traits: the affirmation of life (i.e., a fundamental gaiety or optimism regarding the trials of existence); the presence of jesting in the dialogue or of the comic in action and situation; and lastly, though not invariably, the happy ending. Tragedy, on the other hand, tends to be lacking in all of these.

But in addition to comedies and tragedies in this sense there would appear to be other types of drama, such as historical plays, problem plays, mysteries, popular "who-dun-its" dealing with crime and its investigation, science fiction dramas, others dealing with fantasies, fairies, ghosts, and different forms of the supernatural, as well as musicals and topical reviews whose main concern is with pageantry and spectacle. Even these do not exhaust the possibilities. And while they often combine and overlap as do tragedy and comedy in tragicomedy, nevertheless in many respects they retain characteristic traits of mood, technique, and subject matter, which entitle them to be recognized as distinctive genres.

---

[2] *Encyclopaedia Britannica* (1949), 6, 90.

As with nature, the forms of art appear inexhaustible. The question is where to draw the line. Even comedy itself may be divided into different species, such as the farce, the sketch, the comedy of manners, the romantic, the realistic, or the heroic comedy; or again it may be divided into what is called high and low comedy, according to whether the mood of the play attains penetrating depths or whether it is merely crass and trivial.

Faced with the difficulties of the subject, in a brief treatment such as this the meaning of comedy may best be conveyed perhaps through citation from its greatest masters. In our opinion, almost the whole gamut of comedy is to be found in the plays of Aristophanes, Molière, and Shakespeare. Furthermore its philosophical analysis has been aptly, if less ably, developed in the critical essays of three of their associated countrymen. That a certain relevance or kinship exists between Aristophanes and passages in Aristotle's *Poetics*, between Molière's plays and Bergson's *Le Rire*, between Shakespeare and Meredith's *Essay on Comedy*, few would deny. Accordingly in the present chapter we shall seek to illumine the nature of comedy by considering examples from the work of the three playwrights, followed by discussion of characteristic opinions of the three critics speaking for their respective traditions.

The chief representative of the Old Comedy of Greece, examples of whose work have come down to us intact, and who stands in sharpest contrast to the writers of classic tragedy, is the poet Aristophanes. As the most philosophically interesting of his plays, we have chosen for consideration *The Clouds,* produced at Athens in 423 B.C. More fully than the stage plays of later times Aristophanes' comedy succeeds in satirizing the whole manner of life of his day: dealing in this one particularly with the contradictions emerging between the culture of town and country, between the aristocratic and plebeian classes, the new and the old education, between Sophistical scepticism and traditional religion, self-

ishness and patriotism, conservatism and political radicalism,
virtue and the knavery of imposture.

The plot deals with the fortunes of an old farmer, Strepsiades, who has moved to the city of Athens and taken an
aristocratic wife fond of extravagant society. Their son
Phidippides, brought up in the luxurious tastes of the metrop-
olis, squanders his father's money through his spending on
the race track and horses. Driven to distraction by mounting
debts, the old man finally hits upon a scheme by which he
hopes to escape his creditors. Through learning the tricks of
the new Sophistic logic taught at the Thinking School of
Socrates, Strepsiades believes that he may be able to outwit
them. By making the worse appear the better reason in the
suits brought against him in the courts, he hopes to get out of
paying what he owes. However, on inquiring of a disciple
of the School as to how knowledge may be gained of this art
by which bad lawsuits may be won, Strepsiades is amazed
to hear that its abstruse researches embrace not merely the
art of verbal quibbles but such questions as computing the
broad jump of fleas, the entrails of gnats, and the size of the
celestial globe. Despite his bewilderment at the report of
such subtleties, the old man persists in his conviction that
somehow a course in such impractical nonsense will profit
him in cheating his creditors.

On making his entrance to the School, the old man finds
Socrates suspended in a basket staring at the sun. When
asked what he is doing, Socrates replies:

> I walk on air and contemplate the sun.
> I could not search into celestial matters
> Unless I mingled with the kindred air.
> My subtle spirit here on high. The ground
> Is not the place for lofty speculations.[3]

Addressing his plea to Socrates to teach him how to speak in

---

[3] Edith Hamilton's translation in *The Greek Way to Western Civilization* (New York, W. W. Norton & Co., Inc., 1930, 1942), p. 73.

the law courts, Strepsiades swears by the gods that he will pay any fee however large for the service. To this Socrates replies, "By which gods will you swear? . . . The gods are not a coin current with us." "There is no Zeus." "Whirl-wind is king." Employing concepts reminiscent of Anaxagoras and Empedocles, the philosopher argues that in the endless cycles of the weather nothing is changeless save change itself. If man must ask what causes the rain, his answer should be not Zeus but the Clouds. For who has ever seen it raining without clouds? Unless Zeus can cause rain from a clear sky, he is pure myth. "Henceforward," concludes the sage "rec-ognize no other gods but Chaos, the Clouds, and Tongue, these three alone."

Captivated by such sophisms, the old rustic enters upon his education in the methods of false reasoning, eager, as he says, to gain the reputation of being "a bold rascal, a fine speaker, impudent, shameless, a braggart, and adept at stringing lies, an old stager at quibbles, a complete table of the laws, a thorough rattle, a fox to slip through any hole; supple as a leathern strap, slippery as an eel, an artful fel-low, a blusterer, a villain: a knave with a hundred faces, cunning, intolerable, a gluttonous dog."[4] At this point the parabasis interrupts the story. This is something like the "aside" still occasionally used in comedy in which the artistic frame is broken by a character speaking immediately to the audience. Here the parabasis is a choric interlude addressed directly to the spectators expressing the personal opinions of the author. Aristophanes declares that he regards this comedy as his best, and that posterity will applaud those who find his plays amusing. For unlike his rivals, he urges, his comedies abound in original themes, fresh verses and clever contrivances; also, they attack demagogues (like Cleon) to their faces at the height of their power. Other comic playwrights, by contrast,

---

[4] Aristophanes, *The Eleven Comedies* (trans. published by the Athenian Society, London, 1912), *1*, 323.

are forever plagiarizing, kicking dead dogs politically, and employing stock tricks like having one old codger beat another with a stick to help his poor jokes pass muster. The parabasis ends with a prayer to almighty Zeus for protection, to Athena, patron of Athens, and to Bacchus, god of revelry and joy. Admonitions to sacrificial piety are added; bribery and the extortion of demagogues like Cleon are condemned; while advice on reforming the calendar in accord with the lunar phases is suggested so that the old prosperity may return.

As the story resumes, we find Strepsiades scheming through witchcraft to prevent the new moon from rising so that he may evade the interest due his creditors on that date. Also he has a plan to get rid of his debts permanently by the use of a burning glass which shall destroy the certificates of what he owes. But although the old man has picked up the jargon of the school and a jumble of superficial ideas, his mind is too fixed in a traditional rut to grasp the new subtleties and abstractions. Accordingly Socrates persuades Strepsiades to have his son train in his stead in the new oratory. The son, Phidippides, learns quickly the arts of double talk, of gaining the favor of the mob, of denying justice by cunning shifts, and confounding truth. Having become adept at the new sophistry, and having repudiated the ancient piety and moral precepts that "built the men of Marathon," Phidippides turns fiercely not only upon his creditors but also upon his father. Without warning he cruelly beats the old man, justifying his assault by arguing that just as fathers rightly chastise their children for their own good, so the children may rightly chastise their parents in their dotage or second childhood.

All at once the old rustic's eyes are opened. His dearest wish having been fulfilled, he now wishes it unfulfilled. By a kind of nemesis he now finds himself punished through his own stratagems, strangled in the noose he contrived for others.

The return upon himself of his own knavery in cheating his creditors and violating his oath to the gods brings the truth home to him. His faith in Zeus is restored, and he perceives the suicidal self-contradiction latent in this false logic. Enraged that its seductive phrases have so betrayed his reason, he rushes in fury upon the Thinking School to burn it to the ground. As he stands, torch in hand upon the burning roof, Socrates inquires what he is up to, to which the old man mockingly replies, "I traverse the air and contemplate the sun," while a bystander sagely remarks that the School, having blasphemed the gods, richly deserves its fate.

Thus in the play the teaching of Socrates, as at his trial some twenty years later, is confused with that of the Sophists. He is condemned upon the same charges of corrupting the youth and teaching false gods. In particular, he is mistakenly represented as a physiologer and cosmologist, intent upon physical processes and affirming a cycle of natural causes without divine governance as alone ruling the universe. It is not necessary to labor the point that the heart of Aristophanes' comedy lies in exposure of the contradictions in Athenian life, their danger and destructiveness. Only a most lively scrutiny by the citizens of what goes on can preserve, in his eyes, the city's health and sanity. Yet in indicting unscrupulous Sophists for corrupting the people Aristophanes' scythe cuts too wide a swath. His satire seems to condemn all new discoveries in moral and scientific thought, the very search for more enlightened knowledge. In so doing he violates without being aware of it his own conception of comedy. For comedy in his eyes is a great bulwark of practical liberties, the guardian of free speech, permitting no limits to inquiry, unabashed by indecency, fearless in the teeth of political tyranny. Yet this same comedy in his hands in its attack upon the new philosophy of his day appears as the foe of dialectic and science, and in the name of traditional piety seems to deny to the human spirit its right to an unfettered search for truth.

The suggestion of the primeval revel, the satyric goat song, is still strong in Aristophanes, yet so great is the appeal of his exuberant spirit, his poetry, his comprehensive caricature of his society, the realistic absurdity of his jests, that we are led to forgive him his crudities, his confused conservatism, and even his unbridled license.

In the famous fragment known as the *Poetics,* Aristotle's theory of tragedy was set forth some two generations later, along with his theory of comedy. Though the first finds fuller statement, we may perhaps without straining too much apply some of his remarks on the one to the other, as well as glimpse certain relevances to Aristophanes. "Comedy," in Aristotle's words, "aims at representing men as worse, tragedy as better than in actual life."[5] Both as drama depict men in action; and since imitation, harmony, and rhythm are natural to human nature, we take pleasure in their presentation on the stage, even in the imitation of what is somewhat painful, since to learn something new generally gives men satisfaction.

Whereas tragedy with its graver spirit imitates the nobler actions of greater men, comedy deals with doings of a more trivial sort by meaner persons; that is, with the imitation of persons not in the full sense bad, but inferior in status or possessing some defect or ugliness that is not however absolutely painful and destructive. Thus comedy, which deals with the ludicrous, tends, we may conclude, to deprive men of dignity through selection and exaggeration, minimizing their value so that they are distorted like the comic mask, yet withal not carrying this distortion to the point of the intensely painful and demoralizing, since death, ruin, and loss of the basic conceptions of worth that give life meaning would destroy the perception of the ludicrous itself. Nevertheless personalities and the wellsprings of value within them would appear to be given only surface treatment as compared with tragedy; we are not involved in their inner depths. Human affairs are

---

[5] Aristotle, *Poetics,* II.

viewed with a certain indifference, so that we laugh at the
catastrophes that befall the characters, saying merely "Why
so hot, my little man?"

In comedy, it is suggested, the playwright first constructs
the plot, it being of prime importance, and then inserts the
characters who tend to be general types to fit the action rather
than uniquely developed personalities. Here the author tends
to be guided in his writing by the wishes of the audience,
which often leads to a stretching of the plot to give the spectators what they want, instead of following a deeper rationality.
Nevertheless the playwright, wherever he is able, should prefer
probable impossibilities to *improbable possibilities*; that is,
having presented an absurd or impossible world, he should
abide by its logic in his plot (however at variance with actual
fact) rather than seek to follow rare, unlikely possibilities of
real life.

In comedy, we may infer, a double issue of the plot is a
favorite device. By what is called the license of poetic justice,
opposite fortunes are awarded good men and bad, so that the
villain is paid off with poverty and disgrace while the hero
wins wealth and happiness. This again reveals how the pleasure of the audience enters as a guiding principle. For plainly
such an outcome is often contrived more as "good box office"
and as a sop to the spectators than as the *right* ending found
in tragedy of the first rank, the outcome of an inner struggle
of action and characters involving deep satisfaction of the
moral sense. Still, though the vision of the highest values is
apparently denied, and we are deprived of the stark serenity
and wide horizons of great tragedy, our creaturely desire for
the happy ending with the avoidance of pain and loss of life
is usually satisfied by comedy, so that "the deadliest enemies
. . . quit the stage as friends at the close, and no one slays
or is slain." With some exceptions this tradition of the happy
ending and the avoidance of murder has been observed
through the long history of comedy to the present day, with

the denouement often marked by reconciliations, reunions of relatives and friends, marriages, and a general cancelling of scores. After a proper quota of mishaps (especially to unpopular figures in the play) has been meted out to keep the action going, a generous shower of windfalls (such as success in love, unexpected inheritances, boons, and appointments) is awarded to those characters the audience likes, and the curtain is brought down.

Aristotelian tragedy, on the other hand, affords us no such easy amusement or hedonic satisfaction. To show poetic justice as ruling the world in a larger sense would be a deception; nor does the life of the great hero give him what he wants in the way of natural happiness. Though conventional morality may be seemingly sustained by poetic justice in scoring vice and crime and rewarding virtue, tragic justice is more profound, satisfying our sense of right and truth in far deeper fashion. In great tragedy we find a true hero, yet withal a man like ourselves who through weakness or error suffers a terrible fate that is undeserved or at least disproportionate to his mistakes, but whose life is purged through suffering till we catch gleams of a cosmic justice beyond this world which is far more worthy of approval than the easy poetic sort.

Of course, nemesis is often traceable in comedy in so far as events follow by cause and effect along with a certain retributive action, yet it does not rouse the moral sense to the depths or call forth a catharsis of the emotions through pity and fear as does tragedy. Both, it would appear, make use of the same elements: plot, characters, diction, melody, thought, and spectacle, and should avoid conveying impressions of the monstrous and unreasonable. Even the comedy should be an integral, well-constructed whole, in which the characters have a certain consistency, with the complication and unraveling of the plot possessing some probability, so that the pleasure afforded may be that of the genuinely ludicrous, which is that proper to the comic stage. To be sure, comic plots are generally fictitious (rather than based upon received legends as with classical tragedy); they make free with such devices as word-play, coincidence, surprise, recognition, and the reversal of situations; nevertheless their action should have a beginning, middle, and end and avoid breaking the natural continuity. For of all plots the haphazard and episodic are the worst. Still Aristotle seems to intimate that comedy is more concerned with the probable than the necessary, the latter so marked in the nexus of tragedy. Indeed, in cases in which such dramas deal with the impossible or events quite contrary to fact, as they sometimes do, the skill of the playwright is shown by the air of likelihood and veil of charm which he casts over them so that they appear artistically justified.

It is sometimes said that, whereas tragedy deals with fate, comedy deals with fortune. And although Aristotle has nothing here to say on the subject, and although there are many different meanings attributable to the words fate and fortune, there is some significance in the remark. At least the term fortune calls attention to the looser logic generally operative in comedy, in which superficial, external causes, blind jolts of contingency, accidents of weal or woe, rather than a linked development of the inner structure of the plot and characters, is responsible for the action. Like fortune, fate too is largely beyond prevision and control. Nevertheless fate is held more appropriate to tragedy as suggesting a supermundane power with irreversible action, albeit not wholly determining man's destiny, and certainly not conceived by the greatest Greek playwrights as "a lot fixed without reason." But whereas in tragedy we witness a change from good to bad fortune of a certain magnitude in which a man of high moral nature, though not preeminently just, suffers a downfall for which he is only partly to blame marked by terrible and wonderful scenes, in comedy we are shown mean or middling characters, often quite amoral, in their rough-and-tumble contests with the world. These comic characters remind us of those toy weighted

COMEDY AND THE COMIC

figures beloved of children that right themselves after every upset with a resilient upswing suggesting a buoyant affirmation of life.

At this point, since we are not concerned with the history of comedy we may summarily pass over the Roman, Medieval, Oriental, and near-Eastern traditions in the field, and come at once to its pinnacles in seventeenth-century Europe. If we can make friends with Aristophanes, Molière, and Shakespeare, we may be able to enlarge our understanding to include something like the whole range of comic laughter. Since our hope is to sound the breadth and depth of the subject from a few great examples, we may turn directly from the satiric farce of Aristophanes to the supreme art of the comedy of manners in Molière. Whereas Aristophanes offered something like a full length portrait of his society, Molière's picture is limited by contrast to the life of the French upper class, indeed largely to the great salons and court of Louis XIV in the second half of the seventeenth century. In Molière so much is made of the proper thing to do, of the manner of speech, dress, deportment in the spheres of wealth and fashion, and of the ludicrous contradictions arising from the *faux pas* or improprieties of etiquette made by certain newcomers, that deeper social problems (concerning morals, religion, political justice, love, and the family) are largely neglected.

Despite these misleading appearances, however, as we come to know Molière we find that his heart is in the right place, and that when a rapier pricks his sleeve red blood gushes forth and not ice water. While the necessities of fame and fortune in his day largely determined his subject matter, his eyes were not wholly blinded by his service to *le roi soliel* and the gilded aristocracy. Of the function of comedy Molière remarked that *it is a strange business to make honest men laugh* ("C'est une étrange entreprise que celle de faire rire les honnêtes gens"). By this he meant not that comic perception is a selective principle that makes only those laugh who are

upright, foursquare in their dealings both before and after
seeing the play, but rather that at its best comedy gives its
audience a moment of truth in which they see to the heart
of basic values beyond the shams and trappings of the world.
Through comedy men may pierce to the root of moral verity
by way of that classless common sense that graces the humblest as well as the highest human nature. Though not a re-
publican, Molière is in outlook an Aristotelian, embracing
moderation, the recommendations of common sense, and the
doctrine that virtue is the mean. While for him position, rank,
and class are not the essence of a man, nonetheless a person's
social situation is by no means irrelevant. With Aristotle he
would say that we should consider in regard to an action by
whom it is done, to whom, when, by what means, and for
what end, in judging whether it is good or evil. In Molière's
picture of man in society we find satirized not simply the
fashionable follies of his age, but the characteristic weaknesses inherent at all times in human nature. As Francis Fergusson puts the matter, "His art has an axiomatic quality
which makes it fresh, inevitable, and surprising as the truth
. . . The absurd, the logical, and delightful world of his theater
is always there . . . with the charm and the rare value of
sanity."[6]

Let us choose one of his most famous plays, *The Misanthrope*, for analysis. The plot concerns the misfortunes of an
honest, forthright young man in the fashionable world of
Paris, whose chief talent is to be candid. Coupled with a
highly critical intelligence, his outspokenness in and out of
season contrives to make him a most irritating and irritable
person. Convinced that virtue consists in absolute sincerity
in speech and conduct, he is bitterly disillusioned to discover
the shams, vain compliments, and treachery of the polite
world around him bent on wealth and power. Unfortunately,

[6] Molière, *Plays,* trans. J. B. Poquelin; intro. by Francis Fergusson (New
York, The Modern Library, 1950), Introduction, p. 3.

he falls in love with a worldly young widow, Célimène, a
social climber delighting in the vanities of luxurious Parisian
life and gifted with a satirical wit which spares no one in
slanderous raillery once he is out of sight.

When one of Célimène's suitors who has written a sonnet
in praise of her approaches Alceste to ask his opinion of the
poem, Alceste declares it sentimental trash in such violent
terms that the enraged rival challenges him to a duel, sending
a Marshal of France as his emissary. Alceste, embittered,
buffeted on all sides, finding, as he thinks, true honor and
probity vanquished in a world in which everything goes to
hypocrisy and influence, decides to retire to the country.
Meantime Célimène also has been humiliated in the world's
eyes by writing flattering letters to her suitors, professing admiration of each in turn, while slandering the others behind
their backs, including Alceste. These letters, the suitors in their
boastful rivalry have shown to each other, and, enraged to
discover her heartless coquetry, spurn her as unworthy of
their love. All, that is, except Alceste. He, imagining that this
bitter experience will have purified her heart, offers Célimène
his hand and invites her to accompany him in his retreat to
rural solitude. But Célimène, though admitting her love and
willingness to marry him, if he will stay in Paris, rejects his
offer. "What," she cries "renounce the world before I grow
old, and hurry myself into the wilderness! Never!" So the
misanthrope goes forth from society alone. "Deceived on all
sides," he laments, "overwhelmed by injustice, I will fly from
an abyss where vice is triumphant, and seek out some small
secluded nook on earth where one may enjoy the freedom
of being an honest man."[7]

What Molière seems gayly to be saying is that since it is
natural for man to live in society, it is an absurd violation of
his nature to reject his fellows and the human community.
To renounce society is to renounce being a man. Such isolation

---

[7] *Plays*, p. 236.

goes against human nature, not only in denying the mutual advantages of friendship and political and economic ties, but in contradicting the natural inclination to love and marriage, thereby rendering a man at war with, and untrue to, himself. In declaring that all men are odious and that he will break with the whole human kind, Alceste forgets that he is himself a man. Implicitly in his extravagant raillery he sets himself up as the standard of rectitude without a flaw. In his harsh derision at others' shortcomings he neglects to weigh himself in the balance or to inquire as to his credentials as a censor.

In complimenting himself that he is always sincere and no flatterer, Alceste fails to note that flattery is not the sole alternative to speaking out frankly on all occasions. Indeed, the comic quality of Alceste's character turns on his mistaking contraries for contradictories, on his failure to recognize to his undoing any third possibility. As his friend Philinte points out, the path of discretion and right feeling may often be silence. True integrity involves tolerance, affability, and refrains from offering an opinion on all subjects to all persons at all times, thereby rendering oneself offensive by gratuitous criticism. Genuine virtue consists in achieving the mean or middle way, in attaining the proper line of speech and conduct at the right time, right place, to the right person, and under the right circumstances. As Philinte reminds him, men of the world must conform to the civilities demanded by custom. Plain speaking is in many cases ridiculous. A man must often conceal his feelings, and not tell others what he thinks of them. Why tell a man that you hate him? An old woman that her paint disgusts everyone? X that he is a bore and we are sick of hearing his boasting? We should all be more lenient toward the failings of human nature; virtue needs to be pliable; unbending stiffness requires too great perfection of us mortals; we too may be equally to blame. "Good sense avoids all extremes, and requires you to be soberly rational."[8]

---

[8]*Plays*, p. 180.

In any case, Alceste contradicts himself in declaring that he
hates the human race, since he is in love with Célimène and
exacts no such rectitude from her as he demands from others.
He is divided against himself in being emotionally bound to
a young lady of fashion, particularly given to the arts of social
persiflage, back-biting, and empty compliment. Indeed, it is
Célimène with her sharp tongue that spares no one who gives
the final appraisal of the misanthrope. His melancholy cynicism, she points out, springs from the fact that his nature is
a bundle of contradictions.

> Must he not everywhere display the spirit of contradic-
> tion with which Heaven has endowed him? Other
> people's sentiments can never please him. He always
> supports a contrary idea, and he would think himself too
> much of the common herd were he observed to be of
> any one's opinion but his own. The honor of gainsaying
> has so many charms for him, that he very often takes
> up the cudgels against himself; he combats his own sen-
> timents as soon as he hears them from other folks' lips.[9]

In brief, the misanthrope's splenetic, contentious nature is
untrue to itself, self-destructive by reason of its internal conflict which tolerates no one's opinion save his own, affirming
what others deny and denying what they affirm, even contradicting himself if he hears his views in the mouth of another, forgetting what he has said previously. So the logic of
the hater of mankind is laid bare. In the end we see the hero
and heroine, though of opposing types (the unworldly and
the worldly), brought to the same pass, barred from the favor
of society—the one through excessive fault-finding, the other
through slanderous wit—and both through excess of critical
analysis.

If a requisite of comedy is a happy ending, one may hesitate
to call *The Misanthrope* a comedy, for although the protag-

---

[9] *Plays,* p. 198.

onists achieve fulfillment of their self-conflicting natures, the
ending is far from happy. Alceste returns to a cynical, self-
devouring solitude and Célimène to the cold insincerities
of a life of empty show. One is amused at Alceste's analysis
of the passion of love among other things, so contrary albeit
similar to the verisimilitudes of Shakespeare. He rails at lovers
who see only faultless perfection in the object of their choice:
the lean one as lithe, the stout one as majestic, the silent one
as modest, the chatterbox as good-natured, the slattern as a
careless beauty. On the contrary, declares Alceste, we should
reproach the object of our passion with her faults, not be
blind to them. "The more we love any one the less we ought
to flatter her." "True love shows itself by overlooking nothing."[10] So you, in your contrariness, retorts Célimène bitterly,
would have us rail heartily at those we love! Only from
Philinte and his lady in the sub-plot do we learn the middle
way to happiness, but meantime our spirits are enlivened
with many treasures of insight on man in society.

Unquestionably Molière's comedies are largely intellectual,
free of emotional appeal, while his characters tend to embody
abstract types, such as the misanthrope, the coquette, the
miser, the imposter, the newly-rich man—all points which
serve to remind us of Bergson. Comedy, rather than the comic,
may be said to be the implicit theme of Bergson's essay *Le
Rire*, which brilliantly continues this same French tradition.
The characters of real life, says Bergson, are comic only because they *perform a kind of comedy* before us.[11] We look
down and laugh at their vagaries in the same way that we
look down upon a play from our seat in a box. Yet in appre-
ciating the comic our attitude is not entirely aesthetic, for
instead of being disinterested it is unconsciously utilitarian,
expressive of society's secret intent to correct eccentricity
and enforce conformity to social life. Besides being largely free

[10] *Plays*, p. 199.
[11] Bergson, "Laughter," in *Comedy*, ed. Sypher, p. 148.

of emotion, comedy aims at the general or typical, a feature in which it differs from all the other arts.[12] Indeed, for Bergson it is not too much to say that comedy, in its use of external observation, abstraction, and classification, resembles the inductive sciences,[13] that it stands midway between art and nature as a kind of artifice imitating life—it its lower reaches suggesting children's games played with puppets, dolls, or mechanical toys, although in its higher forms it sometimes approximates to real life so closely that scenes from real life might be transferred to the stage without changing a word.

Nevertheless, as in Molière we still find traces of the popular *commedia dell 'arte* in which each character is identified with a traditional mask (Harlequin with the buffoon, Pantalone with the rich old man, etc.) so in Bergson we find comedy mainly conceived in terms of farcical plots in which we see the wheels go round, and by its repetitive devices are reminded, if not of the Punch and Judy show, at least of the machine analogy. Repetition, inversion, and reciprocal interference, according to Bergson, are the methods of light comedy.

Repetition appears not only in employing simplified types of human nature that can be easily reproduced but in using recurrent phrases, traits, gestures, situations, and even echoing satellite characters in the sub-plot. Comedy is often machine-like in lacking the suppleness of living variety, in employing duplicate molds, and ringing the changes on all manner of automatic contrivances. This makes us laugh because real life never repeats itself. But just as no two thumb prints or leaves on a tree are exactly alike so in real life each character or event is unique and never a replica of another.

Again in comedy the device of *inversion* in situations or roles is a formula sure to produce laughter. By turning the tables in the plot or reversing the usual order of nature, as

---

[12] Bergson, p. 157.
[13] Bergson, p. 170.

when a man is disguised as a woman, a child lectures its parents, or the robber is robbed, we get examples of the world
upside down. Since life is an irreversible process with its rou-
tines rarely infringed, such topsyturvydom is funny.

Lastly, *reciprocal interference* appears in equivocal situations, where as in stage-made misunderstandings an event is
capable of being interpreted at the same time in two opposing
ways. When the ambiguity threatens to be corrected, by some
trick the confusion is renewed and continues to delight the
audience. While such stock artifices abound in the mechanism
of farce, in life itself where the relations of individuals are
unique such coincidences are rare. But all these devices, it
goes without saying, stud the pages of Molière from the inversions and ambiguities of the woodcutter passed off as a
physician to the repetitions of the pious dupe, who, deaf to
his wife's misfortunes, unvaryingly inquires during their
recital "Et Tartuffe?"[14]

According to Bergson, we laugh when we see the living be-
have like the mechanical, the animate like the inanimate, the
voluntary like the involuntary, the free and flexible like an
automaton. We are convulsed when the dignified tumble in
the street or when the orator sneezes at the high point of his

----

[14] The scenario of *Le Médecin malgré lui* affords a typical instance of
Molière's incredible imbroglios, abounding in repetitions, inversions, and
the mechanical linkage of improbable events. In the opening scene a
woodcutter who is beating his wife is interrupted by a sympathetic
neighbor. In return the neighbor is roundly cudgeled by both parties for
his interference. Later, however, the wife, still desiring to revenge herself upon her husband, tells a man who comes seeking a physician that
her husband is a great doctor, although an eccentric one who denies his
medical calling until forced by sound thrashing to admit it. After a
terrific drubbing, the woodcutter is taken to treat a young woman who
is seemingly stricken with dumbness. The make-believe physician learned-
ly diagnoses her dumbness as due to loss of speech. Then accidentally
he learns that her illness is feigned because she is in love with a poor
young man, whereas her father wishes her to marry a rich old one. With
the help of the woodcutter the lovers plan to elope, but unexpectedly
inherit a fortune which resolves all difficulties.

speech—at his spirit suddenly extinguished by the exigencies of matter. We laugh at a *ballet mechanique* or at a march of wooden soldiers on the stage: "the big stiffs," we say, which seems to sum up the whole matter. We are amused, in short, whenever human beings in their behavior remind us of machines—through their wooden gestures, clockwork movements, *clichés*, parrot talk, or cut and dried repetitions of language which suggest a run-down phonograph. For verification one has only to recall many age-old tricks of stage comedy or the contrivances to make children laugh: the stereotyped grimace of the clown, the rigidity of the man on stilts, or the jerkiness of puppets.

Among many variations of such devices we shall here mention only two. First, the coiled-spring, jack-in-the-box effect. We laugh, according to Bergson, when a human being repeats a stiff, comeback reaction like a jack-in-the-box, as when the drunken man felled by the policeman bobs up again *ad infinitum,* or when the endless bore (an animated talking-machine), though momentarily suppressed, breaks forth in fresh torrents of volubility. There are farcical dialogues that always return to the same point as, for instance, one built on the well-known pattern: "What's your dog's name?" "Ask me." "But I did ask you. What's your dog's name?" "Ask me." (*Ask me* is the animal's name.) Somehow our risibilities are released like a coiled spring when we see life taking on the repetitiousness of mechanism.

Again, there is what Bergson calls "the falling-nine-pins effect" under many disguises. This device is often the climax of the familiar theater spectacle known as the march of the wooden soldiers. The line begins toppling over stiffly at one end; each soldier knocks down the next and curiously enough their cumulative overthrow produces loud laughter in the audience. We are amused at observing a serial automatism caused by the animate behaving like the inanimate. More subtly this same one-thing-leads-to-another in what is called a "growing arithmetical progression" affords enjoyment in children's books, in jingles like the House that Jack Built. "This is the dog that worried the cat that killed the mouse that ate the malt that lay in the house that was built by the priest all shaven and shorn . . ."—so the mechanism runs off faster and faster. This is the secret of the plot of many comedies of error, full of unlikely mishaps piled on one another, as one in which a guest rushing into a party knocks against a lady who upsets her tea upon a gentleman who slips against a window pane which crashes upon the head of a constable below who brings out the police force, and so on.

But in our view, as we have said, what is comic in comedy depends far more on the liveliness of the contradictions revealed than upon a standardized world running with meaningless monotony like an inanimate contraption. While at the lower levels of comedy repetitive stereotypes may pass muster, on the whole and in its higher ranges what betrays freshness, diversity, provocativeness of meaning, offers the greatest possibility of the ludicrous. Especially simultaneous assertions of *is* and *is not* in plot and character illumine the irrepressible dialectic in the nature of things and provide endless food for merriment. Such incongruities are of all degrees and kinds from the simple one of a character in disguise (the tramp as a learned judge or a private as an army officer) to the cross-purposes and dubious adventures arising from such things as the concealed marriage, the ill-kept secret, the inadvertent misunderstanding, or again from inverted roles like that of the henpecked husband, the timid warrior, the weakling who floors the bully, or the simpleton who outsmarts the sophisticate. All are ludicrous as tending to contradict reality; while the extreme of absurdity is found in those characters and plots that attain complete self-nullification, as when the villain is caught in his own trap and the scheme recoils on the heads of its authors. Though the elements remain the same, it is the infinite variety of their applications, the ingenuity of their uses that prevents the identification of comedy with any monotonous clockwork of technique.

That repetition often causes laughter we are far from denying; but that this is genuine comic laughter is not so clear. Physiologically, repetition may do no more than wear down nervous resistance, inducing habit formation, so that an audience, having laughed once in response to a stimulus, tends on its recurrence to laugh again. Indeed, this seems to be the secret of many professional comics, whose mere appearance on the stage excites gales of laughter, which is increased by their indulgence in the most familiar patter and routine. Yet noisy, unintelligent responses of this sort hardly signify a genuine appreciation of the ludicrous. Against such tricks, however, stands the contrary, well-known fact that banter and artifices that at their first performance set off laughter fall flat the second time with the same audience, having lost their point. With habituation replacing thought, perception of the point is dulled with consequent failure of the comic reaction. Will Rogers in his autobiography[15] relates how this fact that "a man won't laugh at the same joke more than once" forced him during a long New York engagement at which there were many "repeaters" to set about inventing new jokes for himself each night. To avoid that plague of comedians "ingrown" jests about show business for purposes of advertisement, he tells how he was spurred instead to hunt for a funny angle on the day's news. Unexpectedly in his ruminations upon political events he found a rich lode of comic material. The best prescription for such jests proved to be the contemporaneity of the topic ("A joke don't have to be near as funny if it's up to date"), a grain of truth spiced with exaggeration, an original slant, and sagacity. In his judgment jokes that get the biggest laughs have the least comic value, since they "are generally as broad as a house and require no

---

[15] Will Rogers, *The Autobiography of Will Rogers,* ed. Donald Day (Boston, Houghton Mifflin Co., 1949), p. 39.

thought at all." Rather, the absurdity that makes you think so that you nudge your friend and say "He's right about that!" is the type that Rogers sought after. Incitement to sound thought, fresh insights into life, variety, and not the play of mechanical routine, held for him the secret of the comic stage.

But to return to Bergson. For him there is a sharp contrast between the aims and methods of comedy and tragedy. Whereas comedy even in its higher reaches always approaches human nature from the outside, stressing the life of the body· —men's creature needs and upsets, gestures, and collisions with the rules of society—tragedy approaches human nature from within and tries to lay hold of the inner essence of the individual, the feelings of a man that lend idealism to his life. In short, tragedy seeks to grasp the soul in its vision of the real beyond the surface issues of social status and practical utility. In creating his characters the author of tragedy, while recognizing that souls are impenetrable to one another, enlarges by imaginative analogy upon his experience and upon the possible persons he might have been. Shakespeare, though not himself Macbeth, Hamlet, Othello, or Lear, shared traits with all, and could vicariously imagine the personalities he might have developed had his will consented and circumstances directed him in different ways.

Similarly the spectator in witnessing tragedy plumbs the depths of his own nature and projects it on to the tragic character, while the truth dredged up in the process bears in itself its own power of conviction. In tragedy, according to Bergson, we dip below the humdrum life of business and conventional contacts to lay bare the unique elements in our ego, all that is unrepeatable, atypical, inimitable, hence beyond the scope of comedy. Where comedy deals with the common and repeatable, and for the most part with readymade situations external to character, the tragic poet handles the fires of individual passion, developing his situations as integral to the inner nature of the protagonists. Admittedly the history of stage comedy (though perhaps for reasons different from those Bergson supposes) tends to bear out his criticism. Nevertheless in some of the higher comedies, particularly of Shakespeare and Shaw, unique characters take a hand in the plot and are themselves the source of the fun. In such comedies characters may even grow and develop, while the audience gains wider perspective. At the close the spectators come away feeling more reconciled to life through having seen that what matters in the world's eyes (money, fashion, social status) must have its roots in something deeper, and that, while both are desirable, to have what the world overlooks (love, understanding, loyalty) may be more important.

But it is time to turn from Bergson, who seems to be always thinking of Molière and the comedy of manners, to Shakespeare and a stage that embraces humanity and a deeper philosophic point of view. Even though the Bard's plays belong to the first rather than to the second half of the seventeenth century, we feel justified in placing him after Molière in the order of the development of comedy. For here we have the whole human comedy instead of the fashionable world of convention, a freer, more concealed logic and a range that extends from slapstick imbroglios like the *Comedy of Errors* or *The Taming of the Shrew* to poetic spectacles like *Midsummer Night's Dream*, tragicomedies like *The Merchant of Venice*, heroic comedies like *Henry IV,* and finally romantic ones like *Twelfth Night* and *As You Like It.*

In *As You Like It* we find a tale written with such negligent ease, such masterly freedom of technique, that we may well pause to discuss it. Here is a comedy plainly suggesting Shakespeare's preoccupation with character and theme, coupled with indifference to plot, an indifference however that heeds Aristotle's advice about preferring probable impossibilities to more realistic improbable possibilities. Besides five characters who fall in love with each other at first sight (Or-

lando and Rosalind, Celia and Oliver, Phoebe with Gany-
mede), the fatuous impossibility is employed of having the
heroine disguised as a man consorting intimately with the
hero yet unrecognized by him even while he playfully calls
her by her feminine name. Finally, to crown it all, the happy
reversals of fortune in the denouement turn upon the sudden
about-face to virtue of the chief villains (Duke Frederick and
Oliver) for which we are quite unprepared. On the other hand,
in the play we find several of Shakespeare's finest deline-
ations of character: in the portraits of Rosalind, Jacques, and.
Touchstone; while among the philosophic themes touched on
are the excesses of romantic love, the problems of time, evil,
liberty, and the antithesis of nature and convention as involving the question whether men living out of doors close to the
earth may not gain a wiser, more harmonious outlook that
the mixture of lusts, hates, and envies that plagues them in
cities and courts.

The action takes place in the idyllic forest of Arden where
a banished duke, whose rule has been usurped by his younger
brother, dwells in retirement. Here he with "many merry
men . . . live like the old Robin Hood . . . and fleet the time
carelessly, as they did in the golden world" (I. 1, 15, 16, 18–
19). They live in caves and devote their hours to philosophic
conversation and hunting the fallow deer. Shepherds too dwell
in the forest which, besides its oaks, holly, and spreading
greenwood, its leaping brooks and flowery meadows, harbors
a few poisonous snakes and wild beasts. For the most part,
however, the forest holds no enemies worse than the changing
seasons and occasional rough weather.

Thither to Arden comes Rosalind, daughter of the banished
Duke, together with her cousin Celia, daughter of the usurper,
who has quit her father's court out of love for her cousin.
Thither also comes a young nobleman, Orlando, who has
been denied his inheritance and forced out upon the world
by his miserly elder brother Oliver. The plot, such as it is,

turns upon the various encounters of these and other characters in the forest, the center of interest being the love affair
of Rosalind and Orlando, with the play culminating in a
multiple marriage scene in which eight join hands. The wit
ranges from high contemplation of such subjects as life, government, morality, the advantages of pastoral existence, and
the frippery of courts to joyous banter analysing the passion
of love in all its delightful absurdities. Love, it is said, is a
madness, a lunacy, but so ordinary that it cannot be punished
with the whip, since the whippers themselves are in love. Love
is blind, not only to obstacles, but to blemishes and defects
in the beloved. Like hate (its negative inversion of values) it
is an emotional disposition which blots out certain features,
exaggerating and reinterpreting others. Love is a non-patho-
logical hallucination which endows the beloved with the
highest excellences: truth, goodness, beauty, even adding the
predicate, divine—and all this despite the fact that in the
eyes of the rest of the world the object may appear quite devoid of these traits.

Nobody mocks romantic love and its strange capers more
roundly than Shakespeare; nobody is more keenly aware of
the absurdity of mankind suddenly possessed by a dream,
bisected as it were into one half that runs madly after the
other half, and of the ridiculous trick of nature by which,
once the desired union of halves is accomplished, the whole
process is turned to service of the race, with the sighing
maiden abruptly converted into the practical mother and the
romantic swain into the prosaic husband and father. Yet
Shakespeare has a tenderness for lovers, allowing that the
magic excellences seen by them, though hidden from everybody else, are really there and not mere golden images in-
habiting the souls of those in love. Even in comedy the genuine love affair is for him an experience of the soul, since the
faith inspired by its revelation (for it is a revelation and not
merely hallucinatory) is strong enough to make the lovers

overcome obstacles, suffer hardships, forsake all others, and cleave till death. But in the earlier tradition of the western theater love as involving the soul was largely reserved for tragedy. In the earlier comedy love was for the most part carnally treated as either ridiculous or prosaic; that is, it was viewed either as the slightly obscene jest by which man cleft in twain by the gods remains obsessed with the halves reuniting, or as the bread-and-butter bond governing housekeeping, dowries, and inheritances. In classic Graeco-Roman comedy and the *commedia del 'arte* women appear almost never as real heroines but rather as pawns, dupes, scolds, harlots, jealous wives, or scheming mothers-in-law. In Shakespeare's comedies, on the contrary, women are shown as characters equal with men, while love in its fullest range, high and low, as possessing both body and soul, is presented as a central theme. Indeed, his magnificently penetrating treatment of women and the tender passion must go far to account for Shakespeare's popularity even in a day when boys still played the feminine roles upon the stage. The gods, says an old Hindu proverb, gave man three things—war, gambling, and love— with which to break the tedium of life. And certainly no substitute has been found in the theater for the relation of the sexes as a subject to excite universal interest among high and low, old and young. In Shakespeare to a signally marked degree women characters appear in comic interchange with men on equal footing, free, spirited, and engaged in a love-making that is natural, many-sided, divested of pruriency, and often elevating.

In *As You Like It* it is Rosalind and Touchstone, the fool, both lovers and keen-witted critics of romantic love, who probe love's anatomy for our sympathetic laughter. The spell of love, which falls suddenly upon the victim—"Who ever lov'd that lov'd not at first sight?" (III. 5. 81)—makes poets of plain men, so that they turn versifiers and weary their hearers in their mistress' praise. Rosalind makes fun of Orlando's "tedious homily of love," complaining that she "never was so berhym'd since Pythagoras' time" (III. 2. 157–8, 179–80), while Touchstone parodies the same bad poetry in rhymes as dull as dishwater. " 'Tis not her glass but you that flatters her," says Rosalind to another lover—" 'Tis such fools as you, that make the world full of ill-favor'd children" (III. 5. 54, 52–3). "How many actions most ridiculous hast thou been drawn to by thy fantasy?" (II. 4. 30–1). In their poems lovers feign, swearing false oaths, vowing their mistress' frown will kill them, whereas all the stories of those who died for love, Troilus, Leander, Dido, are false, nothing but old wives' tales. To be sure, lovers are often moonstruck, fantastic, proud, pitiless, impatient, inconstant, full of smiles and tears, changeable; yet, on the other hand, to love is to be "made of faith and service," "All adoration, duty, and observance; all humbleness, all patience, and impatience; All purity, all trial, all obedience" (V. 2. 88, 95–7). It is something "holy and . . . perfect" (III. 5. 99), which pursues a kind of heavenly object by which self-love is overthrown. In short, even in the comedies love appears as an absolute passion, the test and measure of a man, although we must turn to the *Sonnets* (cxvi) for the clearest confession of a Platonism which describes it as

> an ever-fixed mark
> That looks on tempests and is never shaken;
> It is the star to every wandering bark,
> Whose worth's unknown, although his height be taken.

In Shakespeare as in Kierkegaard we have the insight that love awakens men's souls not merely to poetry but to faith in absolute values. It carries a sense of the infinite and the ideal; and whatever weakens faith in love weakens men's faith in other values. Forsaken by faith in the ideal in their most intimate loves, men lose belief in justice, honesty, patriotism, providence, and beauty. So comedy which inverts the value of love through rude farce, denying it as an absolute passion,

almost inevitably treats other values cheaply: the heroic
loses its soul to the mock-heroic, the politician sinks to the
level of a sausage-seller, the soldier becomes a poltroon and
the clergyman a pompous hypocrite. If carried through, the
inversion of values in comedy, by which the sense of the ideal
is converted to the crassly material in a world turned topsy-
turvy, must end by destroying the spirit of the comic itself
which depends on glimpses of objective truth, genuine worth,
integrity of soul, and concord in social relations.

A hint regarding the latent philosophical background of
Shakespeare's plays, the product, it is said, of "a massively
reflective as well as brilliantly opportunistic brain,"[16] is the
suggestion that he had thoroughly absorbed the classic tradition prevalent in his time of "the great chain of being";
that is, the doctrine of cosmic order and harmony in which
everything in nature has its place and degree—with man
occupying an intermediary position as a meeting-ground of
the corporeal and the incorporeal, allied to the beasts in his
sensuality and to the divine in spiritual understanding. The
influence of this philosophy is quite possibly reflected in *As
You Like It*. Its plot turns, as we have seen, upon the unhappy
discord in the characters of the usurping Duke Frederick and
of Oliver, Orlando's older brother, whose love of wealth and
power in both cases leads them to rob and banish their more
worthy kinsmen. Nevertheless in the warfare of opposing inclinations their better natures finally triumph; and in the
forest of Arden, whither they have followed the exiles, all
contradictions of fortune, plot, and character are resolved
through recognitions, reconciliations, and reversals into an inclusive harmony. Meantime much humorous wisdom has been
drawn from the differences between court and country, cour-
tier and shepherd, simplicity and artifice, folly and sagacity,
nature and convention.

---

[16] E. M. Tillyard, *Shakespeare's Historical Plays* (New York, Macmillan, 1946), p. 299; great chain of being, pp. 10–20.

Dwelling in the forest, the banished duke and his friends have leisure to read "sermons in stones" and reflect on how much may be learned from the simple life, even with regard to evil. "Sweet are the uses of adversity" (II. 1. 12), says the Duke, who understands (as Jacques the cynic and libertine never does) that not all suffering and discomfort are bad and that only moral evil is evil. In Jacques, the one thoroughly self-contradictory character, worldly sophistication is combined with blindness to fundamental truths. Viewing life is no more than pursuing the satisfaction of his inclinations, Jacques the hedonist, through satiety and hard knocks, has reached the end of the road in misanthropy, disillusionment, and cynicism. The banished duke, by contrast, finds contentment in the forest far from the hypocrisy of courts. For winter's icy fang is yet no flattery; the hardships of nature teach us what we are, without degrading us as do the feverish vices that stalk the crowded haunts of men. Genuine evil, as the duke understands, lies not in natural calamities but in the misuse of one's free agency, in the penalty paid for perversity of will which fails to win spiritual dignity from the trials of life, losing thereby a revelation of values to be got in no other way. Indeed, the good duke even professes to feel the pang of a usurper at invading the forest and killing the deer, the native burghers of the wood. Unlike Jacques, he is no lover of lawless liberty. The world, as he sees it, is a constitutional, hierarchical order in which creatures must share the goods of fortune according to the measure of their states.

In Jacques, "compact of jars," we have a character whose words (like the fool's) fly free, uncharted as the wind in universal criticism. Life, he views as a spectacle with razor wit and profound detachment, as in his famous soliloquy on the seven ages of man, beginning with the "school-boy with his satchel and shining morning face" and closing in "second childishness . . . sans teeth, sans eyes, sans taste, sans every-

thing." Like the other main characters that furnish the philosophy of the play, he is preoccupied with the mystery of
time, especially its physiological side, by which "from hour to
hour we ripe and ripe, and then from hour to hour we rot
and rot" (II. 7. 26–7). Rosalind's keen, cool mind knows well
the relativity of psychic time which "travels in divers paces
with divers persons," for whom it "ambles withal, . . . trots
withal, . . . gallops withal, . . . stands still withal" (III. 2. 311–
14). It is she who sees in Jacques' divided nature the root of
his black melancholy. His is a restless, discordant spirit that
prides itself on varied knowledge of the world, on being a
sophisticate among innocents; yet for all his brain is crammed
with observations from his many voyages it remains as dry as
a sea biscuit, lacking harmony of deeper understanding.

Then there is the fool, Touchstone, that wise and loyal
heart who uses his folly as a stalking horse for his wit. Satirizing the fantasies of lovers, he is content with the ill-favored
Audrey, "a poor . . . thing, sir, but mine own" in whom
"rich honesty dwells like a miser in a poor house, as your
pearl in your foul oyster" (V. 4. 58–9, 61–2). He it is who
mocks the affectations of the court, its passing obsession with
the pastoral sentiment, its duelling by the book, its semantic
hair-splitting and respect for scholastic pedantry. Aware that
"the wise man knows himself to be a fool," he draws from
the simple Corin the essence of the natural man's view of the
world with the famous question "Hast any philosophy in thee,
shepherd?" The reply, as might be expected, is at first no more
than platitudes, tautologies: "The property of rain is to wet,
and fire to burn . . . good pasture makes fat sheep and . . . a
great cause of the night is lack of the sun"; while "he that
wants money, means, and content is without three good
friends." At such stupidities the man of the world laughs
heartily, yet he can himself do no better than counter with
polite equivocations turning on *it all depends*. Thus the shepherd's life, in so far as it is a spare, simple life, is likable, but

as lacking plenty it leaves much to be desired; as being out of doors and solitary, it is a good life; but in respect it is not in the court it is tedious—it all depends. But at the end we have the priceless authenticity of Corin's speech: "Sir, I am a true laborer. I earn that I eat, get that I wear; owe no man hate, envy no man's happiness; glad of other men's good, content with my harm; and the greatest of my pride is to see my ewes graze and my lambs suck" (III. 2. 73–7).

Here is the voice of honest toil and rural contentment, upstanding, self-respecting, a free spirit which finds its liberty in self-help and mutual regard. Even Touchstone's mocking comment that to live by bringing sheep together and the copulation of cattle is bawdry and damnable sin cannot destroy our fondness for the simple dignity of this rural philosophy. Especially it is the combination of wisdom and foolishness in such speeches that bears the incomparable stamp of Shakespeare's humor.

From the dialogue we may judge that banter, mockery, a kind of verbal play or fencing is the chief pastime of courtly life in the forest. The exchanges of Rosalind and Celia, of Jacques, the fool, and Orlando with the others abound in quick retorts, puns, quips, diversions, and trifling niceties of language designed in pure fun to outdo an opponent. This nimble repartee, the vehicle at times of much salty wisdom, at once disclosing character and furthering action, is what lends such extraordinary verve and economy to Shakespeare's colloquies. Thus Shakespearean comedy is never comedy without the ludicrous, such as is sometimes suggested by describing it as a drama with a happy ending that diverts the audience agreeably. Nor is the mainstay of the comic in his plays to be found simply in the traditional tricks of stage business: stock types, hackneyed situations, reiterated phrases, dumb show (as in repeated blows, falls, salutations), or the entangling and unraveling of imbroglios; for even when (especially in the earlier comedies) Shakespeare makes use of these, there is an inimitable flow of poetic fancy, fresh invention, witty sallies, providing us with deepened insight into the individual characters drawn in opposite ways, at cross-purposes with themselves and the world, thereby extending our knowledge.

Despite its brevity, Meredith's "Essay on Comedy" in its scope, insight, and thistle-down lightness of fancy suggests affiliations with Shakespeare. The flourishing of comedy and the comic idea, says Meredith, provides a test of the civilization of a country.[17] For civilization, as the West understands it, is founded upon the minds of men working in conjunction and accumulating a fund of collective experience known as *common sense*, bred of generations of human perceptions adjusting to each other and conforming to things. To the degree that the individuals of a community become aware of the collective supervision exercised by common sense and accept its sagacity as superior to their own, they advance in culture and perception of the comic. By making us see ourselves in the "general eye," by bringing us to weigh ourselves in the balance against the world, comedy awakens us to our defects as compared with the wisdom of society. It is a discipline by which we come to know the world-as-it-is, to moderate our hopes without abandoning them, and to cure our souls through criticism of their vanity and sentimentalism.

The degree of men's cultural refinement may be judged by what they laugh at, as well as by the specific sound of it. Larger natures are marked by the breadth of their power of laughter, which extends from the delicate and ethereal through the ruminative or digestive to robust, rollicking heartiness. But the test of true comedy is to awaken thoughtful laughter, which need not rob it of emotion, but does mean that the idle, vacant guffaw and soulless cacophony are excluded. Though it takes intelligence to determine what is worthy of laughter, feeling plays a necessary part in the re-

---

[17] George Meredith, "An Essay on Comedy," in *Comedy,* ed. Sypher, p. 47.

sponse. Especially is this the case with humor. Humor—and there should be plenty of humor in comedy along with the comic—provokes not merely a smile but a tear amid boisterous roars that shake the body and occasionally get out of hand. At times humor may be too sentimental, may go too far, become unjust in its partiality, bacchanalian in its excess. Hence the comic spirit must control, since, by contrast, the comic is the expression of men's minds working in conjunction, and is more marked by moderation, good taste, restraint. Laughing through the mind, the comic claims us to high fellowship, to a more select citizenry, in which we feel ourselves at one with many sound, solid characters in the community. Its subject, though topical, is not wholly idle or empty, nor one to leave the audience after the curtain falls to entirely unphilosophical, irresponsible reflections on life.

Nor is the truest comedy bitter satire or crass realism. Far from casting slanderous aspersions on human nature and leaving a bad taste in the mouth, it gives us hope for our kind, a sense of the doggedly upstanding, unquenchable spirit of the absurd human animal with all his weaknesses. Being civilized, its temper is humane, idealizing to a degree upon existence. It lets in the out of doors, seeing below the surface of rank and class (scoring pedant and snob, and in the free play of wit placing women on a level with men), grasping the stuff of humanity.

"In comedy," says Meredith "is the singular scene of *charity* issuing of disdain under the stroke of honorable laughter."[18] At bottom, it shows a kindly heart, an absence of rancor, even while correcting those whose behavior offends against the rights of society. Moral judgment enters into the very spirit of comedy by virtue of its basic common sense and its criticism of all forms of socially pernicious excess—such as conceit, bombast, hypocrisy, self-deception, and violation of those unwritten laws that bind men to consideration of one another.

---

[18] Meredith, *The Egoist* (1879), "Prelude."

As the cultivation of society proceeds, its power of selective discrimination increases; it no longer roars to the echo at empty clowning but demands a moment to think to appreciate subtler wit, more individual characterization. Yet comedy as an experience is always social, requiring a community with other laughers. However, its circle is not restricted to those sharing the same local customs, place, and date. For true comedy is the comedy of humanity, not simply of manners; it is not limited to the fashions, uses, or code of a particular group but is capable of translation from culture to culture, as from language to language, to all men of unfolding taste and insight, being universal in its appeal.

CHAPTER 8

The Paradox of the Comic

FROM the earliest reflections on the comic there has been recognition of a touch of paradox in the experience. Plato compared it to relieving an itch by scratching,[1] to a mixed feeling of the soul involving both pleasure and pain. But why, we may ask, do we find in the perception of the ludicrous these conflicting factors: the agreeable in the disagreeable, an enjoyable effect in defects, an aptness in ineptness, a fitness in the misfit?

Whatever the cause, some see in comic laughter a paradox similar to the hedonic paradox, in which the pleasure seeker is advised that the best way to gain pleasure is not to pursue it. In place of aiming directly at the goal, a kind of "bo-peep" or "sour grapes" method is suggested to the epicurean, by which he is to pretend to look the other way, to claim not to want what he wants, to go west to get east, as it were, to seek by not seeking. Similarly, the best way to the production of laughter, it is sometimes said, is paradoxically not to seek for it. Instead we should affect concern with irrelevant, prosy matters, an indifference to frivolity and the lighter side; then indeed fun will come unsought, take us unawares, whereas, if seriously pursued, it eludes us as a hollow phantom. For just as preparations for enjoyment tend to stifle enjoyment, so calculations for laughter scare off laughter; we find on arrival

---

[1] *Philebus,* 46–48.

that the bird has flown. Moreover, just as an hedonic craving (like hunger) finds in its satisfaction extinction, appreciation of the comic disappears in a twinkling in the very instant of its attainment. In both cases the sequel is held to be indifference or boredom, if not the disgust of satiety. Thus in the amusement industry today its jests are known as "gags," a term vividly suggestive of the revulsion which such trivia inspire in their purveyors. Once in possession, it is said, both pleasure and the comic feeling wither on our hands; even in their pursuit, the pursuit must be denied; while the best way to achieve them is thoughtlessness, spontaneity, since to take thought to ensnare them is a self-defeating enterprise.

But in our opinion, it may be replied, there is no paradox in the comic similar to the hedonic paradox. For while experience of the ludicrous does indeed embrace apparently conflicting factors, and while its charm springs often from its unexpectedness or spontaneity, one cannot rightly say that its pursuit is self-refuting in the sense of hedonism. Unlike the latter, the lover of the comic is directed to a goal with imputed objectivity, to something beyond the subjectivity of the experience itself. Hedonism, on the contrary, centers in the capture of a mood. Since in the pursuit of pleasure the goal is agreeable feeling pure and simple, it may be plausibly argued that any preoccupation with method, with taking pains as to the means to its attainment, tends to drive off the agreeable feeling and to keep the hedonic mood at a distance. And the same paradox, that makes the road to pleasure lead away from it, may seem to weaken the search for happiness since eudaemonism, though in more concealed form, also makes a subjective state the goal.

On the other hand, the search for the comic is not directed simply at experience of the comic; the object of laughter is not merely the enjoyment of laughter. That experience of the comic is more genuinely outgoing, extraneous in its reach, is shown by the fact that its referent (the ludicrous) pertains to situations and different states of affairs and not merely (as with happiness) to the sentience of persons. As to their respective sources, what affords happiness need not itself be happy, but what affords comic appreciation must be assumed to be comic. With happiness or pleasure the sentiment or inner feeling is everything, no matter whence it came. To be sure, happiness is the term usually reserved for the feeling of a well-proportioned mixture of pleasures. Nevertheless it does not, like the comic spirit, reach beyond self-feeling, beyond an inner impression of well-being, to an insight into the structure of things. Moreover, in our opinion, the objection which says that comic appreciation always comes unsought, that it cannot be got by trying to get it, but must be sought by not seeking, does not hold. Admittedly comic insight often comes without warning, like the wind that bloweth where it listeth; yet it cannot be said to lack all possibility of methodological control. On the contrary, the masters of comedy and the comic are experts in repeating their triumphs, and are known for their life-long cultivation of the art.

Sometimes, indeed, seeing the point of a joke has been compared to a religious insight, as similar to a small-scale conversion, in other words to a providential gift or glimpse of ultimates, in which the sudden illumination of the joke claims us for its own. But in neither case, we should point out, does the unexpectedness of the event preclude preliminary effort; for usually the lover of the comic has to fit himself through training for a wider, acuter sensitivity to it, no less than the religious man in a higher sense has to prepare himself through discipline for the moment of revelation. Despite the gulf between the two, in both we should claim there is an ontological insight. In the most trivial jesting one catches an intimation of the objective nature of things. When Khrushchev remarked that anyone who expects that demolishing Stalin's cult of the individual means abandonment of Communism's objective will have to wait until the lobster learns to whistle,

he combined argument with a joke.[2] By arousing the camaraderie of laughter, he sought to convince us that, since the
lobster will never whistle, it is hopeless to try to dissuade the
Communists. Certainly tension is relieved by the jest. Behind
the mirth excited by the absurd notion of the whistling lobster,
the hint is offered that between enemies who can laugh together (thereby admitting the same structure of reason and
nature) differences can be resolved. In comic laughter, as it
were, we salute the sanity of the universe, since in laughing
together we invoke as our common standard the coherence
of truth and reality.

One of the most famous accounts of the ludicrous as based
in paradox and incongruity is to be found in Schopenhauer.
Though at first sight his view appears formidably rational,
this proves to be not wholly the case. Comic laughter arises,
in his opinion, from the subsumption of a concrete instance
under an abstract conception which breaks down in certain
respects, revealing their incongruity. For example, there is the
story of the two lions who broke down the partition between
them during the night and in their rage devoured each other,
so that in the morning there was nothing to be found but the
two tails.[3] Here the experience of the ludicrous turns on the
conflict between *thought* and possible *perception*, and the
correction of one by the other.

"It is possible," says Schopenhauer, "to trace everything
ludicrous to a syllogism in the first figure, with an undisputed
major and an unexpected *minor*, which to a certain extent
is only sophistically valid, in consequence of which connection
the conclusion partakes of the quality of the ludicrous"
(2, 271). But the rectification of the sophism in the ludicrous

---

[2] Irving Levine, *Main Street, U.S.S.R.* (New York, Doubleday & Co.,
1959), p. 52.

[3] Arthur Schopenhauer, *The World as Will and Idea,* trans. R. B.
Haldane and J. Kemp (London, Kegan, Paul, Trench, Trubner & Co.,
Ltd., 1905), 2, 278.

comes, it is to be noted, not from reason for Schopenhauer but from sense perception and the acknowledgment of its infallibility. While the experience involves ideas, the comic effect centers in awareness of the victory of perception over thought. Feeling suffuses our response; we rejoice that "this strict, untiring, troublesome governess, the reason" is "convicted of insufficiency" (2, 280) by sensuous knowledge. Indeed, for Schopenhauer, abstract knowledge is ultimately but a reflex of ideas of perception (1, 76), while "in every suddenly appearing conflict between what is perceived and what is thought, what is perceived is always unquestionably right; for it is not subject to error at all, requires no confirmation from without, but answers for itself" (2, 279). The source of this conflict between the two lies in the inability of concepts to grasp the fine shades of difference of the concrete, so that at best their relation remains only one of approximation, somewhat as a mosaic may approximate to a painting. Awareness of the triumph of perception over thought gratifies the desires of our primitive nature and unconscious will. Yet though we enjoy laughing at the spectacle of this victory with regard to others, we are offended when we are laughed at ourselves, because this suggests that there is a great incongruity between our conceptions and reality. In consequence, "the predicate 'ludicrous' or 'absurd' is insulting" (2, 281).

To hold with Schopenhauer that comic laughter "is occasioned by a paradox" (1, 77) means that it is occasioned by the thought of something seemingly contradictory, incredible, opposed to reason, yet which in a sense may really be the case. Thus when Mercutio replies to his friends who promise to visit him on the morrow, "Ask for me tomorrow and you shall find me a grave man," the jest turns upon subsuming under the concept of a serious man that of a man in the grave by a verbal equivocation. And the joke itself serves to show how the quibbles of the intellect wither before the grim fact of death and inscrutable reality. Analogous to this is the epitaph of a doctor, "Here lies he like a hero, and those he has slain lie around him" (2, 273). In this case, the incongruity of applying the conception of the military hero whose business is to take life to the doctor whose business is to preserve it— though it may produce a momentary chuckle—forces upon us in no uncertain terms the harsh actualities of a bungling medical man's career. To Schopenhauer the incongruities of the comic appear as verbal sophisms exposed in confronting the empirical process. Whereas for the true rationalist the heart of the comic is insight into the falsity of purported contradictions and the ascendancy of rational order, for Schopenhauer laughter marks no more than a passing enjoyment at the ineptitude of our conceptions in their attempts to fit concrete facts. In the ludicrous he sees finally the discomfiture of thought by an inscrutable reality. Where the rationalist finds in comic incongruity awareness of the deceptiveness of conflicting appearances and the triumph of non-contradiction, Schopenhauer finds in it the defeat of reason and the victory of nature's unconscious Will.

In his theory of comedy and its relation to tragedy, Schopenhauer develops most fully his notions of the comic. In comedy we have an artistic representation based upon an apparent yea-saying of the Will to Live as opposed to the nay-saying of tragedy with its denial of the Will. Comedy "declares that life as a whole is thoroughly good, and especially is always amusing" (3, 218); its spectacle keeps us in cheerful humor by turning most of the adversities of the plot into joy. In the end hope and success preponderate, while throughout use is made of the inexhaustible material for laughter of which life is full. With the audience this jocund temper triumphs over any possible reflection as to the defectiveness and unworthiness of the characters, the pains and death that overtake them after the curtain falls, or the thought that the existence of creatures so full of envies, fears, and embarrassments must be some kind of ghastly mistake.

In his treatment of "The Platonic Idea: The Object of Art,"[4] Schopenhauer considers tragedy, the sublime, and the beautiful, but omits discussion of comedy and the comic. His reason for the omission is presumably his conviction that in comedy we experience only very imperfectly that blessedness of will-less perception so essential to the appreciation of art. In enjoying the comic we have a tendency to abandon the Idea and to concern ourselves with trivialities. Impelled by the naive thirst for existence, we are less concerned with the beautiful as an illustration of the Platonic Idea, which is the object of art. As opposed to comedy, which affirms the will to live and in which painful defeats are presented only in passing, while the play ends at a moment of joy, "the tendency and ultimate intention of tragedy" is "a turning to resignation, to the denial of the will to live" (3, 218), and an awakening of the spirit of the beholder to the vanity and worthlessness of life. Thus the satisfaction afforded by the two is radically different. The pleasure of the spectator in comedy arises from a direct reinforcement of the striving of blind, natural volition, whereas in tragedy the satisfaction arises by a reflective act through the denial of this world's goods, which puts us in a mood whereby we find pleasure in what tends directly against the will. "What gives to all tragedy . . . the peculiar tendency towards the sublime is the awakening of the knowledge that the world, life, can afford us no true pleasure, and consequently is not worthy of our attachment. In this consists the tragic spirit: it therefore leads to resignation" (3, 213).

To be sure, even the spectator at a farce may subsequently reflect that comedy points finally to the same conclusion as tragedy, since only the trick of terminating the play at a moment of good fortune prevents us from seeing what came after, whereas tragedy frankly ends in such a manner that nothing can come after. In Schopenhauer's eyes laughter is better with-

---

[4] Schopenhauer, *The World as Will and Idea, 1,* Third Book, Second Aspect.

out cerebration. For presentation of the burlesque side of life shows us man's crudities, ignorance, and embarrassments, that is, much that is ugly, so that if considered deeply comedy awakens distaste and disillusionment—-a sense that for creatures such as these existence was an error, and that it would have been better if they had never been born (*3, 219*).

But this bitter denial of life which may occur to thought after witnessing a comedy is different from the feeling of resignation which comes to the spectator both during and after a tragedy, carrying with it a mood of renunciation of the will to live and of the vital ends one has hitherto followed. And there is another difference from comedy. In the beneficent sense of exaltation or sublimity which comes in tragedy, leading us to prefer non-existence to existence, there is also awareness of *another kind of existence,* although this is only intimated and is quite inconceivable. "As the chord of the seventh demands the fundamental chord; as the color red demands green, and even produces it in the eye; so every tragedy demands an entirely different kind of existence, *another world,* the knowledge of which can only be given us indirectly just as here by such a demand. In the moment of the tragic catastrophe the conviction becomes more distinct to us than ever that life is a bad dream from which we have to awake" (*3, 212–13*).

Thus the paradoxical qualities of comedy and tragedy differ for Schopenhauer in that the conflicts of life are resolved for comedy through the victory of percepts over concepts, that is, of nature over reason, and for tragedy by the movement of the mind through suffering from blindness to vision, that is, from the slavery of the will to liberation, from phenomenal to noumenal insight. Whereas the first proceeds by the suppression of one aspect by the other, the second resolves the opposition by demarcation of spheres and ascent to a higher level. In comedy we are confined to the realm of existence and sensible phenomena, whereas in tragedy we penetrate the veil of Maya and rise for a moment to intuition of a supersensible

world. While comedy is wholly secular and mundane in temper, tragedy treats of first and last things, of the strife of the
Will with itself, and the fate of the soul. In comedy we see
men engulfed in a succession of desires and passions leading
nowhere, with little or no suggestion of their guidance by Ideas
or eternal excellences. But in tragedy we glimpse the Platonic
Ideas as beyond and opposed to the phenomenal world. Still
for Schopenhauer the liberation achieved through the catharsis of tragedy affords but a temporary release, and provides no
ultimate assurance to man of a spiritual framework and destiny.
For Schopenhauer as for Kant, the Ideas have a methodological and regulative function rather than being truly constitutive of reality. Ultimately for him the Ideas (or different
aspects of the Idea), instead of being a self-supporting hierarchy of forms leading to the divine, express but the blind
striving of nature. Even though agreeing with Kant that the
Idea or Ideas offer the most adequate approach that is possible
to the thing-in-itself, Schopenhauer finds them finally indica-
tive of no more than a sightlessly struggling cosmic Will (1,
226–27, 530). But, despite his retreat to a metaphysical naturalism, many interesting insights appear in Schopenhauer's
theory. In witnessing tragedy man seems to attain, along with
painful hints as to the self-devouring nature of existence, for
an instant at least identity with the archetypes, identity of the
atman with Brahman, and consciousness of cosmic universality.

   Still it is obvious that in the end we must disagree with
Schopenhauer. Surely there is something objectionable in
allowing as he does that the Platonic Idea is the object of art,
while failing to admit it as the principle of being and knowledge. Moreover, while tragedy for him attains to insight regarding the relation of phenomena to noumena, comedy is
confined to issues of the empirical world. Comedy, in his eyes,
does not rise above the sensory appearances of stock situations
and types, nowhere glimpsing those elevated, ennobling forms
grasped in the disinterested contemplation of tragedy.

But here, as against Schopenhauer, we must insist that comedy, especially in its higher forms, does penetrate behind appearances to noumena. Already through many pages we have labored the point that by grasping the noumenal order under the Idea of truth (i.e. by revealing contradictions as false, and consequently the noncontradictory nature of things) we lay hold of the laughable in comedy. Our jocund mood we owe basically to the exposure of inconsistencies on the stage, and not simply to the happy ending, horseplay, or patter of empty dialogue. Moreover, there is an ethical effect consequent upon recognition of the fatally destructive action in contradictions like lying, hypocrisy, and conceit, all of which being false must be eliminated. *The Clouds* showed how the advocates of the new theory that everything is a matter of opinion, in playing false to others, found that others played false to them. *The Misanthrope* showed how the divided character, at war with himself and hence everybody else, is inevitably defeated by the world. Even in *As You Like It*, where this kind of exposure of contradiction is not so marked, the moral of the play may be said to be that evil tends to be overcome by non-evil or good. The advance of Shakespeare's play over the first two comedies is, however, that it transcends the phenomenal world not merely by insight into truth but grasps other noumena as well. For here we become intimately acquainted with the character of the lover who finds in one particular face noumena that are hidden from other men. Behind the earthly clay he sees a fair and heavenly form. He enjoys, as it were, a private revelation, finding the lovely in what the world passes by as unlovely, the beautiful in the unbeautiful, seeing beyond the temporal to the timeless, and discovering many noble archetypes mirrored in what to others appears a quite average, undistinguished personality. In the end the paradox of his state as against the verdict of the world is resolved only by admitting the subsistence of different levels of insight and reality. Contradiction is avoided where opposite predicates are attributed to the same subject, in Shakespeare as in Kant, through referring them to different realms, the phenomenal and the noumenal respectively. The upshot of what we are saying is that in the higher reaches of comedy paradoxes are sometimes resolved by the tacit admission of different grades of actuality. Disclosure of this deeper level beneath the comic surface appears sometimes in the relation of friendship, or the devotion of servant to master, or even in loyalty to a high cause lurking in the background, but most frequently in love between the sexes.

In the modern theater the ability to introduce noumenal insight into comedy appears most markedly in certain plays of Bernard Shaw. At the same time, most of us would admit that he is not wholly successful in resolving the paradoxes raised or in handling philosophic problems. Perhaps an early play, *Major Barbara* (1906), best illustrates his brilliant deployment of the contradictions of modern society set forth in an exuberant combination of satirical wit, idealism, radical schemes, and realistic absurdities. The play deals with the reunion of a wealthy munitions manufacturer, Andrew Undershaft, with his family from whom he has long been separated; and centers especially upon his encounter with his daughter, Major Barbara of the title, who has become a zealous officer in the Salvation Army. Each undertakes to convert the other. The father, a self-made, hard-fisted tycoon dedicated to the pursuit of money and power through the manufacture of arms, dynamite, and gunpowder, attempts (by exposing the cynically brutal facts of his business) to destroy his daughter's faith in man's salvation through a gospel of peace, charity, submissiveness, and indifference to this world's goods. Barbara, however, provides a fit match for the wily old Mephistopheles, being endowed with a full share of her father's clear-headedness and drive. In her we find a most earnest, attractive young crusader for lost souls, who marches joyously through city streets to fight the devil with trumpet, drum, and banner.

Hers, as she says, is an army of courage, hope, and love, which has banished the remorse, fear, and despair of the old hell-ridden sects. By its music, free shelters, spare meals, and experience meetings culminating in confessions and sudden ecstasy, the Army, she points out, somehow "picks the waster out of the public house and makes a man of him" or "finds a worm wriggling in a back kitchen" and restores to it the dignity of womanhood.[5] These are miracles done to the humblest to be sure, but performed almost daily. In the scenes in the Army shelter, at once humorous and pathetic, we meet the different types of down-and-outer, victims of the economic system: the ancient soup-kitchener, the drunkard, the outworn workman left jobless, and the radical revolutionary cursing capitalism—all of them paupers on the scrapheap but surrounded by the Salvation lassies working themselves to the bone to kindle new light of hope in them. Along with the derelicts, we meet another of Barbara's converts (in fact, the young man whom she is engaged to marry), a professor of Greek who has found release from pallid scholarship and a brave new life among the Salvationists, revealing to him, as he says, the true worship of Dionysos and sending him "down the public street drumming dithyrambs."

Against them stands the scoffer, Undershaft, the millionaire munitions maker, indifferent to high causes, glorying in the spoils of war, which alone in his opinion are able to bring freedom and power, that is, the command over life and death. To those religious parrots who reiterate "Blessed are the poor," he declares that poverty is the ultimate crime, to escape which he will commit all other crimes. In his youth, he avows, he swore an oath that he would be full-fed and free at all costs, that nothing should stop him except a bullet—neither reason nor morals nor the lives of other men. This is how he has risen to be a manufacturer of mutilation and murder. After

---

[5] George Bernard Shaw, *Major Barbara,* in *John Bull's Other Island and Major Barbara* (New York, Brentano's, 1907), Act II, p. 247.

all, killing, as he sees it, is the final test in life, the only weapon strong enough to conquer the world's might. It is the force that rules the social system, in which the only ballot paper that really governs is one wrapped around a bullet. Who can doubt but that the meekness recommended to the needy in sermons for thousands of years has been but a trick of the powerful to gain mass subservience by removing anger and bitterness from the hearts of the laboring poor? Yet while poverty and slavery have persisted despite the preaching of religious compassion through past ages, they cannot resist revolutionary machine guns. For myself, says Undershaft, I had rather be a murderer than a slave! None of your high-flown religious talk can stand up against my submarines, torpedoes, machine guns, and aerial battleships. "Honor, justice, truth, love, mercy, and so forth" are just "the graces and luxuries of a rich, strong, and safe life." When forced to choose between them and money or gunpowder, "Choose money and gunpowder; for without enough of both you cannot afford the others" (p. 247). This Mephistophelean creed he offers as his counter-religion.

Since all religious organizations, in Undershaft's view, exist by selling themselves to the rich, he proposes to convert his daughter to his side by buying the Salvation Army. Circumstances at the moment are in his favor. Word reaches Barbara that with winter coming on, along with much unemployment and starvation ahead, the shelter must be closed down unless a large sum can be raised. Her father accordingly offers a substantial contribution. This Barbara indignantly refuses as tainted money. Her noble rejection, however, is immediately overruled. The Commissioner of the Army who happens to be standing by at once accepts the money, pointing out that this amount, along with Lord Saxmundham's recent generous gift, will suffice to keep the shelter open. A moment later it comes out that Lord Saxmundham is one of the leading whiskey distillers of the country. At this disclosure, coming on top of the others, Barbara's heart is broken. To her it seems that by taking support from the distiller and the cannon founder, her religion is indeed reduced to hypocrisy and absurdity. Deaf to the Commissioner's argument that the end justifies the means, and that we must accept the paradox by which God in his infinite goodness turns everything—even war and drink—to the work of salvation, Barbara resigns from the Army.

In the next act, Undershaft is conducting a depressed Barbara and her fiancé on a tour of inspection of his arms and dynamite works. The munitions town is a paradise of cleanliness, model homes, churches, sobriety, order, and prosperity. Here good wages from the profits of war have been used to inculate peace, respectability, and abstinence. How different from the world of the Salvation Army, where workmen, surrounded by misery, cold, and dirt, demoralized and starved, are aided only by crusts of bread and dreams of heaven. Why, cries Undershaft mockingly, do good people like yourselves always stand on the side lines and sermonize? Why not get into the fight against poverty, which is the root of all other evils? Conquering society's want and indigence is the only road to salvation. "Are you going to spend your life saying *ought,* like the rest of our moralists? Turn your *oughts* into *shalls* . . . Come and make explosives with me" (p. 301; italics mine).

Awakened by the brutal force of Undershaft's attack, Barbara and her young man are made suddenly aware of their part as accomplices and beneficiaries of the evils of the present system. They can no longer take refuge in the purity of their private motives or label certain funds as tainted, when all incomes (including their own) share the same roots in a social order whose wealth stems from the profits of war, drink, and economic exploitation. Personal righteousness, they find, is not enough. All at once participation in the social guilt of garret, slum, and economic misery descends upon their shoulders.

Your religion of love and peace, continues Undershaft, has now its golden opportunity. If your faith can move mountains, put it to the test. As my heirs you can join me and run a giant munitions industry. Do you dare to make war on war with its own ultimate weapons? To use the sword to destroy the sword? Only that which has power to kill is strong enough to excise the roots of modern society. Have you the courage of your convictions? Will you take the risk?

Being no shirkers but high-minded, energetic young people, Barbara and her young man rise to the challenge. They resolve to seek salvation no longer merely by the easy road of preaching and personal example, but to assume partnership in Undershaft's weapons industry and by fighting the devil with fire to battle for the economic redemption of society. As the curtain falls, they prepare to accept their inheritance and carry on the munitions business in preparation for Socialism and the building of the welfare state. The crusade of the future, they hold, will use the wealth accumulated by the exploiter, distiller, and arms-maker to destroy the evils of poverty, drink, and war forever. In their present defeat they see future victory, since unlike Undershaft and the older generation they are resolved to traffic in evils not for private gain but to win freedom and power for the whole people. At the close, Barbara, her religous faith returned, stands transfigured.

> *Barbara:* Did you believe that I was a deserter? That I, who have stood in the streets, and taken my people to my heart, and talked of the holiest and greatest things with them, could ever turn back . . . Never, never, never, never: Major Barbara will die with the colors . . . Glory Hallelujah! . . .

> *Cusins* (THE FIANCÉ): Then the way to life lies through the factory of death?

> *Barbara:* Yes, through the raising of hell to heaven and
> of man to God, through the unveiling of an
> eternal light in the Valley of the Shadow.
>
> (p. 310)

Here, departing from a long tradition, we find comedy directly grappling with economic and religious problems. Indeed, it is even steeped in Marxian assumptions. The central paradox turns on the contradiction between the moral-religious professions of Englishmen and the facts of their capitalistic society. In our summary of the plot we have sacrificed interesting secondary characters in order to concentrate upon the conflict of father and daughter. For Barbara the world can be saved only through touching the individual heart by religious conversion, whereas in her father's eyes only economic causes count finally since poverty is to blame for mankind's wretchedness. Once poverty, the source of evil, was removed, the world would be saved secularly. As the curtain falls, Barbara has accepted his gospel of the economic means but cleaves dauntlessly to the Ideas and her faith in religious salvation at the goal.

Here is an ideological comedy of argument on abstract issues very different from the concrete wisdom and poetry of Shakespeare's comedies. Whether Shaw's logic borrowed largely from Hegel and Marx is as sound as Shakespeare's may be questioned. Here we have the dialectical method of adopting means contradictory to ends under the impression that the ends justify them. But that signing a pact with the devil in order to defeat him will really work leaves us doubtful. When Barbara accepts her inheritance in the giant munitions industry, we find it hard to believe that such traffic in evils can be converted to good—especially by this innocent young couple, who for all of their religious passion hardly possess the ruthless force, serpentine wisdom, and know-how necessary to transform a system geared to exploitation and death to the ends of peace and social abundance. Still miracles are not excluded for Shaw who, being also a gradualist, has the courage to point out a way and a hope in the face of others' misgivings.

Behind his lively facade of repartee lurk assumptions of economic warfare, class struggle, and gibes at the futility of current political institutions. As might be expected, the fun springs mainly from the contrast of classes and the self-assurance as to their prerogatives displayed by strong personalities. This pride of class extends from the house-painter who gives himself airs before the hodcarrier because he is not "a hewer of wood or a drawer of water," to the self-made munitions king who warns the *grande dame* that it is useless for her to try her aristocratic tricks on him as *he* belongs to the governing class himself, and "it is a waste of time giving tracts to a missionary." Then there is the pride of the classical student, the academic man, who allows "Greek scholars are privileged men. Few of them know Greek; and none of them know anything else; but their position is unchallengeable. Other languages are the qualifications of waiters and commercial travellers: Greek is to the man of position what the hall-mark is to the silver" (p. 219).

Again, there is the young gentleman planning to enter politics who, when asked what he knows, replies simply "the difference between right and wrong." "What!," counters his adversary, "No capacity for business, no knowledge of law, no sympathy with art, no pretension to philosophy; only a simple knowledge of the secret that has puzzled all the philosophers, baffled all the lawyers, muddled all the men of business, and ruined most of the artists: the secret of right and wrong. Why, man you're a genius!" (p. 278). To which the young man smugly replies, "I pretend to nothing more than any honorable English gentleman claims as his birthright." For what governs England, in his opinion, is not business, the professions, the military, or even money—but character, "the best elements in the English national character" (p. 280). And with this as a qualification for governing, he assumes he is well equipped.

Along with much ironical sport at the upper classes goes jovial exposure of the tricks used by the Salvationists' converts who boast of the lies they have told in public confessions in order to get rescued and fed. Same old game! says a veteran. Me pretending to be a bad 'un. I tell how I blasphemed, gambled, and beat my poor old mother, so the lassies can feel good over my salvation and get the money from the meeting!

The playwright whom Shaw delighted to attack was Shakespeare. What led him to do so, aside from a certain natural perversity and a desire to attract attention to himself, was no doubt a feeling of their profound difference from each other. Unlike one for whom ripeness was all, Shaw remained largely an ideologist, tracking causes and panaceas, more than half convinced that by overturning the economic system poverty along with most evil could be wiped out and a millennial era introduced. This rosy future he vaguely anticipated through a dialectical process in which greed paved the way for generosity, ruthless competition for social sharing, class struggle for classlessness, and war for peace. In the temporal process he thought he saw advance through the union of opposites, a secular unfolding in which paradoxically irreconcilables would be reconciled.

But in Shakespeare, writing in a century untouched by Marxism and modern scientific progress, no such faith in unilateral causes, the benefactions of contradiction, and the secular excision of evils had appeared. In his tragedies especially the indication is plain that men cannot count upon the bad as the way to the good. With individuals as with kingdoms in his plays progress seems to occur in spite of, not because of, contradictions. In plays like *Macbeth*, *Henry IV*, and *Richard III*, the hint is plain that means consistent with ends are demanded, that right and not merely might is nec-

essary for genuine advance. Although human frailty and
depravity will presumably always remain, their amelioration
must depend in the future as in the past not simply upon
material causes but upon moral and religious effort, upon
sound laws aided by liberal traditions inherited from good
rulers and the consolidated virtues of the people. Amid the
whirl and strife of the historical flux some impulse to the
Ideas raises men above the battle. In Shakespeare's plays the
intimation of a grand design in history, where one finds one,
instead of being as with Shaw that of a tendency to socializa-
tion of the productive forces through perpetual negation, is
rather that of figures on a cloudy stair ascending the great
chain of being.

As Kierkegaard saw, both "the tragic and the comic are the
same, insofar as both are based on contradiction."[6] But whereas the comic apprehension has in mind a way out, and so
takes the contradiction as finally cancelled and painless, the
tragic apprehension despairs of a way out and in so far remains a suffering contradiction. Nevertheless the levity of
deeper comedy sees man's life as the striving of a finite, eva-
nescent creature against an infinite and eternal background.
Even though comedy turns away from this insight, embracing it as a feeling only in the greatest artists and works, it
must never be forgotten. But these matters we reserve for
further discussion in the next chapter.

------

[6] Kierkegaard, *Concluding Unscientific Postscript*, p. 459.

CHAPTER 9

The Tragic, the Sublime, and the Ridiculous

BROADLY SPEAKING, the tragic may be contrasted with the comic much as the sublime is contrasted with the ridiculous. And by the comparison of dissimilars they throw light on each other. Both the tragically sublime and the ludicrous express a certain victory of spirit over the world; yet whereas the temper of the sublime is one of solemn exaltation, that of the ridiculous expresses a slightly degrading relish for the juxtaposition of opposites. Indeed, relish in the confrontation of opposites plays a part in both, be the mood grave or gay, one of respect or contempt, be the emphasis as in the one case upon the greatness of the theme or as in the other upon the inconsequentially small. In any case, the mood of the ridiculous is not wholly sunny, since narrowly taken as a variety of the comic it inclines (like satire) to demean its object.

In rare instances, the tragic, the sublime, and the ridiculous may be found linked together in a single play as in the *Ajax* of Sophocles. There the hero is a great warrior, a man of peerless valor. Perhaps in history the warrior above all other men most often attains to sublimity. In passing beyond considerations of life and death, in shrinking at nothing, his bravery in battle makes everything else seem small. This was especially so among the ancient Greeks. Nevertheless it is the fate of this great military hero, Ajax, a fate that is self-inflicted (through *hubris*) to fall from the highest to the

lowest state—and through a disturbance of mind to be transformed from a slayer of his country's foes into a mere slayer
of cattle. At Troy, frenzied by jealous rage against the royal
judges, the Atreidae, who awarded not to him but to another
the armor of Achilles, Ajax turns in his madness upon the
helpless flocks, imagining that in butchering them he is destroying his human enemies. The abysmal absurdity of his
act, as he sees when he comes to himself, shames him in the
eyes of the world and renders him forever ridiculous. The
keen, mocking laughter of the Atreidae on whom he sought
to revenge his injured pride, rings in his ears so that he finds
no release from torment but in self-destruction. Represented
in the play is the sublimity of courage, the tragedy of a catas-
trophic fall, and the ridiculousness of a great warrior, a
scourge of men, degraded to the condition of a mere butcher
of defenseless cattle. On the one hand, the catharsis involving
the hero's fall, anguish, and suicide has a sublimity which
wrings the heart while elevating and purifying the spirit. What
a piece of work is man! Yet withal how pitiful! On the other
hand, Ajax in his blind frenzy swinging his sword against
tethered beasts forfeits our respect—as no longer a hero but
a bumbling brute worthy of derision and contempt. Only at
certain heights of Shakespeare and *Don Quixote*, and perhaps once or twice in the modern theater (as in Rostand's
Cyrano de Bergerac), do we catch a similar hint of the fusion
of the sublime and the ridiculous in a single work, at once
tragic and comic.

Yet though occasionally as here we may find the tragic,
the sublime, and the ridiculous fused together, it is well to
examine them separately. Manifestations of the tragic, with
which we may begin, are often said to be found wherever
there is the suffering of calamity. Yet this usage appears to
us too loose, since characters and events are tragic only when
they enact a kind of tragedy, while the term tragedy is employed in a most uncritical sense if extended to include any

human experience of disaster. A truly tragic awareness arises in us, we should say, only when a life or life itself is viewed as a whole and not as a mere discrete succession of experiences in the way it presumably appears to the lower creatures. To be sure, human suffering shares an aspect with animal life which, while cruel, terrible, and involving acute distress, is yet unaccompanied, as we believe, by a sense of wider import and appraisal. The events of the slaughter house, however shocking and pitiful, are not commonly called tragic. Similarly in human life many instances of painful experience or calamity (ranging from the agony of a toothache to mortal illness, from divorce, fraud, robbery to financial ruin or even murder) are not properly dignified by that name. Not all human deaths or intense afflictions, we should maintain, are tragic; nor are all obituaries, accidents, bankruptcies, and crimes reported in the press to be classified as of this genre. To warrant the use of the term the human suffering or disaster must involve (along with some unresolved predicament or final thwarting of hopes) several other distinguishing features.

As has been suggested, both the comic and the tragic center upon contradictions. The difference between the two is not merely that the one resolves its conflicts, finds a way out, whereas the other does not, but that whereas the comic primarily confronts simply logical contradictions, the tragic confronts a moral predicament. Not minor matters of true and false but crucial questions of right and wrong, good and evil face the tragic character in a tragic situation. No enlightenment comes to resolve the fearful dilemma in which he finds himself. He stands at the crossroads compelled to choose his path, without knowing unambiguously which is right but sure that whichever he takes involves suffering and loss. No way out appears to his dark riddle or agonizing perplexity, yet he must act—and his decision, though free, by expressing his character with its imperfections determines his fate. A man

torn between loyalty to his family and his country, a woman
between duty to her parents and her lover, Hamlet's faltering
resolve to kill his uncle, Orestes' quandary whether to revenge
the murder of his father, Anthony's choice between Rome and
Cleopatra, are all examples. Either way lies anguish and the
chooser undergoing the ordeal is racked with misgivings both
as to his standards and as to the alternative to which he commits himself. In the comic experience, we have seen, the
moral and metaphysical frame of life is not usually challenged, the puzzle being mainly one of conflicting appearances, and the solution coming through a kind of compulsive
insight as to the structure of things. But in the tragic experience, moral conflict, metaphysical doubts, painful indecision,
culminating in an action of free will or voluntary choice taken
without any clear-cut intellectual insight is of the essence.
Again, while knowledge comes at the very moment of comic
appreciation, the tragic sense is one of blindness, bafflement,
frustration, with knowledge of the true significance of the
situation coming long after the decision to act—either in
negative, retributive terms or in those of moral purification.

Both comic and tragic experience claim to tell us something about values, the nature of the world and man's relationship to it, and not merely to convey the feelings of the
subject as affected by sensuous representations. To be sure,
the comic insight has largely to do with the value of truth in
a negative way, exposing contradictions as false, and suggesting that despite irrational appearances things have a rational
structure. Tragic insight, on the other hand, shows the world
as a conflict between good and evil forces, shot through with
gleams of holiness, beauty, and justice: by choosing the side
of the right the subject gains serenity as his reward, but if he
makes the wrong choice he reaps terrible punishment.

But whereas appreciation of the comic is generally more
incidental and episodic, aroused by some pertinent but rather
superficial contradictions noted by the way, tragic awareness

turns upon some basic conflict that threatens the whole future. The whole surveyed in this awareness must be a developmental process, stages in the life of a character or characters involving growth, maturity, decline, and often death. Further, the death or decline in which the tragedy culminates must be viewed as a severing of hopes, a loss of earthly fulfillment which had seemed within the individual's grasp, and toward which his potentialities had been directed. The source of the predicament may be sometimes ignorance, heedlessness of the warning: Know thyself. For the tragic figure, like the comic, appears often like a sleepwalker possessed of a dreamful conceit of himself, unaware of his true nature or that of the world around him. Self-knowledge comes with awakening to the disparity between pretension and fact, between how one seems to oneself and in the eyes of the world—as some ridiculous pedant or would-be gentleman, or again as with the tragic consciousness of Oedipus, engulfed by a terrible fate through blindness as to his own nature. Yet in a way, as we have said, comic perception seems wiser than tragic in apprehending more clearly that suffering is part and parcel of the nature of life. As the jester (whose skin is thicker) puts it, "If it isn't one thing, it's another! *C'est la vie.*" Once you get rid of this trouble or annoyance, there is always another waiting. On the other hand, tragic perception, though especially concerned with pain and distress, never fully grasps the truth that suffering is essential to existence—at least not until the tragedy has issued in catharsis, if it ever does. Instead the subject construes his life as something distinct from the misfortune that befalls it and imagines that if the misfortune were removed he would be quite happy. In failing to recognize that life involves inexpugnable difficulties, struggle, pain, and loss, so that "ripeness" and "readiness" are "all",[1] tragic awareness is less profound than the humorous, being farther removed from the religious, unable (to borrow Kierkegaard's

---

[1] Shakespeare, *King Lear*, V.2.11; *Hamlet*, V.2.226.

expression) to "understand the secret of suffering as the form of the highest life, higher than all fortune and different from all misfortune."[2]

Again, the perceiver of the comic tends to retain mastery over himself and the situation, whereas in tragic awareness the individual is overcome with despair at man's inadequacy to resolve the problems of life. While the tragic sense, as we have said, focuses upon personal responsibility and the question of a moral order, the comic attitude surmounts the ethical problems by a swing away from the individual to the species, excusing one's weakness or failure with the thought "all men are like that." In tragic drama there is often, along with an ambiguous sense of guilt, an awareness by the protagonist of some mysterious power in the universe which has put an incubus upon him by which he brings upon himself a doom inherent in the potentialities of his situation and character. In so far as his suffering springs from an ancestral curse or external misfortune, at first the hero feels no guilt, although he may assume moral responsibility and say with Hamlet, "The times are out of joint, O cursed spite that ever I was born to set them right." As he proceeds, however, he acquires a sense of guilt from his failure and helplessness to resolve the painful dilemma, or from his sense that he has made the wrong choices in his attempt to escape. On the other hand, the comic outlook sees the laughable incongruity in the perpetual preoccupation of men with petty questions of preferment, wealth, and status, as against their unmindfulness of their total contingency, their obliviousness to the brevity of life and their progress toward the grave. The humorous man sees life as a joke; and he is in on the joke, as it were, like a spectator watching brokers in the market eagerly buying and selling stocks which he knows to be worthless, or watching fish swimming gaily to and fro in a net, unaware that they are caught.

The contrast between comedy and tragedy as dramatic

---

[2] Kierkegaard, *Concluding Unscientific Postscript*, p. 398.

forms is worthy of further remark. Whereas comedy usually involves acceptance of the generally received frame of values, jesting in action and dialogue the affirmation of life and a mundanely happy ending, tragedy is wanting in these, questioning the worth of existence as well as those basic conceptions that lend it meaning and value. The tone of tragedy is sombre, with action turning on the moral decisions of the chief characters in the face of trial, leading to an unhappy ending in downfall or death. While both forms of drama require a certain consistent organization, the demands are stricter for tragedy. In it, incidents flow from character and plot with a close-knit necessity, whereas in comedy a looser, episodic treatment of plot together with more surface depiction of character, tend to be the rule. Where comedy skates over the crust of things in a gay, sociable mood, tragedy deals with the lonely voyage of the soul in the troubled depths of life. Its appeal is to a select group, to men of reflective sensibility on the whole, as against the wider, more superficial appeal of comedy. Generally it is enough for the public if the comedy is amusing, but the tragedy must satisfy its moral sense. Usually less feeling is awakened by comedy, though it may excite in the audience much laughter, clapping, and noisy behavior;—in contrast to tragedy, which, while more quietly received, may arouse sympathy, pity, and fear of great intensity.

Both have a paradoxical quality which raises the question why we should find pleasure in the unpleasing, or enjoy the spectacle of much that is painful or repulsive. With comedy the answer is not so difficult, since there we remain more external to the frame; we see through the problems that plague the characters, anticipating a termination to their misadventures, and their finding a way out. With tragedy, where the problem is deeper, the suffering more extreme, the case is harder. Aside from the aesthetic euphoria arising from the technical skill of the work and its presentation, we may be solaced in our existential anxiety at seeing the terrible enigmas of life faced dauntlessly, energetically, without illusions. For some it is enough that the hero did as his ambition or passion dictated, providing the audience thereby a vicarious outlet or safety valve for dangerous emotions. Macbeth, Ajax, Othello are such heroes marred with great imperfections. As has been said,[3] tragedy forces us to live for the moment in blackness, uncomforted, without supports, to be, as it were, *agnostic*. But if this were all, appreciation of tragedy would not harbor a sense of the objectivity of values. And one of the oldest traditions has it that tragedy discloses a worth outside ourselves and provides, not a happy, but the *right* ending. Admittedly, we should say, at the tragic climax we stand (like the hero) with nothing to sustain us, bereft of all guidance and solace; nonetheless with catharsis come hints of a larger scheme. As the business of comedy seems to be to make honest men laugh —i.e., to give them for a moment the gift of truth, of seeing things as they are—so the business of tragedy seems to be to make them weep through affording them a glimpse of cosmic justice and the relation between men's actions and the highest values. For while the conclusion of tragedy is not poetic justice, not the mere allotment to characters of mundane penalties and rewards, yet it carries with it intimations of a balance of opposites and of things worth while, like goodness and mercy, beyond any earthly scale of requital.

Although comedy as a dramatic form covers a wide variety of works from rough-and-tumble farce to the heights of romantic and heroic comedy, tragedy admits no such range of degrees from low to high. Low tragedy is a contradiction in terms: the agonizer, thriller, tearjerker, and melodrama are denied the right to the name. A somber mood coupled with calamity and a fatal ending is not enough; nor does the merely sensational play exciting the emotions by a rapid succession

---

[3] I. A. Richards, *Principles of Literary Criticism,* (New York, Harcourt, Brace, & Co., 1925). p. 246.

of lurid, shocking, or pathetic happenings qualify. Skillful craftsmanship, poetic artistry, penetrating development of characters and plot, delineation of the soul in the critical decisions of the hero, whose fate awakens philosophical reflections, all these seem to be necessary. Against this, the play that is out of sight out of mind, that awakens no moral reverie as to the worth and meaning of existence, is not tragedy.

However, a prime requirement of tragic drama handed down from Aristotle, a requirement which is challenged today, is that of catharsis. This liberation and purification of the emotions by means of art, characteristic of the greatest Greek dramas, is usually missing from modern tragedy. For the modern stage, inclined to boast of its emancipation from belief in fate, supernatural religion, and a universal moral order of retributive justice, presents many so-called tragedies fraught with causal nemesis but without catharsis, in which heredity and environment override the efforts of their victims to escape, and innocent characters suffer unjust lots in a blindly indifferent world. While sometimes it is hard to draw the line in regard to a particular play as to whether or not it is to be classified as tragedy, nevertheless it seems to us not too much to say that those plays are in a fuller, more genuine sense tragedies that convey, besides a heightened feeling of pity and fear at the spectacle of human defeat, a sense of wider illumination and purgation. In its higher reaches tragedy passes beyond the unfolding of nemesis (by which a nexus of actions and partly free motivations leads to the fall of the hero) and attains a catharsis, bringing with it a sense of revelation and purification to the protagonist and spectators, not unlike a religious experience. In this connection a gradation of levels may be distinguished in the tragic worth of such works as Racine's *Phèdre*, Goethe's *Faust*, Part I, Ibsen's *Ghosts, Hedda Gabler*, or *Peer Gynt*, Eugene O'Neill's *Anna Christie* or *Mourning Becomes Electra*, Aeschylus' trilogy of the *House of Atreus*, Sophocles' *Oedipus Rex, Antigone*, and *Oedipus at Colonus*, and Shakespeare's *Macbeth, Othello, Hamlet,* and *King Lear.*

Thus *Macbeth,* we should say, is more of a melodrama and morality play, showing with supreme literary skill the nemesis of evil deeds and that crime does not pay, than a tragedy in the grand sense of *Hamlet* or *King Lear*—or even in the lesser sense of *Othello* or the *Ajax* of Sophocles. For these latter are military heroes flawed with a single fault, whereas Macbeth appears from the outset as a cool schemer, a bloody ambitious warrior, whose unspoken thoughts are aroused at the first encounter with the witches, and who is able to anatomize and reject the moral reasons that should deter him from Duncan's murder as coolly as if it were a matter of balancing accounts.[4] Potentially from the start Macbeth is a preeminently bad man, one whose downfall springs from his own deliberate acts of villainy and not from error or ignorance as with Othello and Ajax, although, as with them, bravery, which has been his prime virtue, remains with him to the end. But whereas Othello and Ajax through repentance and through destroying themselves win pardon in men's eyes, and by their deaths achieve a purification which ennobles their memories and lifts them to a higher plane, Macbeth forfeits all pity by his continued crimes. Even at the end, though weary of life and faced with a meaningless world, he suppresses remorse (being of tougher fiber than his wife), morally he seems no wiser than at the beginning, still imagining perhaps that if things had fallen out differently he might have happily succeeded in his schemes. He has not learned through suffering; in place of redemption we have his continued decline, increasingly evil deeds, and black extinction. Instead of causing us to pity Macbeth, his cumulative crimes forfeit our sympathy and freeze our blood. With the hero, the audience having "supped full with horrors" may also "gin to be aweary of the sun."[5] Of course, by the fury of the dramatic nemesis they may have

---

[4] *Macbeth,* I.7.
[5] *Macbeth,* V.5.13, 49.

been made wiser in the lesson that "the wages of sin are death" and been weaned from the impulse to go and do likewise. But aside from this psychotherapeutic action, their vision may be narrowed by a sense of men as puppets; and instead of an enrichment of values, they may be left with a feeling of heaviness at the scope of evil and a certain emptiness of life.

For the full, the highest tragic effect, on the contrary, catharsis is necessary for both protagonist and audience in a more positive sense. In it, the pattern of the origin of drama in Greek religious rite can still be traced symbolizing the struggle (*agon*) of light against darkness, the sequence of sacrifice, death and new life, of sorrow followed by ecstasy, of conflict by reconciliation. While the hero may suffer from a moral infirmity which conduces to his disgrace, in the highest tragedy there is a release from blindness, an expiation, an enlightenment. Through his sacrifice and downfall, he atones for his imperfection, and having lost all in this world, wins (so the audience is made to feel) redemption and acceptance by the universe. Catharsis includes besides liberation and exaltation a sense of retributive justice; for despite much unmerited suffering (which remains an enigma), our moral sense is not offended at the outcome (being reconciled by our metaphysical intuition), since in some measure the hero has deserved his fate, although through his atonement our blame has been turned to compassion. In the *Orestiea*, the great trilogy of Aeschylus, the catharsis is delayed until the last play, in which Orestes is acquitted of guilt by a divine jury. Similarly the *Oedipus Rex* of Sophocles fails of full tragic effect without the *Oedipus at Colonus*, when as a blind saint or wandering seer he is finally led in peace by the gods to holy ground.

Some there are who agree with Schopenhauer that catharsis is no more than a spirit of resignation. Plays like the *Antigone* of Sophocles or *The Trojan Women* of Euripides, it is said, can be fitted into no other tragic pattern. Since in neither case are the protagonists culpable, it may be urged, they can undergo no moral atonement and regeneration; our overwhelming sense of pity and fear is roused by the slaughter of the innocent, by the dignity of the victims in their submission, rather than by any judgment of them as guilty agents in the drama.

In answer to this negative theory of pure resignation, it may be said that in *The Trojan Women* we weep for the woes of the world through war, of which we are all guilty, and for which the powers that be exact unending atonement. True, in the scenes before us the women are primarily patients rather than agents, effects rather than causes, their sins of pride and collusion in Paris' theft forgotten in the horror of a war in which, having lost homes, husbands, children, country, they are being led away into slavery. In a sense the whole play is a kind of purifying sacrificial rite of catharsis through suffering, while in the background one feels nemesis tracking the Greeks for their violation of the temples of the gods in the madness of war. In the *Antigone*, with its conflict between lower and higher law, the state and individual conscience, the heroine is guilty in one sense, innocent in another. From one point of view her tragic choice is made early in the play, the remainder constituting her tragic expiation of it; while from another point of view, her steadfastness in moral defiance, her refusal to appeal to Creon's mercy, is a continual choice that intensifies her spiritual grandeur, making her active rather than passive throughout, although the exaltation that sustains her is revealed by silence rather than words, and in the tragic emotions of the spectator.

In tragedy there is the spectacle of personal loss and collapse that is final. Such irreparable overthrow brings home the transiency of man, his inexpugnable defects, yet also a heightened sense of the worth of noble individuals and acts. So we are led beyond concern for the particular sufferer to a universal sweep, a new depth of ideas, to a paradoxical intimation that perhaps somewhere, through sacrifice atoned,

such dauntless spirits still abide, such priceless things are safe;
that perhaps, in A. C. Bradley's phrase, this tragic world is
but a fragment of a whole beyond our vision.[6] This is the
mood of catharsis which yields exaltation and reconciliation.
Butcher is wrong in suggesting that it is "in . . . [a] transport
of feeling which carries a man outside his individual self, that
the distinctive tragic pleasure resides."[7] With it goes, as Schopenhauer saw, demand for another world,[8] a different kind
of existence, another plane of being. Again, as Hegel saw, in
tragedy is found a "satisfaction of spirit" and reconciliation
of forces through which "our emotional attitude is tranquil-
lized on a true ethical basis."[9] Or to put the matter in language still appreciable by many who lived through the last
world war, those who rise to the challenge of great tragic
experience may find that sacrifice can reveal the glory of life,
its "finest hour."

If indeed catharsis is necessary to tragedy in the full sense,
then it would seem that mere aesthetic illusionism induced by
skillful literary execution or dramatic verisimilitude to real life
are not enough, but that ethical and metaphysical insight are
essential. Further, naturalistic assumptions would seem inimi-
cal to catharsis—as witnessed by its absence in most modern
tragedies. For admission of a sense of sublimity and purification in viewing a tragedy would appear to involve acceptance
of a world of values outside ourselves, whereas the naturalist
denies the authenticity of such meanings, reinterpreting the
pity and terror aroused in catharsis as simply a contagious
shiver of fellow-feeling at personal danger, and even constru-
ing the joy which he is forced to allow as "strangely the heart

---

[6] A. C. Bradley, *Shakespearean Tragedy* (2nd ed. London, Macmillan,
1919), p. 39.
[7] S. H. Butcher, *Aristotle's Theory of Poetry and Fine Art* (2nd ed.
London, Macmillan, 1898), p. 262.
[8] Schopenhauer, *The World as Will and Idea, 3,* 212.
[9] Hegel, *Philosophy of Fine Art,* trans. Osmaston, *4,* 321.

of the experience" as no more than "an indication that all is right here and now in the nervous system."[10]

Admittedly something like fear enters as an ingredient, as Aristotle saw, into the catharsis of tragedy. Yet on closer inspection such awesome dread is seen not to be the same as personal alarm. As Kant rightly remarks, "He who fears can form no judgment about the sublime . . . just as he who is seduced by inclination and appetite can form no judgment about the beautiful."[11] While Kant is speaking here of the sublime in nature, his words apply no less to the catharsis of tragedy in which the fall of the hero, though serving as a solemn warning against a possible analogous danger to ourselves, instead of exciting personal alarm, makes us aware of something in us that surmounts concern with existence, apprehension for our life and goods.

Yet Kant is mistaken, in our opinion, in limiting the sublime wholly to the mind of the judging subject, to his sense of superiority over nature, and the moral dignity of the human soul in its destination.[12] Along with it goes also, in our view, a metaphysical insight into a supersensible or spiritual dimension of the universe as well—an insight that is distinct from any mere deification of nature or *pantheism*. In the sublimity of Greek tragedy, it will be recalled, a sense of cosmic meaning is awakened that suffering is inscrutably intertwined with good, and that a great soul is fitted by purification to an all-embracing object. At the same time, this hint of the cosmos as involved in the background is not of its involvement as a mere collection of facts but as a standard or arbiter of value, as the arbiter of existence rather than existence itself.

---

[10] Richards, *Principles of Literary Criticism*, p. 246.

[11] Kant, *Critique of Judgment*, p. 100.

[12] Kant, p. 96: "The feeling for the sublime in nature is respect for our own destination, which, by a certain subreption, we attribute to an object of nature (conversions of respect for the idea of humanity in our own subject into respect for the object)."

It is hard for us to doubt that in the experience of sublimity, especially in tragedy, something authentic is communicated regarding the grandeur of the whole, which is apprehended not as blind, aimless, futile, and going nowhere, but, despite its agonies and wastage, as patterned, worthwhile, suggesting an overarching order.

In its disinterestedness, our experience of the sublime is indifferent not merely as to whether its particular object is phenomenally real or a mere imaginative representation ("only a play," a fictitious picture of characters and events) but also regarding our own existence. By attaining a certain indifference regarding our creature jeopardy in a hazardous world, we gain insight that the worth of our personality lies in its rational autonomy and moral core. But great as is Kant's insight here in finding a locus of the sublime in the moral ideas of the subject, he is wrong in our opinion in denying to the experience any metaphysical revelation and in limiting awareness of the sublime wholly to our consciousness of our superiority over the natural world. "Who," asks Kant incredulously, "would call sublime, e.g., shapeless mountain masses piled in wild disorder upon one another with their pyramids of ice, or the gloomy, raging sea?"[13] Lovers of mountains and mountain climbers would be fools, he intimates,[14] to attribute sublimity to peaks and precipices themselves, which by their desolation, disorder, and immensity serve merely to point up by contrast man's spiritual grandeur, though against them in bodily terms he is nothing.

But sublimity, we should say, is to be found not only in the human subject with courage to measure himself against the apparent almightiness of nature but in natural objects themselves in their magnificence. The starry heavens at night, the Andromeda nebula, vast cloud effects, the desert, storms at sea, earthquakes, giant redwoods, the inexhaustibility of space

---

[13] Kant, p. 95.
[14] Kant, p. 105.

and time are but a few examples. That greatness pertains to manifestations of the sublime is a notion widely accepted. Nevertheless this grandeur is not necessarily inherent in the spatial magnitude or dynamic power of the object, which overwhelms the spectator. Sublimity may appear in such minutiae as the sands of the sea, the complexity of the atom, or again in the bravery of some small creature in defending its young, or in the majesty of death. In the experience of sublimity we learn something not merely regarding the soul of the subject but also regarding the object; we catch some word as to the ground plan of the world that surrounds us, of nature as the garment of the divine. Many have found in high mountains glimpses of a geometry so pure, perfect, aloof, as to permit them in these lofty solitudes acquaintance for a moment with "the flight of the alone to the alone." Far from perceiving mountain scenery as formless, chaotic, wild (as did the eighteenth century), we may discern in its sublimity an appropriateness suggesting, however briefly and cloudily, a higher order in which we somehow have a part. Indeed, the adjuration "Live as on a mountain" intimates that we should view the world as from a distance, surveying the whole of its wondrous configurations rather than confine ourselves to human subjects and the study of personal relations. As our domestic pets (as William James noted) now and then look up and seem to catch an arc of meaning, a flash of significance from our higher human drama, so in our experience of the sublime we may ourselves catch for an instant hints of the pattern of a loftier action on a cosmic scale.

In summary, it may be remarked that in our awareness of the sublime we notice, in addition to a sense of inspiration, expansiveness, and reverence akin to religious veneration, a feeling of one's creature insignificance together with almost a dread of the object. Very different from this is the perception of the ridiculous, which in contrast to the peak of sublimity appears as a kind of reversal or nadir of descent in the scale of values. With our perception of the ridiculous goes a swing to negative feeling, to anticlimax, an evaporation of mystery and worth, and an attitude of irreverence, even scorn, of the object. Also with it goes a sense of self-congratulation on our part quite contrary to the deep humility (albeit combined with spiritual exultation) instilled by the sublime. Whereas the sublime object is regarded as majestic, solemn, exalted, the ridiculous one is taken as laughably trifling or futile. The sublime insight is cloudy; that of the ridiculous is clear; in the one the subject loses himself in admiration of the object; in the other he stands alienated and aloof. In the experience of the sublime we gain (aside from aesthetic appreciation) a sense of cosmic spirituality—as opposed to a self-satisfied perception of absurdity in the ridiculous.

Where the scope of the two is limited to tragedy and comedy, the sublime effect of the first is found to arise from the spectacle of a hero who "dies that he may live, . . . falls that he may rise, . . . suffers that he may learn,"[15] while the ridiculous effects of comedy spring from the undignified behavior, misunderstandings, errors, accidents, and verbal badinage of the characters in an action terminating without serious eventuality. What is ridiculous differs further from satire and the satirical in that, whereas the latter refers primarily to the expressive form of disparagement, the former has to do with the state of affairs that is indicated. Narrower in meaning than the comic, what is designated as ridiculous is that which is *worthy of ridicule* through laughter and the lowest esteem. Through the centuries men have drawn from great tragedy spiritual illumination, a sense of sacredness and ascent to a new life from the aesthetic semblance of darkness, death, and suffering. On the whole, no such ennobling influence is attributable to comedy, though in tending to wean men from errors it is not lacking a civilizing function. Gen-

---

[15] Herbert Weisinger, *Tragedy and the Paradox of the Fortunate Fall.* (London, Routledge & Kegan Paul, 1953), p. 271.

erally avoiding such solemn themes as anguish, death, and atonement, comedy deals lavishly in pratfalls, inconsequential actions, and misadventures from which characters often rebound to good fortune beyond their deserts. Nevertheless in the background of the genuinely comic, as of the tragic play, there is awareness of the ideal—at least in its discrepancy from the actual. But while tragedy faces the ideal in catastrophe, comedy by its laughter seems to turn its back on it. When carried to the limits of the sublime and the ridiculous, the two indeed in their conflicting attitudes of exaltation and debasement, acceptance and rejection of their objects, represent opposite extremes of evaluation. Yet rarely both may appear in the same work, suggesting the possibility of their origin in a single source, and that the author of the greatest tragedy and comedy may be one and the same.

But having dwelt upon the philosophic and aesthetic import of the ludicrous so long, it seems time to turn in the opposite direction, as it were, to the question of the origin and genesis of laughter as considered by natural philosophers.

CHAPTER 10

The Genesis of Laughter

NOTHING is more familiar than casual reference to the "sense of humor" or for that matter to the "moral sense," "the sense of beauty," or to "common sense." Yet the metaphorical character of such usage is obvious the moment we ask ourselves whether we are employing the term in the same way as when we refer to the basic *five*—to the senses of sight, smell, taste, hearing, or touch (with its organic, cutaneous, and kinaesthetic subdivisions)—capacities possessing end organs through which impressions of the physical world are produced. Without a differentia the word "sense" may be used with almost any range of significance. But in default of attachment to a terminal nerve network adapted to a specific sensation, its meaning is hardly more than that of an irreducible branch of experience of some sort. Not only this, but unlike the generally recognized bodily senses, humor and the experience of the comic seem to be historically more complex, drawing into themselves various simpler, more primitive tendencies reflecting earlier stages in the life of the individual and the race.

Among those who have felt such difficulties are especially evolutionary thinkers. These approach the problem of the ludicrous largely through observation of bodily behavior, and by study of the neuro-muscular processes involved in laughter they seek to find out its biological origin and basis. Because their whole interpretation is under the influence of the hypothesis of evolution, their interest centers on the development and functional utility of laughing as discoverable by genetic psychosomatic analysis. The complete responsibility of the existential forces of the environment for the consciousness, feelings, and thoughts of living creatures remains their general assumption. Reason is held to be derived from non-rational sources; in consequence, conceptions drawn from the empirical sciences rather than from logic or the import of reflective thinking are relied upon for their conclusions. Their concern is with the efficient causes of phenomena—with what came out of what, with questions as to advantage to the species and practical use rather than with considerations of ground-consequent, intrinsic meaning, or the thought content of the ludicrous. In this group Darwin and Herbert Spencer, and to a lesser degree Freud and perhaps even Bergson have a place. Indeed, if one were not to draw a line, a long list of names like those of James Sully, C. W. Kimmins, William McDougall, and many others might be included.

But unquestionably the most influential discussions of laughter from the evolutionary point of view are those of Spencer and Darwin. While Spencer's well-known essay on "The Physiology of Laughter"[1] was published earlier (1860), Darwin in his *The Expression of the Emotions in Man and Animals*[2] (1872) by his favorable references to Spencer's treatment of the subject and by his absence of criticism indicated his general agreement with Spencer's theory. Their discussions

---

[1] Herbert Spencer, *Essays: Scientific, Political, and Speculative* (New York, D. Appleton & Co., 1892), 2, 452ff. This essay on laughter was first published in *Macmillan's Magazine* in 1860.

[2] Charles Darwin, *The Expression of the Emotions in Man and Animals* (New York, D. Appleton & Co., authorized edition). However, Darwin (p. 9, note 11), in referring to Spencer's treatment of the subject, remarks, "I may state, in order that I may not be accused of trespassing on Mr. Spencer's domain, that I announced in my *Descent of Man* that I had then written a part of the present volume: my first manuscript notes of the subject of expression bear the date of the year 1838."

differ in range, however. While Spencer deals with the physiological processes, Darwin, the great naturalist, offers a most careful behavioral description of laughter and the expression of associated emotions. This is supplemented by reports from skilled students on the laughter of children, savages, and mentally defective persons, together with accounts of apparently analogous manifestations of joy and play in animals. We can vaguely see, Darwin concludes, how in a large part of the animal kingdom the utterance of certain sounds became associated with pleasurable experiences; nevertheless we do not know why the sounds which men utter when pleased have the peculiar character of laughter.[3] Despite this, he provides us with much valuable information regarding the probable evolution of laughter and its individual development.

In contrast, Spencer, in dwelling on the physiological problem, expresses regarding psychosomatic relations a franker, more sweeping agnosticism. "In the production of consciousness by physical agents acting on physical structures," he declares, "we come to a mystery never to be solved."[4] But concerning laughter "the real problem," he says, is "How comes a sense of the incongruous to be followed by these peculiar bodily actions? . . . Why, when greatly delighted, or impressed with certain unexpected contrasts of ideas, should there be a contraction of particular facial muscles and particular muscles of the chest and abdomen?"[5]

The answer to this question, according to Spencer, is briefly as follows: Excitation of nerve centers in human beings leads to a state of tension which may be discharged in one or more of three ways. (1) If the excitation is not strong, it may be passed on to other nerve centers which have no direct connection with the bodily members, thereby causing emotions and ideas; that is, liberated nerve force in an inscrutable way

---

[3] Darwin, *Expression of the Emotions,* p. 205.

[4] Spencer, *Essays, 2,* 455.

[5] Spencer, *Essays, 2,* 452–53.

may produce in us sensations and states we call feeling and quiet thinking.[6] (2) Or again the current of nerve force may be expended in the excitation of motor nerves, and so cause muscular contractions; (3) or the current may pass on to the nerves which supply the viscera (heart, stomach, intestines) and may stimulate one or more of these.[7] Rarely does the disturbance expend itself in one direction only, but often, though in different proportions, in all three.

That the nervous excitement at any moment present to consciousness as feeling must expend itself in some way means further that, since the quantity of energy is limited, the closing of one channel increases the discharge through the others. In consequence, according to Spencer, since "the suppression of external signs of feeling makes feeling more intense"—it being reflected back as it were and increased—"the men who . . . have the keenest appreciation of the comic are usually able to do and say the most ludicrous things with perfect gravity."[8] We should remark that there is a difference of opinion here, however, as to whether the best appreciators of the comic maintain a solemn mien, as intimated by Spencer, Freud, and Mark Twain, or whether, on the contrary, they sympathetically reveal by their own laughter their relish of the joke; the first would seem to operate by contrast, the second by suggestion and the association of similars.

In any case the discharge of arrested feelings into the muscular system as laughter occurs only when the escape of excess energy is denied other adequate channels. This theory of laughter as a sudden overflow of surplus energy (formulated by Spencer, accepted by Darwin, Freud, and others) rests on the adoption of energy as an inclusive concept embrac-

---

[6] Darwin notes with approval (*Emotions*, Ch. I, note i, p. 27) the "clear distinction" drawn by Spencer between emotions and sensations, the latter being "generated in our corporeal framework," adding "he [Spencer] classes as feelings both emotions and sensations."

[7] Spencer, *Essays*, 2, 455.

[8] Spencer, 2, 457.

ing notions like "nervous energy," "psychic" or "mental energy" (with mass and intensity), as well as physical energy of well recognized mechanical, thermal, electrical, and chemical types. Along with admission of the general principles of the conservation and degradation of energy, together with the evolutionary assumption that mental life is causally produced by, and intimately dependent upon, its physical nexus, the supposition is accepted that, when there is a surplus of stored or available energy in an organism, there is a tendency (unless obstructed) for its conversion to kinetic forms. Thus when the supply of energy summoned to meet the actual occasion is found to be in excess of that required (or when, as Spencer would say, consciousness is transferred suddenly from great things to small), the excess energy becoming superfluous is released as laughter. But if the energy summoned for use is adequate and no more, it is consumed in relation to its object. On the other hand, if after a seemingly insignificant event something very great suddenly and unexpectedly occurs, the emotion called *wonder* results, involving an increased absorption of nervous energy into mental channels and a diminution of its outflow into the muscular system, as shown by a dropping of the jaw and a relaxed grasp. Finally—if we may be permitted to repeat Spencer's major point—if in expectation we have mobilized a large quantity of nervous energy and find ourselves confronted with a small, unworthy object, the superfluous force is discharged in the form of certain half-convulsive facial and respiratory contractions known as laughter. Thus laughter appears as a physiological act serving as an automatic means of restoring our momentarily disturbed psycho-physical equilibrium.

Turning to Darwin, we find him agreeing with Spencer not only that nerve force generates feeling while feeling generates bodily action, but that a certain quantitative equivalence may be traced in their manifestations. Accordingly, a "general law" is discovered by which an overflow of nerve force, undirected by any motive, takes the most habitual routes; and, if these do not suffice, will next overflow into the less habitual ones.[9] Hence the facial and respiratory muscles, being those most used, are first likely to be brought into action; next those of the upper extremities; then those of the lower; and finally those of the whole body. Thus in laughter the discharge of energy passes most frequently into movement of muscles round the mouth, of the jaws, tongue, lips, and organs of speech, then through changes of respiration, circulation, then movements of the viscera, limbs, head, and spine. The smile, with visible characters similar to but less marked in degree than the laugh, is silent. But "the sound of laughter," says Darwin, "is produced by a deep inspiration followed by short, interrupted, spasmodic contractions of the chest, and especially of the diaphragm."[10] Its audible expression is apparently the antithesis of cries of distress, where the expirations are continuous and prolonged, with brief interrupted inspirations. In his extremely detailed description of laughter, Darwin notes how the corners of the mouth are drawn backward and upward through the contraction of the great zygomatic muscles, how the upper lip is raised drawing the cheeks upward, how wrinkles form under the eyes which tend to sparkle brightly, and in extreme laughter are suffused with tears. Not infrequently the circulation is increased, the body shakes, the head nods, the lower jaw quivers, and the teeth are bared. In the pleasurable excitement or high spirits, which is often accompanied by laughter, the color rises, the brain is stimulated by an increased flow of blood, the mental powers are enlivened, and the affections are warmed.

Although Darwin professes ignorance as to why feelings of pleasure and laughter go together, he suspects habit and long continued association fixed through many generations. Everyone admits, he declares, citing Bain and Huxley, the power of

---

[9] Spencer, 2, 458 f.; Darwin, *Expression of the Emotions,* pp. 9, 71.
[10] Darwin, *Emotions,* p. 200.

association. Yet unlike Huxley he does not describe it wholly
in terms of ideas or mental representations, but as a correlation of mental states with bodily movements.[11] Indeed, to this
principle of conditioning, as we should now call it, he attaches
primary importance in the expression of the emotions. Of the
three principles utilized by Darwin to account for emotional
expression in men and animals, subsidiary place is given to
antithesis or contrast, and *direct action* due to the constitution
of the nervous system, as compared to the great weight which
he attaches to *associated habit*.

In addition to a wide range of material drawn from the
observation of what we should call clearly comic laughter,
Darwin considers analogues and precursors of it among lower
animals, primitive men, human infants, as well as among abnormal, defective types, such as idiots and imbeciles. While
he construes the movements and sounds apparently anticipating laughter in the lower animals as probably mere expressions of joy, Darwin goes so far as to claim to recognize
in the dog on certain occasions the germ of what he calls "a
sense of humor."[12] This he finds especially in the dog's teasing behavior, as distinct from mere play, when retrieving a
stick. Often the master throws a stick and the dog, instead of
returning it, will carry it away a short distance, squatting on
the ground with it close beside him. When the master comes
up to take the stick, the dog will seize it "and rush away in
triumph, repeating the same manoeuvre, and evidently enjoying the practical joke."

Initiating a tendency followed by later evolutionary students, Darwin pays close attention to the phenomenon of

---

[11] "Certain complex actions are of direct or indirect service under certain
states of mind, in order to relieve or gratify certain sensations, desires,
etc.; and whenever the same state of mind is induced, however feebly,
there is a tendency through the force of habit and association for the same
movements to be performed, though they may not be then of the least
use." (Darwin, *Emotions,* p. 28.)

[12] Darwin, *The Descent of Man* (New York, 1879), p. 71.

tickling, noting that anthropoid apes utter a reiterated sound corresponding to laughter when tickled, especially under the arm pits. "The imagination," he remarks, "is sometimes said to be tickled by a ludicrous idea; and this so-called tickling of the mind is curiously analogous with that of the body."[13] Nevertheless there is a difference. Whereas the laughter arising from being tickled by a light touch is a reflex action, that arising from a ludicrous idea, though involuntary, is not— since, in the latter case, not only must the mind be initially in a pleasurable condition, but the laughter-producing idea itself cannot be of grave import.

"Laughter," says Darwin, "seems primarily to be the expression of mere joy or happiness"[14]—as shown by the incessant laughter of children at play and even by that of idiots and imbeciles. That man laughs when he is pleased appears to hold of all races and to be possibly a native or instinctive tendency developed through association, as suggested by cases like that of Laura Bridgman since in her case congenital blindness and deafness ruled out learning through imitation. Hardly anything in Darwin's opinion arouses laughter more easily than mimicry,[15] both among primitives and modern Europeans. Further, the laughter of adults, Darwin observed, is excited by considerably different causes than those which suffice during childhood, being frequently employed by them in a forced manner to mask other states of mind than happiness, such as shyness, shame, anger, or derision (in which we have a hybrid expression combining amusement and contempt). Basically and genetically, however, laughter is the natural expression of joy, cheerfulness, high spirits, and even sympathy. In sympathetic emotion the identification with others' feelings may occur either with persons in real life or with those in fictitious situations, as in reading a novel or

---

[13] Darwin, *Expression of the Emotions*, p. 199.
[14] Darwin, *Emotions*, p. 196.
[15] Darwin, *Emotions*, p. 207.

watching a play—in which cases the reader or audience shares
the satisfaction, distress, or comic attitude appropriate to the
action of characters for whom he feels no real affection. Besides sympathizing with others' happiness or distress, even
though imaginary, we may also upon occasion be said to
sympathize with ourselves in comparing our present with our
former lot in life.

Among various kinds of laughter, such as that due to tickling, hysteria, sardonic emotion or mental distress, or again
to the mere overflow of pleasurable feeling, there is also distinctively comic laughter. "Something incongruous or un-
accountable, exciting surprise and some sense of superiority
in the laugher, who must be in a happy frame of mind," according to Darwin, appears to be its "commonest cause."[16]
Spencer, who carries the analysis somewhat further, recog-
nizes that there are perceptions of *non-ludicrous incongruity*,
such as wonder which, although involving unexpected feeling
of equal quantity and intensity, have muscular effects the reverse of laughter. But while the emotion of wonder arises from
the experience of an *ascending* incongruity (when after something insignificant something great occurs unexpectedly),
laughter at the ludicrous "naturally results only when consciousness is unawares transferred from great things to small—
only when there is what may be called a *descending* incongruity,"[17] as when at a concert the pause between the *andante*
and *allegro* of a Beethoven symphony is broken by a loud
sneeze. An illustration from my own experience, closely parallel to another example given by Spencer, may further clarify
the point. Some years ago I remember that while witnessing
a serious Siamese drama in Bangkok dealing with legendary
princes, princesses, and demons, a large tomcat wandered on
to the stage and began caterwauling disconsolately. At first
the native audience was too intent upon the dramatic action

[16] Darwin, *Emotions*, p. 198.
[17] Spencer, *Essays*, 2, 463.

to notice him, but in a few moments the spell was broken by an outburst of laughter. According to Spencer the train of emotions or, physiologically speaking, the nervous tension induced by the dramatic ideas was suddenly checked and a new channel opened by the appearance of the cat; but as this new outlet was a very small one insufficient to carry off the arrested excitement, the overflow was discharged as laughter.[18]

With both Spencer and Darwin incongruity is interpreted psychosomatically rather than logically, by equating quantitative notions of energy with simple *contrasts* of feeling. With Darwin especially laughter is treated as predominantly an expression of the emotions. That psychological surprise is always necessary seems to us contradicted by the practical joke, in which the audience that laughs has usually been in on the trick and seen the point from the beginning. Further that comic laughter requires a *descending* incongruity, by which consciousness is transferred from great things to small may be questioned. For instance, our laughter at a cartoon in the *New Yorker* with a sign in the foreground labelled "Lovers' Leap" extending over a chasm, while descending in mid-air we see a bearded, turbaned Turk with five veiled ladies in balloon pants, is not due to a decreasing incongruity, since a polygamous love affair leading to a collective suicide seems certainly a greater, more serious incongruity than one involving a mere duo. Broadly speaking, the difficulty with Darwin and Spencer is that, although they cursorily mention incongruity as a common cause of laughter, by translating it

---

[18] Or, as Darwin puts the matter more generally, "If the mind is strongly excited by pleasurable feelings, and any little unexpected event or thought occurs, then, as Mr. Herbert Spencer remarks, 'a large amount of nervous energy instead of being allowed to expend itself in producing an equivalent amount of new thoughts and emotions which were nascent is suddenly checked in its flow . . . the excess must discharge itself in some other direction, and there results an efflux through the motor nerves to various classes of the muscles . . . producing the half-convulsive actions we call laughter.' " (*Expression of the Emotions,* p. 198.)

into psychological and somatic terms, they rob it of logical efficacy. In their hands, logical distinctions are existentialized: incongruities are viewed as feelings of contrast, as phenomenal events in the experience of human perceivers, but without implications of intellectual insight or objective axiological significance.

Our objection to the reduction of the category of incongruity, as well as of thought itself, by evolutionists to basically existential terms goes very deep. For where, as with evolutionary theorists, ideas and reasoning are ultimately attributed to non-ideational, non-rational origin and control, the ludicrous (along with other problems of our world) becomes impossible of intellectual comprehension. For if logical relations are held to be the result of a temporal alogical process, what criteria (logic being excluded) have we for testing the scientific account of the evolutionary process? Actually a framework of logical standards is presupposed as the basis of the natural sciences and the physical, biological, and psychological realms they deal with; acceptance of the existential world of science presupposes and rests on assumption of the validity of the non-existential world of logic. Science can be true, if and only if, logic with its distinctions is valid. [19]

A point against the incongruity theory of the ludicrous mentioned by Spencer and Bain, which needs to be disposed of here, is that not all incongruities cause laughter; and that often the most intense feeling may be aroused by the perception of quite non-ludicrous incongruities. In a famous passage, Bain remarks:

> A decrepit man under a heavy burden, five loaves and two fishes among a multitude, and all unfitness and gross disproportion; an instrument out of tune, a fly in ointment, snow in May, Archimedes studying geometry in a siege, and all discordant things; a wolf in sheep's cloth-

---

[19] M. C. Swabey, *Logic and Nature*, pp. 21 ff.

ing, a breach of bargain and falsehood in general; the multitude taking the law into their own hands, and everything of the nature of disorder; a corpse at a feast, parental cruelty, filial ingratitude, and whatever is unnatural; the entire catalogue of the vanities given by Solomon are all incongruous, but they cause feelings of pain, anger, sadness, loathing, rather than mirth.[20]

That there are different types of incongruity, some of them non-ludicrous, is a point, in our opinion, well worthy of emphasis. Indeed, in our view, all values are forms of concord or coherence, and all disvalues are forms of discord or incoherence. Yet just as there are many *values* (truth, goodness, beauty, righteousness, holiness) so there are many *disvalues* (falsity, evil, ugliness, unrighteousness, unholiness) with corresponding different forms of congruity and incongruity. In the ludicrous we have a value of an odd, paradoxical kind, positive but with an admixture of negative, which reveals congruity through incongruity, sense through nonsense, order through disorder, concord through discord. Grasp of the ludicrous involves an insight of feeling and thought of no great practical concern, in which some logical incompatibility is confronted and then penetrated and resolved. That Bain's so-called incongruities are non-ludicrous is not to be wondered at since none of them clearly involves a logical contradiction. Rather they are instances of things out of place, of situations contrary to custom, marked by a certain existential unfitness or unsuitability (as a corpse at a feast or five loaves and two fishes to feed a multitude). Some instances—e.g. the fly in ointment or the instrument out of tune—are mere trivial notations of factual annoyances and so unworthy of laughter; while others—pub-

---

[20] Quoted by Spencer, *Essays, 2,* 463. Spencer holds that because the state of consciousness suddenly produced in all these instances, though totally unlike, is not inferior in mass to the preceding one, the conditions of laughter (descending incongruity) are not fulfilled. Bain holds to a degradation theory.

lic disorder, cruelty, ingratitude—involve discordances of so grave a nature as to arouse strong revulsion. Genuine comic perception, we would say, belongs neither to the domain of the inconsequential nor to the gravely consequential, being removed from the former by containing a logical incongruity, and from the latter by avoiding all serious challenge of the basic framework of values.

That those who take the evolutionary approach to the comic through the study of animals, children, and primitive men do not stress the perception of logical incongruity almost goes without saying. What is remarked in both children and savages is the tendency to spontaneous laughter free from reflection or ideation. In its earliest stages laughter is said to appear as a sign of pleasurable excitement or the sudden increase of it. Often among evolutionary students the proto-type of the comic attitude has been traced to the response to tickling as a kind of play. That is, they have been led to wonder whether our sense of fun may not have sprung from these "funny sensations," from a series of light tactile stimula-tions yielding a mixed agreeable and disagreeable feeling tone. That tickling may be regarded as one of the earliest forms of play, as a social activity similar to *teasing*, is readily seen. It takes its rise apparently from a simulated threat of blows by one participant, and defensive movements to ward them off on the part of the other. In being tickled, as Sully points out, there is often a slight shock of fear shown by the recipient at the approach of an alien hand for an unknown purpose, which dissolves into nothingness at a harmless light touch.[21] Repeated attack and defense movements in this make-believe or mimic combat establishes a clear pattern of play activity. Laughter comes to be associated with it probably not merely as an expression of joyous feeling but as a sign, essential for its un-derstanding by the other party, that the contest is merely a good-natured game of make-believe. Indeed, some students

---

[21] James Sully, *Essay on Laughter*, pp. 77, 82 ff.

maintain that in animals like the dog or monkey behavior analogous to laughter is both a manifestation of pleasure, the antithesis of hostile attack, and a form of *communication,* a signal from one member of a group to others that "all is well" and they may relax from tension with safety.[22] Thus when the dog "laughs with his tail" or the approaching tickler smiles or chuckles, he says in effect "Have no fear of me, I will not hurt you." In tickling, as in play in general, a certain amount of self-control is present (even in the play of a cat with a kitten) and with it something like a divided or two-level consciousness. It is therefore conceivable that from tickling as a generic type, the many varieties of teasing may have developed, together with the manifold playful forms of social activity found in games, sports, pranks, and practical jokes. Eventually we may suppose, as the intellect of the higher mammals grows and matures, its expressions will become more involved, until word-play, mind-play, and subtle ideational complexes lead to full-fledged appreciation of the comic.

However it is too much to claim that the detailed stages in the genesis of laughter have as yet been satisfactorily traced, although it has been widely noted that love of play, mimicry, teasing (pretended but harmless attacks), and so-called practical jokes are common among children and primitives, and that in general these precede developed control of the mind and laughter due to elaborate ideation. While in a primitive African tribe, for instance, one member may take delight in scaring another by imitating the roar of a lion, among civilized children the game may take the form of "bo-peep" or of making faces with the very young, or of jumping out of dark corners crying "boo" with the older. That feelings outweigh ideation in the psychic content accompanying the earlier stages of laughter is generally agreed. But whether at these earlier

---

[22] P. Hayworth, "The Social Origin and Function of Laughter," *Psychological Review 35* (1928), 367–84; P. T. Young, *Emotion in Man and Animal* (New York, John Wiley, 1943), p. 327.

levels we have what may properly be called laughter at the ludicrous is by no means so clear. Granted that an overflow of pleasurable feeling mixed with a sense of something slightly disagreeable, together with an element of surprise (Sully's main cause of laughter) and a suggestion of two-level consciousness is usually present in teasing, playing, and laughter, nevertheless all this describes simply factual states of physiology and psychology. The defect in such accounts in our view is their failure to deal with the expression of the ludicrous as an evaluation, as not a fact but an import, as not an existent but a significant insight.

A related and much favored theory, locating the comic in a psychological attitude of self-feeling, attributes laughter to the emotional exuberance (or "sudden glory") arising from a sense of superiority of oneself to others and the impulse to degradation of the object. Hobbes and Bain are the classic exponents of this view, which centers appreciation of the ludicrous in a self-feeling of pride and power, in a delight expressive of malicious contempt or the desire to take someone down. "Laughter," says Hobbes, is a "sudden glory arising from some sudden conception of some eminency in ourselves by comparison with the infirmity of others, or with our own formerly."[23] While a certain rather cruel joy of triumph in getting the better of others is often noted in the laughter of primitives and children (and even dogs, Westermarck noted, dislike being laughed at), this is far from being invariably the case with civilized adults. Here again the old saying that the origin is not the essence is worth repeating, since the soil or matrix from which something emerged—astronomy from astrology, chemistry from alchemy, or appreciation from the ludicrous perhaps from teasing—must not be mistaken for its distinctive nature, just as the temporal order of its emergence must not be confused with its order of logical dependence. The obvious

---

[23] Hobbes, *Human Nature,* IX, 13. *The English Works of Thomas Hobbes,* ed. Sir W. Molesworth (London, J. Boun, 1840), *4,* 46.

weakness of such a view, which translates laughter to terms of egoistic feeling, is that it denies the possibility of sympathetic laughter and of intellectual laughter expressive of a disinterested outlook. In so doing it overlooks those experiences of identification of vicarious sharing with the comic object, in which our sense of kinship with the victim adds to our comic appreciation of his plight. Again, a detached, disinterested standpoint is involved in one's ability to laugh at a joke on oneself or at the spectacle of those universal frustrations common to everybody. Finally, while the superiority or degradation theory would seem to cover fairly adequately many cases of small misfortunes, awkward situations, personal defects, and the exposure of hypocritical make-believes, it fails to cover various kinds of mental and verbal play with incongruities (as in puns and novel word associations), where no one's dignity is at stake.

Passing over the maze of views and suggestions dealing with the genesis of comic laughter, it seems best to conclude our chapter with some further remarks on two well-known thinkers already mentioned, who while continuing in the general direction of Darwin and Spencer have sought to modify and supplement their earlier trend. Thus Freud, the first of these, finds that Spencer's "view of the mechanism of laughter . . . fits our own realm of thought excellently."[24] Like Spencer, for Freud laughter is evidence of the discharge of a psychic irritation which has met with a hindrance; and he quotes with approval Spencer's remark that "laughter naturally results only when there is what we may call a *descending* incongruity." Nevertheless Freud modifies Spencer's thought to fit his own theories of submerged psychic life or depth psychology. In defending the quantitative treatment of "psychic energy," Freud maintains that the larger, more important portion of psychic life is to be found, not in the content of consciousness,

---

[24] Freud, *Wit and Its Relation to the Unconscious*, p. 22.

but in the unconscious. But despite his having learned, as he thinks, the practically indestructible character of psychic traces, and how psychic energy can be displaced from one idea to another along certain association channels, he makes no attempt to represent these psychic paths by particular cells and fibers of the nervous system.[25] In Freud, Spencer's and Darwin's notion of liberated nerve force taking the most habitual route possible becomes more clearly formulated as the principle of the economy of psychic energy. For him psychic energy tends to take the simpler, easier, and shorter path. We naturally seek to save psychic expenditure, to save work, words, thought, material, and trouble. Finding multiple associative connections is the technique that aids in this by helping, among other things, toward the manifold applications of the same material.

To unravel Freud's meaning and to follow through his doctrine of the discharge of surplus psychic energy is often difficult. But that in general he adopts an evolutionary cosmology, using a psychogenetic method, and finding the roots of the comic in the primitive, the infantile, and in biological need, can hardly be questioned. In his view, there is a close relation between the comic and the infantile, according to which we find the nature of the comic in the foreconscious association with the infantile,[26] in a comparison by which I find the child in others or in myself. For instance, in his immoderate energy of movement and inferior mental development, the clown may seem like an over-active youngster, or the bad person may appear like a naughty child. Again we may find the comic in others through our identification with what seems their childlike embarrassment, repetitiveness, imitativeness, lack of dignity, etc. But while the child laughs continually from sheer pleasure and playfulness, it has itself no feeling for the comic. The feeling for the comic, according to

---

[25] Freud, p. 228.
[26] Freud, p. 366.

Freud, arises only with education as one acquires a standard in one's own ego for comparing the different energy-expenditures of the grownup and the child. That is to say, in himself the child is not comic, but only in comparison with the grownup. At first the infant or toddler acts through imitation; then teaching or instruction exercises its mandate "So must you do it!" Gradually the norm becomes a personal possession, an inner monitor, and the active ego, comparing itself with others, says "He has not done it right; I can do it better."

By way of summary we may repeat that, according to Freud, comic possibilities appear when we are brought back to the level of childhood through a comparison dealing with others and myself, or altogether with others, or altogether within myself. Indeed, the largest number of experiences of the comic proceed from our identification with the apparently juvenile action of others (as in the comic of situation, exaggeration, imitation, degradation, or unmasking). Thus our sense of the comic situation usually arises from some form of embarrassment, in which we feel again vicariously the helplessness of the child; the comic of exaggeration from people's exhibiting the immoderate behavior, the uninhibited imagination, and ignorance of quantitative relations of the child; again the comic often turns on the love of imitation (said to be the child's best art—in his desire to be like the big fellows); while degradation and unmasking correspond to the child's delight in seeing the adult, voluntarily or involuntarily, lowered to his own level. But the most difficult cases to explain by comparison with juvenile psychology are those of the comic of expectation. Obviously the child has not developed much concern for the future or power of reflective anticipation. However jests of this sort may be interpreted as laughing at discovery of the child in oneself, at one's innocent gullibility, and the frequency with which one is disappointed by the unexpected turn of events. Although Freud claims a certain hesitancy as regards the universal applicability of his theory that "every-

thing is comic that does not fit the grownup," the impression
left by his remarks is that "everything comical fundamentally
depends on the degradation to the level of the child."[27] Nevertheless, far from indicating any depreciation of the comic by
such comparisons, Freud's evolutionary concern with the
earlier, undeveloped stages of life seems to express rather the
longing for some secure primordial home, for the womb, or
for return to some biological Eden of pleasurable innocence
as a wish-fulfillment.

The fact is that the roots of the comic extend for Freud
beyond the play life of the child to the nursing of the infant,
the embryonic, and the unconscious. Indeed, the most distinctive element of his psychology in his emphasis upon the unconscious, together with man's longings for reversion to infancy and the embryonic stage, longings, which reveal themselves in adult life in wit, dreams, and psychoneuroses. In
general, childhood expresses a heedlessness, love of play and
experimentation, unrestricted by reason, morals, and society,
while adult life represents attainment of discipline of the
impulses, which suppresses these amoral, asocial, alogical fantasies. The comparison of the two, brought out in laughter,
contrasts the sensible, inhibited, consecutive mind of the
grownup with the nonsensical, free, inconsecutive feelings of
infancy and adolescence. Thus the adult laughs at himself or
others, as we have said, when he notices in them the un-
repressed extravagances, the ignorance, thoughtlessness, and
heedlessness that mark the young. On the other hand, witticisms, according to Freud, often embody man's primal, childlike revenge against reason by expressing, through what
appears a free play of thought and words resembling a dreamlike fantasy, our unconscious modes of thinking. In these,
ideas may appear simply next-to-next, with an entire lack of
relevance or "either–or," neutralizing each other and the laws

---

[27] Freud, pp. 369–70.

of thought, as in the story of the borrowed kettle.[28] Wit and laughter establish a mood unfavorable to reason, in which one enjoys the free disposal of his psychic activity unhampered by logic, as in the dreamy play life of the child. To be sure, even this is not purposeless but tends to satisfy instinctive, biological sources of pleasure. But reason inhibits the emotions, frowning upon childish fairy tales and the disconnected imagery of capricious fancy. Still even Freud, for all his irrationalism, has to distinguish between wit and nonsense—going so far as to deny the name of wit to those pseudojests for which he has no appropriate name, but which today we call "shaggy dog stories." Whereas true wit has sense behind its nonsense, these on the contrary have no sense hidden behind their nonsensical facade, although they lead us to expect it: as, for instance, the story of the dinner guest who, after putting both hands in the mayonnaise ran them through his hair, and to the exclamation of his astonished host replied, "Oh, I thought it was spinach."[29] Such anecdotes fall into the same class apparently as riddles with no answer—as when the funster, who sets people guessing with the question: Why is life like a suspension bridge? on being asked for the solution replies, "How should I know!" Instead of affording pleasure, such tricks serve more as blank cartridges to deceive and annoy. It hardly needs to be added, as against the irrationalism of Freud, that in our view the comic in all its forms offers a rewarding challenge to our mental acumen, awakening our intellect from somnolence, and correcting our faults of logic. Far from expressing the wish to escape the strictures of critical reflection, to return to infancy and the lawless limbo of the unconscious, appreciation of the ludicrous betrays a tendency to check the topsy-turviness of uncritical perception against the norms of pure reason.

Paradoxically, for Freud our appreciation of the ludicrous

---

[28] Chapter 6, p. 118 above.
[29] Freud, p. 212 f., note.

seeks to recover a state in which we had no perception of the
ludicrous. The three forms of it which he distinguishes (wit,
the comic, and humor) are all attempts to regain the euphoria
of childhood, to recapture the bygone state in which we
enjoyed life without work and exercised our psychic processes with the slightest expenditure of energy. In all its
types, the principle of economy or least means is at the heart
of the matter. As Freud puts it, "The pleasure of wit originates
from an *economy of expenditure in inhibition,* of the comic
from an *economy of expenditure in thought,* and of humor
from an *economy of expenditure in feeling.*"[30]

As already remarked, the saying "Brevity is the soul of wit"
refers to this principle. In Freud's eyes, the creator of witticism may achieve apt expression in a condensed form of words
of a natural impulse (like sex or aggression) that society ordinarily represses in the interest of public order. Wit, like
dreams, springs from the unconscious and deals in large part
with *forbidden topics*—so-called "tendency wit." Since much
energy is expended in the repression of these impulses, witty
ideas only get past the "censor" (or inhibiting force) by
using disguises, displacements, or deception. That the author
of the witty remark himself fails to laugh at it is due to the
fact that in the work of its creation and in overcoming the
inhibition to its utterance, he has already utilized all the psychic energy at his disposal. But the hearer of the witticism
laughs, and laughs in the exact amount that his psychic force
is liberated by the suspension of the inhibition energy. Especially the third party or congenial onlooker, who serves not
as the butt but as the public arbiter of the joke, laughs and
laughs freely only if no expenditure of mental work is exacted
of him in grasping the allusions.

While wit is made, says Freud, the comic is found. But
though the comic is usually discovered in social relations, unlike wit it may be enjoyed by oneself alone without imparting

---

[30] Freud, p. 384.

it to anyone else. Generally in its genesis the comic requires two people: the finder of the comic and the one in whom the comic is found. Unlike wit, it does not essentially demand a trio and linguistic expression. Further, the comic is said to belong by its very nature to persons (their actions, shapes, psychic peculiarities, and mental qualities), albeit it may be extended to other objects through their personification. Comic pleasure has its source in a "quantitative contrast" which arises when we compare, by a kind of ideational mimicry, our outlay of force with that of another under similar circumstances. The standard is always our own innervation expenditure, but we laugh on observing our own superior economy of thought in achieving a certain end, as against that of our (childlike) neighbor or of a stage character who expends more energy than is necessary.

Although "release of painful emotions is the strongest hindrance to the *comic* effect,"[31] in *humor* on the contrary painful effects are often the occasion of laughter. The humorist laughs at what earlier or as a child he would have wept over, saying by a kind of elevation of the ego, "I am too big to have these causes affect me painfully now." Unlike wit, which tends to be heartless, humor is sympathetic, despite the fact that it *economizes the expenditure of feeling.* For it uses laughter as an antidote to feelings of suffering, overcoming the sense of misfortune to a degree by liberating energy as comic pleasure. Though as a rule involving others, humor may be enjoyed by oneself alone, being indeed the most self-sufficient form of the comic. In "gallows humor," for instance, we recognize something akin to greatness of soul in the ability of a man under the most trying circumstances to economize his painful feelings by turning some psychic expenditure into the channels of a joke. The man on the scaffold who requested a scarf for his neck to avoid taking cold, clinging to his precautionary habits to ward off despair, presumably appreciated no less than the

---

[31] Freud, p. 371.

bystanders the absurdity at the end of taking thought for the future.

To expand our criticism of Freud in full detail would not be profitable. In general we must protest his tendency to psychoanalyze and biologize the realm of meaning and values. We must deplore his obscurantism, which takes refuge in such cloudy, explanatory concepts as the unconscious, psychic energy, the censor, the id, and the superego. While as a psychiatrist he professes to free man's personality from control by forces of which he has no knowledge, the fact remains that his technique accounts for human psychic behavior in terms of which we have least accredited information. To treat "psychic energy" as if it were a measurable, physically observable quantity like mechanical energy is absurd. To treat the unconscious as if it were something distinct from the physiological, as well as different from vague, inattentive awareness (yet at the same time as something whose existence can be known only through awareness) is to embrace the equivalent of an *unconscious consciousness*, something that is quite incomprehensible. To split up the unity of the self, the individual subject, into three phenomenally distinguishable objects also has its difficulties. But especially his picture of the world as a blind, irrational process undermines our confidence in the power of human intelligence (construed as a late, restricted comer) to authenticate its construction of a genuine "scientific" cosmology. In stressing the wild vagaries of the early stages and in limiting the presence of logical and moral order to the "maturation" of the individual and the race, Freud destroys our assurance of man's ability to grasp the creative process of its unfolding.

Without realizing it, Freud in his frame of thought makes contradictory claims: on the one hand, nature as an inclusive, arational totality is assumed as the standard and ultimate term; while, on the other, rationality as a late, local product is offered as the final criterion and referent. A not dissimilar conflict appears in the attempt to find a norm in some one of the different temporal stages of life, leading to a war of preference as to the superiority of the standpoint of the adult or of the child. On the one hand, *maturation* is used in a laudatory sense as the attainment of comprehension, moderation, self-control, and all manner of goods; while on the other, *infantilism* with its feelings of ease, security, uncritical pleasure, not to mention its freedom from the inhibitions of adult life, is often suggested as the more desirable state. Attempting to face both ways leads to schism, even though the verdict is sought finally in terms of the pain-pleasure principle without consideration of objective values. In any case, to Freud wit and the comic appear predominantly as enemies of reason, as attempts to mobilize racial and subliminal resources; whereas in our view appreciation of them turns upon exposing faulty thinking, and so is rational at the root.

As Freud points out, Bergson is another genetic thinker who "seeks to trace the comic to the after-effects of childish pleasure," in particular to youthful games and "the blurred memories of childish toys."[32] Such blurred recollections of dolls, marionettes, the jack-in-the-box and punch-and-judy associate automatism with laughter and give rise to his theory of the comic as the mechanization of life." Accordingly, Bergson may serve as our final example of an evolutionary thinker, since like the others he construes higher mental life in terms of a changing historical process, and offers a psychogenetic interpretation of comic laughter.

But, unlike Freud, Bergson's emphasis is not upon the generic and unconscious but rather upon the conscious memories of the individual as a child. Many of our adult pleasures, he suggests, turn out upon examination to be nothing more than recollections of our youthful ones. "After a certain age we become impervious to all fresh and novel forms of joy," so that we find the core of our present laughter in "revival of

[32] Freud, p. 361.

the sensations of childhood."[33] Along with its indebtedness to childhood memories of happy games and especially of mechanical toys, laughter in Bergson's eyes expresses the discipline of the group. From his evolutionary standpoint it performs the important life-conserving function of social correction. "In laughter," he says, "we always find an unavowed intention to humiliate, and consequently to correct our neighbor . . . a secret or unconscious intent, if not of each one of us, at all events of society as a whole."[34] For the comical in a person reveals something lifeless, automatic, that is, his likeness to a thing. While the *élan vital* or evolutionary process is supple, creative, ever-changing, at times there appears within it a propensity to backslide into a clockwork of rigid routine or inert mechanism, which demands rebuke. Laughter singles out such tendencies for repression as threats to the race endangering its survival.

But to constrict laughter to cases in which life simulates mechanism, as Bergson often seems to do, is to construe the ludicrous as something wooden, unimaginative, lacking a third dimension. Actually our comic amusement is often induced, as we argued earlier, by the discovery of people's unexpected resourcefulness, their nimble alertness, and feats of catlike agility in adjustment. Surely we appreciate the mischievousness of the youngster who outwits the grownup *on its own account*, and not as a mere contrast effect to the latter's inflexibility. Moreover, for many of us the great joy of childhood came not from dolls and mechanical toys, but from association with animal pets, who stand out in memory as unique, living companions.

Instead of simulated mechanism, Bergson's analogy of the comic to playing a game is more apt. For much as a game creates a mock domain based upon a set of conventions demanding conformity, so does comedy. Indeed, living itself would

---

[33] Bergson, "Laughter," in *Comédy*, ed. Sypher, pp. 104–05.
[34] Bergson, p. 148.

seem to involve adopting many different frames of precon-
ceived ideas and promising to abide by them: as in joining a
club, taking a wife, speaking a language, or becoming a citi-
zen. Sharing any of these different worlds means accepting
their various requirements as the condition of harmonious
social relations. Initially we take for granted that their multiple
codes are consistently interrelated and are not in themselves
contradictory. But comedy arises often with the discovery of
conflict in their claims—as when in *Love's Labour's Lost* or
in Tennyson's *Princess* a rule of life (celibacy) is adopted
which contradicts the principle of life itself, condemning the
code to comic failure. Again there is the endless confusion of
spheres as when youth counterfeits age, the numskull passes
for a scholar, or the unconventional conventionalist, like Mrs.
Malaprop, violates the rules to which she seeks to conform.
In comedy a duality of feeling appears in our attitude toward
the "rules of the game," an impulse sometimes of obedience
and sometimes of transgression. This two-fold sentiment in
social life, which is sometimes a partisan of the code, and
sometimes on the side of the rebel or violator, has much to do,
in our opinion, with man's unfolding sensitivity to the comic.

In the interpretation of laughter, Bergson's great error is
his duality in attributing its sources both to the demand for
conformity and to an anti-mechanistic impulse, which he assumes do not conflict. On the one hand, in its conservative
biological function, laughter appears to him primarily to exact
homogeneity, conformity with the herd, adherence to custom
as making for social cohesion. This, for Bergson, would seem
to be in evolution its main effect. But on the other hand,
as a protest against lifeless inertia, laughter appears to place
suppleness, resourcefulness, initiative at a premium. Indeed,
evolutionists agree that continuous change is the law of evolution and that the unadaptable perish. Hence laughter must
have biological utility also as a protest against routine, uniformity, and social dominance, and in favor of independence

and individual variability. Considering Bergson's recognition (in his *Two Sources of Morality and Religion*) of two levels of evolution, we might suppose that he would recognize these conflicting functions of laughter by referring them to different evolutionary levels: laughter at the lower stage serving as a life-conserving corrective of non-conformity, and at the higher as an encouragement to fresh individual insight and creative novelty. But such is not the case. As far as he has treated the subject, laughter as social criticism wins out over fresh, innovative, individual laughter. Deviations are made fun of as threats to solidarity and collective survival. For Bergson laughter would seem to be a recessive trait, functioning at the lower evolutionary stage, characteristic of the closed rather than the open society. For as evolution advances, direct responsiveness to the stream of life increases, and men come to be swayed more by the warm instincts of the heart than by the rule of custom and group solidarity. Instead of guidance by social pressure with its penalties, men are fired by enthusiasm—especially for great leaders who seem to embody in their persons the spirit of the *élan vital*. At the higher level of evolution under the power of these spiritual leaders, concern with the life of the soul overshadows questions of biological survival, with the result apparently, in Bergson's eyes, that fellow-feeling triumphs over repression and sympathetic intuition replaces the caustic bite of laughter.

Admittedly the biological utility of laughter is differently construed by different evolutionary naturalists. While they apparently agree that hilarity serves the health of the organism through the discharge of surplus energy and springs from an affective urge, they differ as to whether its function is predominantly positive or negative. Darwin found in it largely a generic expression of joy and friendliness, the antithesis of hostile attack. With Spencer the exposure of incongruity was emphasized, something neglected by Freud and Bergson, in whom laughter became more clearly the enemy of reason.

Since laughter springs from the primal and the childish, the contrast with these can never die out. Sometimes it is the revenge of the adult group upon infantile impulse, and sometimes the revenge of the infantile upon the adult group. But although for Freud laughter often expresses an explosion of anarchic primal impulse, for Bergson its function is chiefly conservative, expressing the weight of tribal displeasure against deviations of its members.

But perhaps an interpretation of laughter which did not treat it predominantly as an instrument of society and its customs might be a truer evolutionary view. To many, laughter seems a double reaction, sometimes choral, protective of the group, ridiculing all departures from common practice, and sometimes individual, independent, rebellious, expressing defiance of the reigning code. Perhaps in the historical process both are useful, just as institutions depending on mass subservience to conservative customs need to be supplemented by new ideas and inventions put out by the radicalism of froward individuals.

Broad conjectures as to the evolution of laughter suggest a pathway from a bodily to a mental reaction, from a compulsion to a freer response, from social to individual expression. On this subject Sully especially has many helpful hints.[35] The primal laugh, we might suppose, was a quasi-reflex reply to a stimulus like tickling, as void of ideas as a yawn or a cough. Gradually, perhaps through the long process of natural selection and differentiation, community laughter arose tending to the self-conservative ends of tribal life. Further evolutionary advance may have come with man's passage from dominance by the group with its customs to increasing guidance by ideas. For human societies and the environment are not only persistently repetitive in their patterns but subject to constant flux. Yet novel adaptations to change come usually from ingenious individuals who originate new inventions, "laugh their

---

[35] Sully, *Essay on Laughter,* Ch. IX.

own laughs" and are not mere echoes of the group. The continuing utility of laughter would seem to require mirthful approval of such innovators who make for advance and not mere hilarious disapproval of whatever threatens tradition. Along with childish imitativeness and communal resonance, a more ruminative kind of laughter appears. Instead of merely doing what others do, through the action of mind man becomes critical of the world around him and of himself. With the growth of reflection he is led to perceive defects in his culture, absurdities in tribal life, while self-scrutiny discloses discrepancies in his own actions and professed beliefs. In the institutions that surround him he comes to distinguish between mere fashions of the day—capricious, short-lived manners of dress, speech, deportment—and those techniques and ideas with more lasting justification genuinely to be called improvements. Consequently sometimes he laughs in delight, applauding innovations, censuring the laggard group. Thus with growth in discrimination and in the widening range of objects seen to be comic, the comic spirit gains in independence and uniqueness of expression. However whether the evolutionary utility of laughter lies more in encouraging novelty or in promoting conformity can perhaps never be finally decided even by posterity in retrospect.

CHAPTER II

The Comic and Other Values

SOONER or later our repeated references to congruity and incongruity as descriptive of the comic must raise the question as
to how we distinguish the ludicrous from other values such as
the beautiful, the morally good or right, the true, the sacred
or holy. All of these values are very commonly, and in our
opinion rightly, conceived as different forms of concord, congruence, consilience, or harmony. Yet the discrimination of
their differences from one another, but especially from the
ludicrous, however philosophically necessary, is no easy matter.

The comic, being generally regarded as an aesthetic value,
is referred to the sphere of aesthetics, which is concerned with
the realm of the beautiful. Yet the comic from Aristotle on has
been taken as participating in the ugly. Whether the inclusion
of the comic judgment in aesthetics is owing to its concern
with the satisfaction of pure sensuous form, as Kant holds, or
whether it is because it deals with the same subject matter as
the beautiful (though far removed in degree toward the other
end of the scale) need not delay us here. The point is that,
though often associated with the ugly, the comic is generally
rated as a predominantly positive, though mixed, value—and
not as a disvalue like the ugly, the evil or the false—seeming
to indicate thereby that in the comic judgment in a paradoxical
way pleasure takes captive displeasure, and a sense of the
congruous overcomes that of the incongruous.

However, it is notable that the comic despite the fact that it is accorded positive worth has no direct *contrary* or negative disvalue corresponding to it (after the fashion in which evil corresponds to good or ugliness to beauty) but only a featureless *contradictory*, the *non-comic*. While weeping is the behavior commonly opposed to laughter, one cannot offer the tragic in similar contrast to the comic, since the tragic is not wholly a disvalue but has worth in itself. Rather, the opposite of the comic is the non-comic, a sphere which, besides blank neutralism and non-existence, would presumably include both heaven and hell, since in neither of these is to be found that paradoxical admixture of the agreeable and the disagreeable known as the comic. There are no jokes in the Bible or other great religious scriptures featuring realms of perfect beatitude or utter torment and depravity, since neither the worlds of pure goodness, beauty, and holiness, on the one hand, nor those of pure evil, horror, and blasphemy on the other, have place for that delightful yet irreverent combination of ingredients known as the ludicrous.

Nor is the tragic, as we have said, the true contrary of the comic. For the tragic like the comic affords satisfaction, heightened vision, and something positive, although its worth is mixed and largely suffused with painful negation. Indeed, tragic vision is achieved only by a kind of rebirth, after fear, suffering, and volitional struggle, through being finally forced to accept that which one had previously been most averse to. To comic perception, on the contrary, the contingencies of life appear more external, the will remains unbroken, and the outcome is more readily accepted and understood. Both provide enlargement of spirit, but whereas the tragic experience despite its elevation leaves us weaned from the world by life's buffetings, the comic, on the other hand, leaves us hale, hearty, and full of zest. Somehow by its shrewdness the comic triumphs over misfortunes and successfully scouts the general lay of the land.

As compared with beauty as a value, the comic, we have suggested, has a paradoxical character, whereas the total impression of the beautiful is one of consonance or harmony. Nevertheless the negative element in the comic shown in our awareness of something awkward, blundering, inept, is not so marked as to destroy our satisfaction or conviction of its worth. For shadowing the foreground of comic incongruity there is always a latent aura of congruity no less essential to its nature, of which we have frequently made remark.

Aesthetic judgments deal with forms of sensibility, and as such are transcendental and disinterested. Thus appreciation of the comic or the beautiful requires one to be *detached*, above the battle so to speak, rather than wholly of it, or *engaged* in the struggle. Were comic perceptions merely sensory, linked in causal sequence, they would not be oriented upon form. Rather they would center in appetencies, in matters of selfish, organic concern, in the satisfaction of particular tastes, smells, hues, tints, sounds, tactilities regardless of the pattern of colors or lines, the order of tones, the configuration of words, movements, or gestures. Besides this detachment from the immediate fulfillment of organic desires, perceptions of the comic and the beautiful are characterized by a kind of *illusionism*, an indifference as to whether their objects exist in the actual, historical world, a preoccupation instead with their "aesthetic surface," mold or essence. To be sure, the spell of a scene of majestic redwoods may be broken by considering the commercial value of the timber, just as the comic appreciation of tumbling clowns may be interrupted by concern for their safety; but so long as the experiences continue as they are, such practical concern with existence does not intrude. What is comic or beautiful is contemplated for its own sake, without raising questions as to its use, possession, or actuality in the realm of everyday life. Whether the value pertains to Falstaff or to a real fat man met in the street, to Imogen or to this year's Miss America, is no matter. Nevertheless both claim objectivity, *viz.*, that the comicality or beauty genuinely belongs to its object, so that the evaluation is one on which all men would agree being universally acceptable to humanity. Actually, owing to divergences of space, time, and circumstance, men differ in their aesthetic appreciations; yet underlying these differences is a common referent, a basic agreement presupposed in our perception of the ludicrous, and in our recognition of the beautiful, in certain works of nature, drama, and other arts which stretch across widely separated cultures, continents, and centuries.

But before pursuing further the question as to what the distinctiveness of the comic as opposed to other values consists in, we must pause to consider briefly the general nature of values. Plainly, in addition to aesthetic values (such as the comic, the beautiful, the sublime), there are moral values (the good or the right), religious values (the sacred or holy), the value of truth, and use values (such as those of economy, efficiency, and health), to mention only the main ones. *Value* is the term used to designate either the *activity* (of valuing) or the *referent* (that which is or should be prized or esteemed as of worth). Whether the term basically indicates a substantive essence, a quality, a relation, or simply an affective organic activity is a matter of interpretation. But in any case values are generally classified as *intrinsic* (estimable for their own sake), *extrinsic* (estimable for the sake of something else), or both.

The fact is that wherever we think and act we find ourselves selecting, that is, preferring something to something else in the light of certain criteria of worth, certain standards or goals. In so doing, in grading or ranking states of affairs in a hierarchy of levels or degrees, we are said to be appraising their value. Our interest in things turns not simply upon *what is the cause* of this or that in the world but upon *what is the good or worth of it?* And it is to the degree that objects partake of worth of some sort that they are said to be rendered estimable or valuable. Thus an act is morally right in so far as it accords with righteousness as a standard, a statement is true in so far as it partakes of verity, and an object is beautiful in so far as it shares or participates in beauty.

In philosophical discussions of the subject, disregarding minor differences, there would seem to be three theories of the nature of values distinguishable. The first views them as immediate and indefinable. The second regards them as instrumental (i.e. as means of satisfying desire or of furthering human life or of both). The third construes values always and everywhere as forms of coherence. In this essay we have defended the third view of value, which explains it everywhere in terms of systematic articulation, congruence, or harmony. Accordingly, the true, the morally good, the beautiful, and the comic are in a sense one, being all taken as forms of coherence, although differing from one another as species in ways which we shall attempt to delineate.

The first view, which regards values as immediate or intuitively self-evident, is here rejected for several reasons, the chief being that it becomes impossible to explain, or even to admit, errors of value. To us it is not enough to claim that the mere existential givenness of an intuition is sufficient authentification of the *value* of what it imports, any more than one can say that the inexplicable feeling of the jokiness of a joke is what entitles it to be accepted as truly comic. To be sure, there is an element of the unique and incommunicable in every experience; only the man who has eaten roast venison knows exactly how it tastes; only the man who is not blind and has seen the color is fully acquainted with yellow. Similarly with the meaning of values. Yet if we maintain that all axiological terms are indefinable, in the last analysis our world becomes like a dictionary whose root definitions are in terms of words undefined in this or any dictionary, or like a language incapable of being translated into any other, or like a collection of signs whose significance is incommunicable. Actually, how-

ever, our world of meanings and values is explicable, capable
of cross-rendering, transmissible, and, though separated into
subsystems, all of a piece. Worths are conveyed from one
individual, community, or civilization to another through
their embodiment in acts, words, ideas, technologies, scientific
formulae, music, architecture, literature, but especially in the
characters of men. Through the strength of personalities and
traditions, through schools, universities, theaters, philanthropic
institutions, courts of justice, works of art, temples, and
churches, the spirit of truth, the right, the comic, the sacred,
and the beautiful lives on in the world. The forms of excellence incubated in all these are passed on from generation to
generation and group to group through their power of stimulating in diverse individuals unique yet common kinds of appreciative experience.

The second view, instead of holding values as intrinsic and
indefinable, regards them as definable and worth having but
only for the sake of something else. This outlook includes utili-
tarianism, pragmatism, positivism, cultural relativism, and all
those views that treat values in terms of desire or translatable
into terms of the factual sciences. From this standpoint, all
valuations are instrumental, means of satisfying wants, expressions of wishes, commands, or feelings in deceptive grammatical form. The way in which they are set forth in language
is misleading because to say "Lying is wrong," "Stuttering is
comical," "Crabs walking sideways are ludicrous," etc. seem
to indicate states of affairs certifiable by some accepted mode
of procedure. Actually, it is contended, value sentences have
no verifiable referents with accepted designations ("beautiful," "comical," "estimable"). For instance, "Lying is wrong"
should be translated either into some imperative such as "Stop
lying!" or into some descriptive type of expression such as "I
dislike lying," "I wish that lying were punished," or else into
an expression of opinion with regard to the undesirable and
destructive effects of lying on society. Again, in declaring

"Stuttering is comical" and in laughing at the stutterer, you implicitly command him to "Stop stuttering!" expressing both your dislike of it and your pleasurable sense of superiority as a non-stutterer. Indeed your laughter expresses a tacit reprimand of stuttering as a detriment to efficient communication. Similarly laughter at the crab could be exfoliated linguistically to express one's self-congratulatory appreciation of one's own straightforward movement toward a goal, combined with disparagement of the crab's ineffective, sidelong shuffling and of the silly irrelevance of such evasive tactics.

Evaluations, on this view, are always directed to the satisfaction of wants or self-feeling. As Bertrand Russell puts it, "I shall always act from desire, and the desire is necessarily mine."[1] Of course I may feel that the satisfaction of others' desires is a condition of the satisfaction of my own, so that I may talk, as does the utilitarian, as if all values were instrumental to community living or the general welfare; but in all this my creature constitution is such that I serve others basically to serve myself, and seek to gratify their wants as a means to gratify my own. What this comes to is that things are valuable because desired, and not desired because they are valuable. And whether a given state of affairs is desired or not is something to be settled by the scientific criteria of biology, psychology, and sociology. That is to say, they are determined, or at least claim to be, by publicly observable, factual conditions and responses without attributing any objective validity to the value judgments themselves.[2]

---

[1] Bertrand Russell, *Human Society in Ethics and Politics* (London, Allen & Unwin, 1954), p. 84.

[2] A. J. Ayer, *Language, Truth, and Logic* (2nd ed. New York, Dover Publications, Inc., 1946), pp. 170-71: "Our conclusions about the nature of ethics apply to aesthetics also. Aesthetic terms are used in exactly the same way as ethical terms . . . words such as 'beautiful,' 'hideous' are employed, as ethical words are employed, simply to express certain feelings and evoke certain responses . . . As in ethics [there is] . . . no sense in attributing objective validity to aesthetic judgments, and

Such a view as this, which reduces value sentences to factual sentences, the normative to the descriptive, terms of significance to those of existence, and axiological references to mere attitudes for or against, must be rejected. For the whole realm of factual assertion and verification presupposes a different kind of affirmation and procedure involving values and validity. As we see it, value assertions imbedded in structures of inference underlie and certify factual ones, but factual ones cannot certify valuations. When science and common sense accept certain statements as verified, they do so because of their demonstrable congruence with certain data of sense experience, which congruence is taken as *significant, worthwhile*, a reliable index of something about the world. What we learn here is not mere matter of fact but something about the disposition of facts. This disposition is described by such phrases as "becauses," "therefores," "patterns of evidence," and "relational structures" which constitutes a kind of knowledge very different from the compulsory deliverance of sensory givenness or existent fact. The whole frame of knowledge, including the natural sciences, rests upon acceptance of *values* (like truth, utility, fitness). In the sciences we are constantly distinguishing states of affairs into those which are more or less relevant, important or unimportant, useful or useless, reliable or unreliable. And these appraisals with their criteria and ordering principles, while controlling the structure of psychology, biology, sociology, etc., are not themselves part of the data of the sciences.[3] Rather they are

no possibility of arguing about questions of value in aesthetics but only about questions of fact. A scientific treatment of aesthetics would show us what in general were the causes of aesthetic feeling, why various societies . . . admired the works of art they did, why taste varies as it does within a given society, etc. . . . . ordinary psychological and sociological questions . . . Aesthetic criticism purposes not to give knowledge but to communicate emotions."

[3] M. C. Swabey, *The Judgment of History* (New York, Philosophical Library, 1954), p. 250.

assumed without empirical proof as the precondition of natural knowledge. In brief, facts presuppose but do not certify values, although values certify facts. The system of positive knowledge rests not simply upon givenness through empirical observation, but upon different forms and tests of coherence. And if the charge be made that coherence is itself a mere fact, our answer is that since coherence is the only theory of value that is self-tested (the others merely asserting their existence), it would seem to hold a privileged position of validity. For whereas coherence presupposes the laws of logic, these laws are themselves established by the test of coherence: by the operation of the *reductio* and reaffirmation in denial. (That is to say, by *reductio* in that since denial of the laws of thought leads to contradiction, their denial is false, while in complementary fashion, the attempt to think through their denial reaffirms them.)[4]

This brings us to the third and final theory of values, the one here accepted, which locates them in various types of congruity or coherence, and which construes relevance, consistency, convergence, and sufficiency as pertinent criteria. Everywhere men are constantly comparing, rating, and building a structure of valuations, dependent upon their employment of standards of worth that are not mere palpable sensa, existential givens, or matters of immediate feeling but archetypes, principles of systematic order or excellence invoked throughout life. Man alone among creatures apparently grasps such guiding norms of relational unity behind the sensory many. He alone discovers not only laws of motion, sound, heat, color, electricity, but regulative notions of truth, beauty, goodness, and holiness. While none of the latter is revealed without reflection, they awaken in addition to such insight an emotional response and a sense of ontological significance. They are grasped not as impenetrable givens but as radiant congruences, as forms of teleological pertinence and illumination.

---

[4] M. C. Swabey, *Logic and Nature,* p. 143.

According to one of the oldest and most honored traditions, in becoming aware of recurrent patterns of our sensory deliverances we also awaken to the higher patterns of moral and aesthetic perception, to the true and the divine as interrelated aspects of a harmonious whole.

In contemplating the heavens, Plato points out, the sense of sight reveals a harmony in the motions of the heavenly bodies akin to the operations of ideal reason found within our souls. Values appear through the meeting of like with like; the discovery of systematic articulation in the world outside helps to dispel discords within us, and to bring us into concord with ourselves and the universe. Similarly agreement is found to hold between the sense of hearing, the deliverances of sound, the kinaesthesis of rhythm, and the music of the spheres. A single passage from the *Timaeus* must suffice to suggest how for Plato the human soul passes from sense experience to cognizance of the highest values and their union through grasping them as different types of harmony or coherence.

> God . . . gave us sight to the end that we might behold the courses of intelligence in the heaven, and apply them to the courses of our own intelligence which are akin to them, the unperturbed to the perturbed; and that we, learning them and partaking of the natural truth of reason, might imitate the absolutely unerring courses of God and regulate our own vagaries. The same may be affirmed of speech and hearing . . . For this is the principal end of speech, whereto it must contribute. Moreover, so much of music as is adapted to the sound of the voice and to the sense of hearing is granted to us for the sake of harmony; and harmony, which has motions akin to the revolutions of our souls, is not regarded by the intellectual votary of the Muses as given by them with a view to irrational pleasure . . . but as meant to correct any

discord which may have arisen in the courses of the
soul, and to be our ally in bringing her into harmony and
agreement with herself; and rhythm too was given by
them for the same reason.[5]

That the senses are revelatory of hidden patterns and proportions, and of an unseen world of values interwoven with
one another, expressing a divine appropriateness or perfection,
is the final message of this philosophy. From its standpoint,
modern tendencies in science and art which construe the
deliverances of the senses as finally chaotic and unintelligible
are inherently false and conducive to the destruction of man
and the world.

Although perception of the comic likewise requires intelligence for its determination in dealing with the forms of sensibility, as compared with the perception of a value like the
beautiful, that of the comic involves more overt bodily effects
(such as laughter), more marked relief from tension, and
show of healthful exuberance. Nevertheless in both—as indeed
in all experience of values—there is a sense of recreative
power, exhilaration, insight, wider horizons, freedom, and
serenity, although liberation is possibly a more marked feature
of the comic as against the serenity of the beautiful. In relation to both (as in all valuations) one may be either an
agent or a *spectator*, that is, one may create beauty or perceive it, or both, just as one may make fun or perceive the
funny in things, or both.

Furthermore, whereas perception of the comic involves, as
was said, a kind of mixture of the lovely and the unlovely, of
positive and negative, whereby in deviating from a standard
we encounter a certain disharmony or discord, perception of
the beautiful grasps its sensuous object as a more direct, immediate embodiment of harmony or the Idea.[6] Perhaps as

---

[5] Plato, *Timaeus* (Jowett trans.), 47.
[6] Schopenhauer, *The World as Will and Idea, 1,* 270–71.

Plato suggested in the *Phaedrus* (250), "Beauty alone among
the forms is seen in the world of becoming as she really is."
In the experience of beauty we seem at the goal of our striving,
the material is immaterialized, and we seem to glimpse a unity
of the celestial forms suggestive of the religious experience.

While all perceptions of values are revelatory, that of the
comic as compared with the beautiful appears more intellectual, whereas that of the beautiful relies more on sensuous
representation, the given, surface qualities of things, which yet
serve as signs, symbols of ideal essences in another world. Both
types of aesthetic acquaintance point beyond the sensible to
the non-sensible; both take their objects as vehicles of a larger
meaning. But whereas the comic insight turns on the falsity of
contradictions in the world, appreciation of a thing as beautiful rather involves grasping it as the felt hieroglyph of some
vast import beyond intellectual formulation, expressed rather
than represented (though still using representation) by the
sensuous sign. In our view, it goes without saying, art must
employ a language and forms of representation not wholly ab-
stracted from the world of objects of organized perception,
intellectual sanity, and integrated experience. In this, our outlook frankly diverges from that of many so-called artists of
recent decades for whom art is simply the deliberate creation
in a sensuous medium of works expressive of any kind of
human feeling or ideation however bizarre, without requiring
of them conformity to such criteria. Such "artists" who turn
away from beauty, classical harmony, objective representation,
and, comprehensibility to the expression of the abnormal,
chaotic, and subjective, we can only dismiss with the familiar
jibe, "Those who paint such pictures in bad faith are
frauds; and those who paint them in good faith need to see
a doctor."

The close relationship of the beautiful and the holy, so explicit in Plato, reappears in Hegel's view that beauty is the
manifestation of the divine to the senses, expressing the in-

sight that spirit alone is the true content of the world. In the
experience of the beautiful there is a tendency toward the absorption of the subject in the object, which is distinctively
mystical, suggestive of the religious vision. We find something
wondrous about the object, a nimbus or halo, an enchant-
ment that draws us on. This way, we feel, lies final consum-
mation, our spiritual home. The experience hints at knowledge of some vast reality, a parting of the veil, by which the
lost is found and we enter the ideal world. To be sure, the
sensuous representations of the paradise of the beautiful differ
in their content with differences of fashion and locality in
space and time. In an art like painting, for instance, styles
change in depicting the paradise of the beautiful from the
Graeco-Roman classicism of eighteenth-century Europe, to
the romantic medievalism of the ninteenth, to the archaic
neoprimitivism of the twentieth[7]—much as styles vary in presenting the comic in comedy from delight in teasing, horseplay, and slapstick, to preoccupation with verbal quips and
quibbles, or again to the subtle humor of character revealed
in action and gesture rather than words. But despite changes
in the lineaments of the dream of beauty in different periods,
the core of its disclosure (of some sensuous perfection with
mysterious significance) remains the same. While both appreciation of the comic and the beautiful involve sensuous, affective, and intellectual elements, and yield disinterested
satisfaction, the sense of teleological fitness, of mutual adaptation of man and nature to each other, is stronger in the beautiful. In contrast to the comic, whose datum as involving
contradiction is always flawed, imperfect, the datum of the
beautiful is more marked with a sense of appropriateness and
mysterious harmony.

Distinctively religious experience, we should say, centers in
recognition of an unseen power or powers as the source of

---

[7] Edwyn Bevan, *Symbolism and Belief* (New York, Macmillan, 1938),
pp. 280–81.

value and control of the universe. Generally this higher power is of a personal sort, expressing the relations of a supreme person or souls to lesser ones through direct acquaintance or spiritual law. The holy or sacred is the sentiment in which we clothe our sense of worship for mind (or spirit) as the source of value and the supreme value. However, some would say that this mystical, reverential element in our appreciations is only a projection of our own creature feelings into mindless nature, *and not religion*. When, for instance, the Confucian scriptures say that the *chungtze* (the moral man) exemplifies the *chungyung* (the moral order of things), and that great music expresses the harmony of the universe, this may be taken by naturalists as no more than a mystical gloss read into the interpretation of nature. But to say that a vague sense of the sacred colors our appraisals of existence is certainly far less than is meant by Platonists, Oriental sages, and Spinoza in holding that nature is the garment of God. For to all these, while existence is held to be a product of the divine, the reverse is not the case, and the divine cannot be taken as a mere aspect, offshoot, or product of nature. Especially in Platonic thought the distinctively religious notion is brought out clearly that, while in all valuing experience there is some sense of perfection, some sense of the ideal unity of all excellence as the generative, normative, attractive first principle of the cosmos, this insight concerns the ground of being as distinct from being—the spiritual, formative agency of existence as distinct from existence itself.

When the religious spirit is compared with the comic spirit, one sees that in different degrees both are metaphysical, that both intimate what the universe is, that it involves a basic coherence overreaching passing incoherences, an order superseding disorder, and enveloping cosmos beyond the semblances of chaotic detail. Yet both include a kind of paradox: the religious consciousness, as Santayana says somewhere, feels that "it is right that things should be wrong, yet it is wrong

not to strive to right them" whereas the comic spirit, though it
lacks a fervent sense of providential control and moral obligation, is nevertheless torn between delight in the incongruities
confronting it everywhere and a sense of challenge to resolve
them. In the comic experience as in the religious there is a
momentary escape of the prisoner from life; he stands outside
as in eternity. Yet while the spirit of the religious man remains submissive, reverential, worshipful of a providential
power, that of the comedian remains disobedient, irreverent,
and disrespectful. To be sure, in the religious consciousness
obedience to the divine may lead to a teleological suspension
of one's duty to man, that is, the bond to the metaphysical
may supersede the ethical, but in the comic experience, on the
other hand, the sense of freedom, of liberation got in our droll
perception of the foolishness of mortals, marks the high point
of the experience rather than any sense of our subservience
to the ultimate. Admittedly also the sense of teleological fitness
is far more marked in the perception of religious value and in
that of the beautiful than in the comic; in them our appreciation is like that of participating in a dance in which the
rhythm and harmony of the dancing have a purposiveness
without purpose (*Zweckmässigkeit ohne Zweck*) and are their
own excuse for being, at once the process and the goal.

In comparing the comic with the good, a preliminary distinction must be drawn between *pleasures* (as subjective satis-
factions of sensation, centering in ourselves), *happiness* (as
awareness of our total creaturely satisfaction as an organic
person), and the *morally good* or *right*. In connection with
the discussion of the hedonic paradox, it was pointed out that
both pleasure and happiness pertain solely to the inside or
psychic experience of persons and cannot be attributed to
situations or impersonal objects, although happiness is a more
active, complex, other-regarding mood than pleasure and not
confined to the field of the special senses. Happiness is a
euphoria involving intelligence and feeling, requiring self-

control and judgment in the ordering of impulses, and leading
to a sense of everything within us being in its place—of fitness,
well-being, fulfillment, and health. The right or the morally
good, on the other hand, though it also refers to the personalities or actions of rational beings, is more than self-feeling,
being in the full sense a genuine value (i.e. an *objective worth*
disclosed through a still more active attitude of will and enlightened intelligence). Happiness is a natural, creaturely
quality adhering to man's experience as a product of living,
growing, and adjusting to the existent world. But moral goodness or righteousness belongs to men only as they exhibit a
higher dignity betokening possession of a spiritual center or
soul responding through free determination to an ideal moral
law. With this something new appears in the world that is
normative but not factual, true but not tangible, exemplifying
the ought to be instead of things as they are.

What is morally good or right expresses in human action a
universal, consistent standpoint, in which we treat others' cases
as like our own. Morally good acts and characters embody
harmony as their implied standard, exemplifying a coherence
in words and deeds which suggests the Golden Rule. In short,
ethics, which deals with finite persons, presupposes in their
relations to each other, despite gradations of worth in their
acts, a certain reciprocity and equivalence. That is, between
such selves a certain equality is assumed, a fundamental dignity
or intrinsic value in each, beyond measurement, requiring
that one be respected as another. That men have worth
in themselves is implied in their nature as rational beings. And
the categorical imperative as a principle of equivalence requires that *rational beings should be treated rationally*. Basically this means that we should act toward this man as toward
any man, toward one as another, regarding them always as
ends in themselves and not as mere means or as exceptions.
That is to say, it is as contradictory to treat a post as a man,
as in fetishism, as it is to treat a man as a post by denying

him rights, as in slavery, serfdom, or dictatorship—where many men are regarded as hardly better than *things*, being used as doormats, rubber stamps, pack horses, cattle, shovels, hands, animate machines, or mere apparatus of technology. If it be asked how it can be shown that the rule of willing for others what in principle one wills for oneself, or how universalizing the maxim of one's action can be shown to yield systematic coherence, without the test of empirical consequences, the answer, as has been said, is the indirect certification of the *reductio, viz.*, that to treat rational beings as non-rational is contradictory, as objects not subjects, as bound not free, as mechanisms of cause-and-effect rather than as responsible, imputable selves, which is absurd.

Nevertheless the comic spirit, unlike the moral and religious consciousness, is less attached to the fate of its subject matter and does not emphasize the sacredness of personality, its power as a first and final cause, to the same degree. Often it treats men as objects more than as subjects, more as means, butts, or targets for some rather cruel joking, as hardly more than flotsam and jetsam on the tide of events. Needless to say, the comic spirit is largely centered upon the imputations of existence, the fortunes of this life and its episodic situations, to the neglect of eternity and the soul's destiny beyond. Yet, despite this, the comic spirit is not entirely lacking in recognition of the spiritual self, the moral law, and cosmic significance. Against the view that the comic consciousness centers in an atheism regarding spirit and values, in a cynical sense that "nothing matters," we have already protested. Far from expressing blind negation to the effect that "nothing is of any importance or account," it harbors at bottom a positive insight of genial, comradely assent. In comic appreciation there is a glimpse of congruity as the arbiter of incongruities, a unifying glimpse of truth (as Molière saw), a reference to oneness, kinship, order, and mindedness in the nature of things. Still, admittedly, the comic spirit does not penetrate as far beneath the surface as does the religious, as regards the indefeasible dignity of the soul, the obligatoriness of the moral law, or cosmic mind as the source of value. Nevertheless in higher comedy a certain originative power and imputability is allowed to the characters, so that their actions are not merely mechanical, their shortcomings not mere quirks of nature, tricks of physiognomy, blunders, and stupidities for which they are not responsible. In such comedy the lineaments of the plot may even show how *hubris* is met with *nemesis*, how men get what is coming to them in a rough and ready way, in that those who fail in their obligation to justice, who make no due return or proper requital to their fellows for their services, suffer on their side some painful penalty or *quid pro quo*. Of course this is far from the clear recognition of duty to others as souls or centers of intrinsic worth found in ethics, just as it is far from the infinite concern and compassion shown by the divine for its creatures in the higher religions. Pains are less serious in comedy, where men's failings are less matters of imputable choice and their sufferings almost never accompanied by moral remorse or the consciousness of sin against divine law as in religion. In comedy, the action is largely a chapter of accidents with the actors focused on their own ingenious schemes, mundane triumphs, and reverses; in religion, on the contrary, where the chips are down and everything is at stake, man is oriented beyond his natural self in his dependence upon cosmic mind and forces.

As for the disvalues (such as ugliness, unrighteousness, wickedness or sin, impiety, evil, or falsity), all these to the extent to which they occur involve inconsistency or incoherence. The ugly appears in a sensible distortion or disfigurement that has a disagreeable effect upon our sensibilities. Unrighteousness (or moral wrongdoing) centers in the action of will and practical choice—in yielding to hedonic desire in defiance of the obligation to consistency in the relation of selves to each other. Iniquity or sin, on the other hand, stresses the violation of divine law (a vertical rather than a horizontal transgression, one might say), thereby rejecting the genuineness of cosmic significance and ultimate value. In the narrower sense, blasphemy or impiety do the same, save that they are especially directed to the repudiation of divine mind as the source of excellence. As for evil, in so far as it is claimed to possess non-human subsistence, it must be located in a certain chaotic, disorderly strain in the universe. Falsity as a disvalue further indicates a state of affairs which, when offered as a description of evidence for something, stands in contradiction with the referent of which it claims to be evidence. To say that man is a quadruped, for instance, involves a factual contradiction; to assert that a man is not a man, a self-contradiction; while to break a law one has sworn to abide by is treacherous action in being false to trust. Untruths may take the form of misrepresentation through outright lying, incorrect statements through ignorance, or appear in non-propositional fashion as deeds like breach of contract or the inculcation by practice of erroneous beliefs in others.

Lastly, truth as the value which underlies other values may be described as abstract coherence or validity. Keats' famous dictum that all we need to know is that "truth is beauty and beauty truth," affirms not only the unity of values but that the archetypes, far from being illusory dreams, are authentic and trustworthy. A specific truth may be said to consist in the integration of a systematic pattern of evidence with the referent of which it is evidence. Thus the probable truth of evolution consists in the totality of patterns of evidence (paleontology, embryology, comparative anatomy, etc.) in relation to the referent (the evolutionary process itself). It consists in a coherently connected relationship rather than in a factual state of affairs in itself, or in the coincidental matching (correspondence) of such a state of affairs with the propositional statement of the evolutionary theory, which remains dependent upon the knowledge and verbal expression of particular minds. The rationale of truth as a relationship, in our opinion, depends only on mind as such but is independent of particular existent intelligences, since there are admittedly many un-discovered and forgotten truths.

In brief, verity is never a mere factual matter of corre-spondence, a matter of natural belief (a compulsory attitude of our constitutional make-up), or of propositional statement. Rather it inheres in a clear and distinct nexus of reflective appraisal of the harmonious disposition of facts. Truth is the intellectual value par excellence, by which the rational pattern of thought authenticates the being of its object. In most cases (like that of evolution) the truths that we know are only probable; but in a few cases, necessary truths are discovered: i.e. the rationale of thought fully guarantees the reality of the object, as in the instances of the self, the perfect, or truth in general. *What must be, undoubtedly is.* For just as the denial of truth claims truth, and the denial of self presupposes the self of the denier (the doubt implies the doubter), so the denial of the perfect (a self-contained and self-tested stand-ard of value) reasserts such a standard, and hence is impos-sible of rejection, being reaffirmed in its very negation.

As distinguished from beauty, truth is non-sensuous, and the satisfaction it affords is far removed from pleasure; in-stead, like the moral consciousness, it often carries a sting. Yet, unlike the issue of righteousness, it does not imply the action of the will as agent, the dignity of the self, and the conflict with desire to the same extent. Truth is an excellence seen by the intellect rather than by the whole man. In contrast to the religious insight, it does not involve a fusion of feeling, will, and reflection, nor does it like the appreciation of holiness culminate in the absorption of the subject in spirit as its ob-ject, or in the conviction of supreme spirituality and inexpres-sible beatitude.

In contrast to these other values, as we have seen, the comic puts incongruity in the foreground, although its grasp by the intellect is shadowed by a sense in the background of an enveloping coherence. Still, because the ludicrous exploits pretense and falsity, there are those who, forgetful of the pre-supposition of truth as its criterion, aver that it conduces to scepticism and disbelief in all genuine worth. Satire and irony, it is said, in our modern world have destroyed belief in abso-lute values. The art of debunking morals, religion, beauty, even scientific knowledge, has brought about a widespread sense of meaninglessness and emptiness. A creed of relativism pervades our thinking, in which objects of esteem are taken as mere subjective projections, a screen of passing pleasures hid-ing from us for a moment our deeper agnosticism and despair. Only the hollow laughter of cosmic irony remains, in which men find their values proven cheats, no light behind the veil, and all nothingness and vanity. In *Brave New World* we saw the farcical absurdity of our dreams of scientific progress and the perfect society ending in the perception of the best as like the worst, and the suicide of the main character at the use-lessness of the struggle.

To this charge, in our opinion, the resilient spirit of the comic provides the fittest answer. Though a mixed value, the negative side of the ludicrous can never overrule its positive aspect. Let satire and irony do their worst, there still remains the jollity of the comic spirit, the serenity of humor. Undeni-ably, a chief function of laughter is to help sweep the world free of shams, superstitions, outworn customs, and false beliefs, a process which leaves us with a chill sense of fewer supports to lean on. Nevertheless along with this goes—even in the exchange of common, street-corner jesting—a fresh conviction of the camaraderie of truth, a renewal of hope, of springtime in life, which despite all reverses finds the world good, reason in its heaven, and man eager to fare forth on new adventures.

Index

(Italicized numbers indicate major discussion.)